Lineum crystals

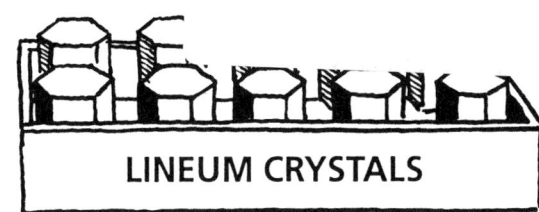

1. Lineum crystals are stored in boxes of 10. How many boxes can be filled using
   (a) 80 crystals   (b) 250 crystals   (c) 1500 crystals?

2. Find mentally, one tenth of
   (a) 340   (b) 570   (c) 4760   (d) 22 000   (e) 10 760

3. Mike earns one credit for every 100 crystals mined. How many credits did Mike earn in each of these months?

Month	January	March	May	July	September
Crystals mined	8700	15 400	21 000	30 000	107 600

4. Find mentally, one hundredth of
   (a) 6800   (b) 9000   (c) 39 200   (d) 90 300   (e) 350 000

5. One thousand lineum crystals weigh one galactogram (gg). What is the weight of
   (a) 6000 crystals   (b) 26 000 crystals   (c) 705 000 crystals
   (d) 290 000 crystals   (e) 80 000 crystals   (f) 800 000 crystals?

6. Find mentally.
   (a) 5300 ÷ 10   (b) 15 000 ÷ 1000   (c) 7600 ÷ 100
   (d) 41 000 ÷ 100   (e) 10 100 ÷ 10   (f) 900 000 ÷ 100
   (g) 600 000 ÷ 1000   (h) 300 000 ÷ 10   (i) 110 000 ÷ 1000

7. 320 crates of crystals are divided equally among 8 transporters. How many crates are loaded onto each transporter?

8. Find mentally.
   (a) 240 ÷ 6   (b) 300 ÷ 6   (c) 240 ÷ 8   (d) 240 ÷ 4   (e) 350 ÷ 5
   (f) 280 ÷ 7   (g) 270 ÷ 3   (h) 700 ÷ 10   (i) 420 ÷ 7   (j) 720 ÷ 9

Transporters

Place value: hundreds of millions
Heinemann Mathematics P7
Textbook pages 13 and 14

5

1. A message transmitted from Star Lab X-4 takes **twelve million, eight hundred and forty-two thousand, six hundred** galactoseconds to reach transporter *Zarco*. Write this number in figures.

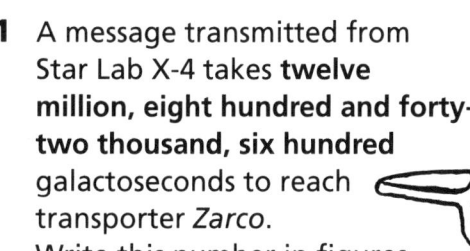
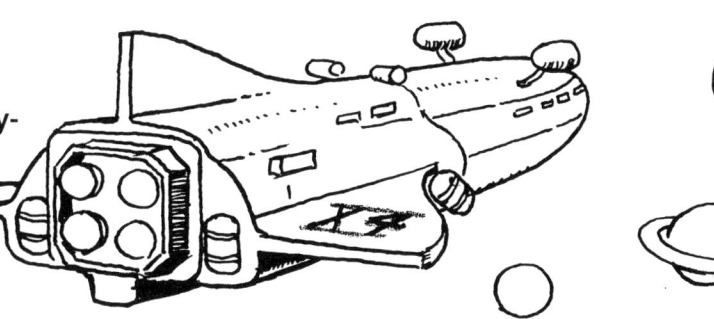

2. Write in figures the transmission time to each of these transporters:
   (a) *Nina* — one hundred and three million, four hundred thousand galactoseconds
   (b) *Marco* — ninety-four million, twenty-four thousand galactoseconds
   (c) *Maria* — three million, one hundred and five thousand, and fifty galactoseconds

3. Write **in words** the transmission time from Star Lab X-4 to each planet.
   (a) Ag — 32 405 000 galactoseconds (b) By — 143 240 700 galactoseconds
   (c) Cob — 7 046 350 galactoseconds (d) Dal — 100 307 060 galactoseconds

4. The gauges show the total distance in galactometres travelled by each transporter. Write the value of each arrowed digit.

   Zarco   *Nina*   *Marco*
   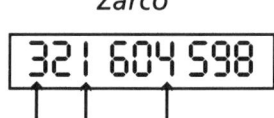 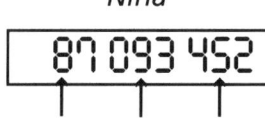 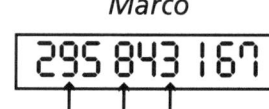

5. Which transporter gauges show a number that has
   (a) a thousands digit greater than 3
   (b) a millions digit less than 7
   (c) a hundreds of thousands digit of zero
   (d) a hundreds of millions digit less than 3
   (e) a tens of millions digit greater than 5?

6. Galactic storms affect some numbers on the distance gauges. The change in *Zarco's* number is **−100 000**

   Find the change in each of these numbers:

   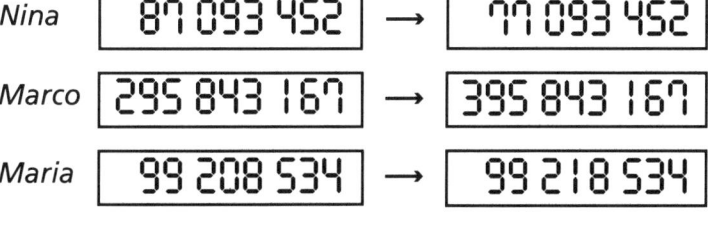

Fruit and veg

Division: calculator, exact remainders
Heinemann Mathematics P7
Workbook page 4, Textbook page 16

1. Some of Dr. Martha Thomas's experimental fruit is ready to be transported to Earth. The laboratory staff pack the fruit in boxes. Complete to find the number of
   - **full** boxes
   - fruits in the partly filled box.

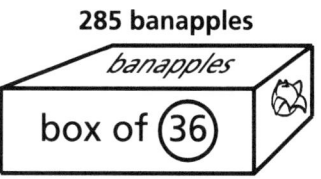

285 banapples
box of 36

285 ÷ 36 = _____ → _____ full boxes
____ × ____ = _____ banapples
____ − ____ = _____ banapples in the partly filled box

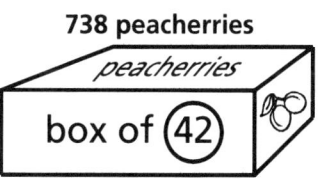

738 peacherries
box of 42

____ ÷ ____ = _____ → _____ full boxes
____ × ____ = _____ peacherries
____ − ____ = _____ peacherries in the partly filled box

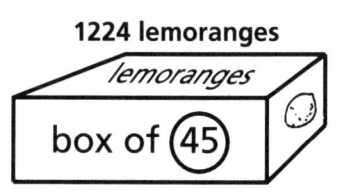

1224 lemoranges
box of 45

____ ÷ ____ = _____ → _____ full boxes
____ × ____ = _____ lemoranges
____ − ____ = _____ lemoranges in the partly filled box

2. Dr. Thomas sends some of her vegetables to the Camp Zog Diner. Complete the table.

	Caulipeas	Potarrots	Carronips	Carroots	Parsnibeets
Number of vegetables sent	438	2187	148	263	1234
Number in one full box	18	50	32	12	44
Number of full boxes					
Number of vegetables in partly filled box					

3. Dr. Thomas packs turnions in boxes of 70. Zandra needs 1650 turnions for the Diner.

   How many full boxes should Zandra order? _____

   How many extra turnions will she have? _____

© SPMG 1996. Restricted copyright cleared.

Heinemann Mathematics 7

Droids on Planet Ag

Calculator: checking answers
Heinemann Mathematics P7
Textbook pages 17 and 18

7

1. (a) Explain how, without calculating the answer, the droid can tell which of the possible answers must be wrong.
   (b) Which answer could be correct? Check.

   128 × 982
   Possible answers
   125 698   125 696
   125 702   125 700

   Three of these answers must be wrong.

2. Find each answer and show how to check it using the droid's method.

   (a) 1046 + 7204
   Check by subtracting.

   (b) 21 462 + 7014
   Check by adding in reverse order.

   (c) 763 × 367
   Check by dividing.

   (d) 4 162 008 ÷ 3434
   Check by multiplying.

   (e) 123 × 456
   Check by multiplying in reverse order.

   (f) 9876 − 5432
   Check by adding.

   You can also check an answer just by repeating the calculation.

3. Find each answer and check it in **two** ways.

   (a) Transporter *Nina* is being loaded with minerals on Planet Ag.
   What total weight, in galactograms, of Lineum and Ambal is being loaded?

   (b) When the Zelac is also loaded the total weight of the cargo is 30 650 gg. What is the weight of the Zelac?

   (c) One buggy-load of Mignon weighs 195 galactograms. What is the total weight of Mignon in 160 buggy-loads?

   (d) The total weight of minerals carried by transporter *Nina* on 6 journeys from Planet Ag is 210 000 glactograms. What is the mean weight carried on the 6 journeys?

   Lineum   7045 gg
   Ambal   16 375 gg
   Zelac

   Planet Ag

Mosaics

Fractions: equivalence, simplification
Heinemann Mathematics P7
Workbook page 5, Textbook page 21

8

1 Write equal fractions for each pair of Kitbits mosaic designs.

(a)

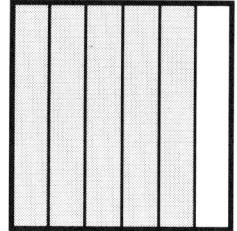

(b)

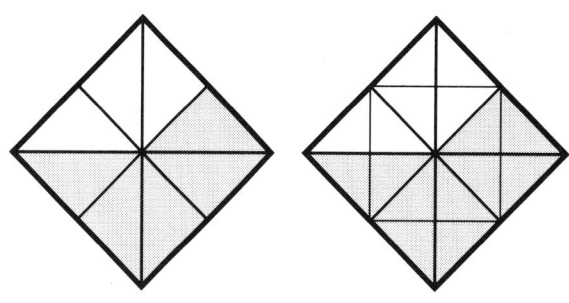

2 Copy and complete.

(a) $\frac{3}{5} = \frac{\square}{10}$ (b) $\frac{1}{3} = \frac{5}{\square}$ (c) $\frac{7}{8} = \frac{\square}{16}$ (d) $\frac{7}{10} = \frac{\square}{50}$

(e) $\frac{1}{2} = \frac{6}{\square}$ (f) $\frac{3}{4} = \frac{\square}{16}$ (g) $\frac{5}{6} = \frac{20}{\square}$ (h) $\frac{9}{50} = \frac{\square}{100}$

3 Write equal fractions for each pair of mosaic designs.

(a)

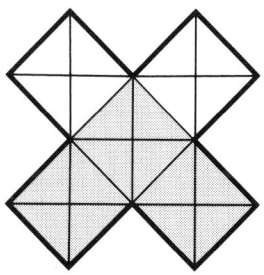

(b)

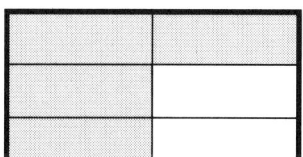

4 Copy and complete.

(a) $\frac{9}{12} = \frac{\square}{4}$ (b) $\frac{8}{20} = \frac{\square}{5}$ (c) $\frac{35}{50} = \frac{\square}{10}$ (d) $\frac{30}{42} = \frac{5}{\square}$

(e) $\frac{27}{36} = \frac{3}{\square}$ (f) $\frac{12}{32} = \frac{\square}{8}$ (g) $\frac{63}{81} = \frac{\square}{9}$ (h) $\frac{14}{35} = \frac{2}{\square}$

5 Find the missing numbers.

(a)

(b)

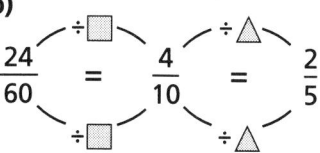

(c)

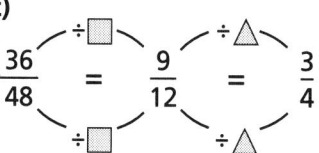

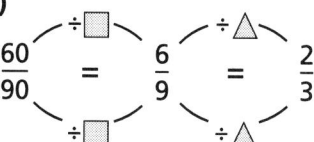

6 Simplify.

(a) $\frac{15}{60}$ (b) $\frac{42}{56}$ (c) $\frac{42}{70}$ (d) $\frac{36}{60}$ (e) $\frac{32}{80}$ (f) $\frac{60}{150}$

(g) $\frac{36}{96}$ (h) $\frac{20}{60}$ (i) $\frac{120}{160}$ (j) $\frac{240}{300}$ (k) $\frac{210}{270}$ (l) $\frac{400}{480}$

Kitbits Shapes packs

Fractions: of a set, mixed, improper
Heinemann Mathematics P7
Textbook page 22

9

1 Kitbits *Shapes* packs are made in a range of sizes.
What fraction of the shapes in each pack are triangles?

Size	small	standard	medium	large	extra large
Number of triangles	7	8	15	30	20
Total number of shapes	14	20	30	75	30

2 What fraction of the pack is each type of shape?

(a)
10 circles   60 squares
30 rectangles   20 triangles
Contents 120 shapes

(b)
20 circles   40 squares
12 rectangles   108 triangles
Contents 180 shapes

3 Write what each diagram shows • as a mixed number • as an improper fraction.

(a)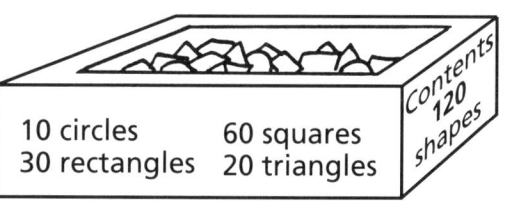

(b)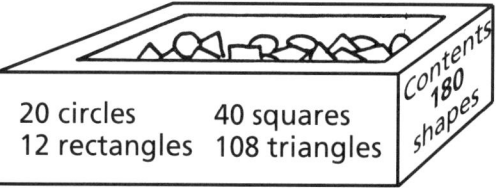

(c)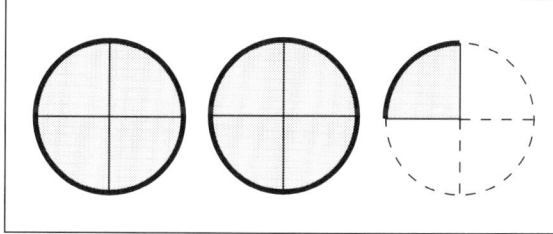

(d)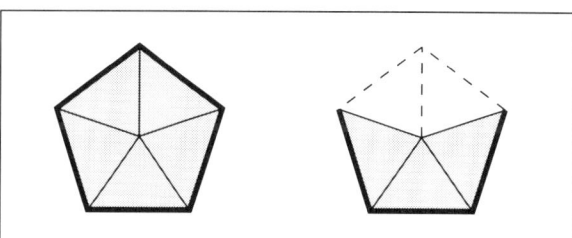

4 Write each mixed number as an **improper fraction**.

(a) $1\frac{7}{8}$ (b) $3\frac{3}{5}$ (c) $2\frac{3}{8}$ (d) $4\frac{2}{5}$ (e) $2\frac{1}{3}$ (f) $3\frac{7}{10}$ (g) $2\frac{5}{6}$

5 Write each improper fraction as a **mixed number**.

(a) $\frac{10}{3}$ (b) $\frac{15}{4}$ (c) $\frac{17}{5}$ (d) $\frac{23}{6}$ (e) $\frac{10}{4}$ (f) $\frac{14}{6}$ (g) $\frac{28}{8}$

(h) $\frac{24}{9}$ (i) $\frac{12}{4}$ (j) $\frac{20}{15}$ (k) $\frac{19}{7}$ (l) $\frac{30}{6}$ (m) $\frac{40}{7}$ (n) $\frac{57}{9}$

Kitbits colourama

Fractions: addition and subtraction
Heinemann Mathematics P7
Textbook pages 23 to 25

10

1 Tom mixes $\frac{3}{10}$ kg of red paint powder with $\frac{9}{10}$ kg of blue powder. What is the total weight of powder in Tom's mix?

2 (a) $\frac{2}{5} + \frac{2}{5}$ (b) $\frac{3}{8} + \frac{1}{8}$ (c) $\frac{1}{6} + \frac{3}{6}$

   (d) $\frac{7}{10} + \frac{4}{10}$ (e) $\frac{3}{8} + \frac{7}{8}$ (f) $\frac{3}{4} + \frac{1}{2}$

3 (a) $\frac{4}{5} - \frac{2}{5}$ (b) $\frac{6}{7} - \frac{3}{7}$ (c) $\frac{7}{8} - \frac{5}{8}$ (d) $\frac{7}{10} - \frac{3}{10}$ (e) $1 - \frac{4}{6}$ (f) $1 - \frac{4}{10}$

4 Mia adds $\frac{5}{8}$ l of water to $1\frac{1}{8}$ l of yellow paint. What is the total volume of the paint?

5 (a) $2\frac{1}{3} + \frac{1}{3}$ (b) $3\frac{1}{4} + \frac{2}{4}$ (c) $2\frac{1}{6} + \frac{1}{6}$

   (d) $1\frac{3}{10} + \frac{3}{10}$ (e) $2\frac{3}{8} + \frac{1}{8}$ (f) $3\frac{1}{6} + \frac{3}{6}$

6 (a) $1\frac{3}{5} + \frac{3}{5}$ (b) $2\frac{3}{4} + \frac{3}{4}$ (c) $3\frac{4}{5} + \frac{3}{5}$ (d) $4\frac{5}{7} + \frac{6}{7}$ (e) $2\frac{5}{8} + \frac{7}{8}$ (f) $1\frac{5}{6} + \frac{1}{6}$

   (g) $2\frac{7}{10} + \frac{8}{10}$ (h) $2\frac{3}{5} + \frac{4}{5}$ (i) $3\frac{9}{10} + \frac{7}{10}$ (j) $1\frac{3}{8} + \frac{7}{8}$ (k) $2\frac{5}{6} + \frac{5}{6}$ (l) $3\frac{1}{2} + \frac{3}{4}$

7 A drum contains $2\frac{4}{5}$ kg of green paint powder. Tom uses $\frac{2}{5}$ kg in a paint mix. What weight of powder is left in the drum?

8 (a) $2\frac{5}{8} - \frac{2}{8}$ (b) $3\frac{4}{5} - \frac{2}{5}$ (c) $1\frac{5}{7} - \frac{2}{7}$

   (d) $4\frac{5}{6} - \frac{1}{6}$ (e) $3\frac{7}{10} - \frac{3}{10}$ (f) $2\frac{1}{2} - \frac{1}{4}$

9 (a) $3\frac{2}{5} - \frac{4}{5}$ (b) $2\frac{2}{7} - \frac{5}{7}$ (c) $4\frac{1}{6} - \frac{2}{6}$ (d) $2\frac{5}{8} - \frac{7}{8}$ (e) $1\frac{7}{10} - \frac{9}{10}$ (f) $3\frac{1}{4} - \frac{2}{4}$

   (g) $1\frac{3}{8} - \frac{5}{8}$ (h) $2\frac{4}{9} - \frac{7}{9}$ (i) $4\frac{3}{10} - \frac{7}{10}$ (j) $2 - \frac{3}{4}$ (k) $1\frac{3}{7} - \frac{6}{7}$ (l) $3\frac{1}{2} - \frac{3}{4}$

Orlando

Decimals: notation and place value
Heinemann Mathematics P7
Workbook page 6, Textbook pages 29 and 30

11

This display shows the weight, in kilograms, of a box being stored in the *Orlando's* main hold.

The box weighs **13·209 kg** or $13\frac{209}{1000}$ **kg** or **13 209 g**

1 Write each of these weights in **two** other ways.
   (a) 4·716 kg   (b) 2·310 kg   (c) 15·003 kg   (d) 0·097 kg

2 Write these weights in **grams**.
   (a) 5·574 kg   (b) 14·010 kg   (c) 75·5 kg   (d) 0·25 kg   (e) 7 kg

3 Write these weights in **kilograms**.
   (a) 3070 g   (b) 444 g   (c) 2003 g   (d) 3000 g   (e) 59 g

4 Write these weights in order, starting with the **heaviest**.

5 These are the distances between the *Orlando* and some holiday locations.
Write the **shorter** distance in each pair.
   (a) Volandia 32·123 km, Zergovia 32·3 km
   (b) Kolos Islands 110·919 km, Botundi 110·09 km
   (c) Port Tropic 100 km, Sun River 99·999 km
   (d) Dolphin Bay 42·555 km, Blue Isle 42·5 km

6 This display shows an engine pressure reading.
The value of the arrowed digit is shown.
Write the value of each arrowed digit in these displays.

7 hundredths

(a) 6·367   (b) 67·402   (c) 30·019
(d) 55·555   (e) 112·011   (f) 98·524

© SPMG 1996. Restricted copyright cleared.

Heinemann Mathematics P7

All at sea

Decimals: first and second places, addition and subtraction
Heinemann Mathematics P7
Textbook pages 31 and 32

12

This extract from the ship's log shows how many kilometres the *Orlando* sailed on each morning of a cruise.

Week 1: morning distances (km)	
Sun	62·4
Mon	47·3
Tue	56·7
Wed	58·5
Thu	39·9
Fri	61·0
Sat	70·1

1 What was the total distance sailed on these mornings?
  (a) Sunday and Monday
  (b) Tuesday and Thursday
  (c) Thursday and Saturday
  (d) Sunday and Thursday
  (e) Wednesday, Thursday and Friday

2 What were the differences between the distances sailed on these mornings?
  (a) Sunday and Monday   (b) Tuesday and Thursday
  (c) Tuesday and Friday   (d) Monday and Thursday
  (e) Wednesday and Saturday   (f) Friday and Saturday

The table shows the times, in seconds, taken by some children to put on their life-jackets.

Time in seconds	Gavin	Tanya	Jerome	Flo	David
First try	63·29	61·06	60·72	49·90	46·18
Second try	54·01	59·99	62·00	50·19	45·50

LIFE-JACKET DRILL
TARGET 1 MINUTE

3 What was the **total** time taken, in seconds, for **both** tries by
  (a) Gavin (b) Tanya (c) Jerome (d) Flo (e) David?

4 What was the **difference** between the first and second times of
  (a) Gavin (b) Tanya (c) Jerome (d) Flo (e) David?

5 Who beat the 1 minute target at the first try?
  By how many seconds?

6 (a) 3·08 + 40·93   (b) 23·01 + 19·19   (c) 17·06 − 9·9
   (d) 25 − 0·18   (e) 44·3 + 20·91   (f) 40 − 24·57

© SPMG 1996. Restricted copyright cleared.

Heinemann Mathematics P7

Team games

Decimals: multiplication
Heinemann Mathematics P7
Textbook pages 33 to 35

13

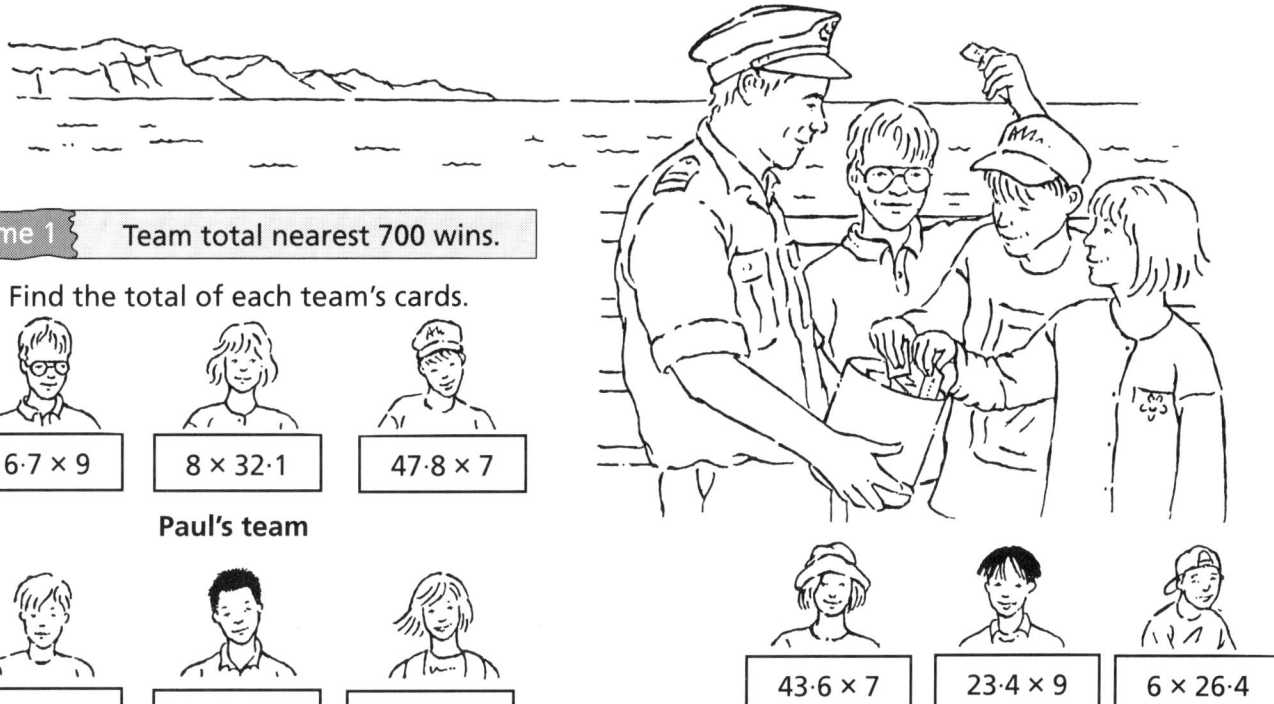

Game 1 — Team total nearest 700 wins.

(a) Find the total of each team's cards.

Paul's team:
- 16·7 × 9
- 8 × 32·1
- 47·8 × 7

Leon's team:
- 6 × 38·2
- 9 × 14·7
- 8 × 45·9

Jan's team:
- 43·6 × 7
- 23·4 × 9
- 6 × 26·4

(b) Which team won Game 1?

Game 2 — Add any **two** cards. Team score nearest to 100 wins.

Find which team won Game 2.

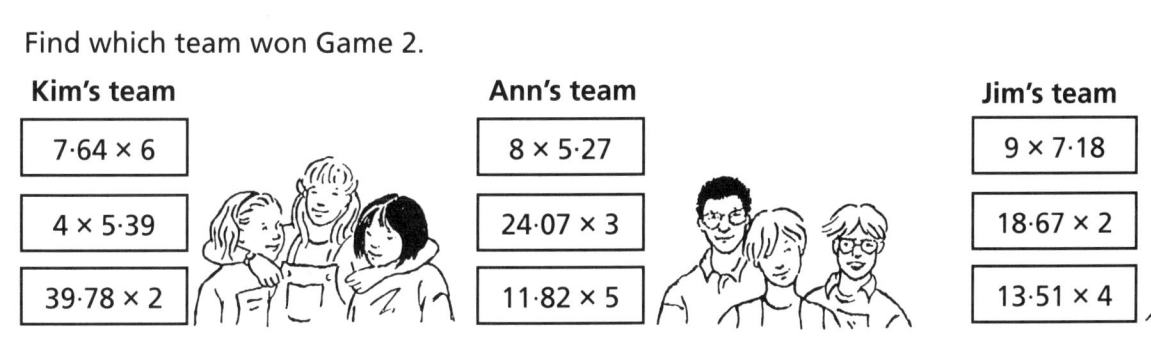

Kim's team:
- 7·64 × 6
- 4 × 5·39
- 39·78 × 2

Ann's team:
- 8 × 5·27
- 24·07 × 3
- 11·82 × 5

Jim's team:
- 9 × 7·18
- 18·67 × 2
- 13·51 × 4

Game 3 — One point for each correct answer. Highest team score wins.

For each team, copy the multiplications **which are wrong** and give the **correct** answers. Which team won?

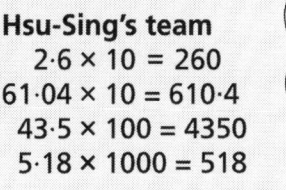

Hsu-Sing's team
2·6 × 10 = 260
61·04 × 10 = 610·4
43·5 × 100 = 4350
5·18 × 1000 = 518

Joe's team
3·15 × 10 = 315
2·4 × 100 = 24
3·7 × 1000 = 3700
43·6 × 1000 = 4360

Niall's team
23·61 × 10 = 236·1
6·14 × 100 = 6140
5·18 × 1000 = 5180
38·47 × 1000 = 38 470

Children's club

Decimals: division
Heinemann Mathematics P7
Textbook pages 36 to 39

14

1 The children make party decorations. For each group, find the average length of paper-chain made by each child.

(a)
Total length 34·8 m

(b)
Total length 35·4 m

(c)
Total length 31 m

2 (a) 4)14·68   (b) 6)29·22   (c) 5)30·45   (d) 3)28·02
     (e) 19·44 ÷ 8   (f) 31·14 ÷ 9   (g) 22·05 ÷ 7   (h) 50·72 ÷ 8

3 Some children buy presents to take home.
Find the average cost of each child's presents.
   (a) Tom buys 5 presents for £34.
   (b) Jo buys 4 presents for £45.
   (c) Ann buys 8 presents for £60.

4 (a) 5)91·85   (b) 8)89·92   (c) 7)71·82   (d) 6)88·32
     (e) 90·27 ÷ 9   (f) 193·2 ÷ 8   (g) 173·4 ÷ 5   (h) 277 ÷ 4

5 (a) 10 children share equally 2·5 litres of cola.
What volume, in litres, do they each receive?
   (b) 100 children share equally 3·4 kg of raisins.
What weight, in kg, do they each receive?

6 (a) 64 ÷ 10   (b) 205 ÷ 10   (c) 3·8 ÷ 10   (d) 16·3 ÷ 10
     (e) 30·4 ÷ 10   (f) 16·43 ÷ 10   (g) 8 ÷ 10   (h) 1·85 ÷ 10

7 (a) 286 ÷ 100   (b) 714 ÷ 100   (c) 352·8 ÷ 100   (d) 234·6 ÷ 100
     (e) 65·4 ÷ 100   (f) 8·9 ÷ 100   (g) 7 ÷ 100   (h) 0·6 ÷ 100

8 (a) 12·3 ÷ 10   (b) 19·84 ÷ 10   (c) 627·1 ÷ 100   (d) 84·3 ÷ 100
     (e) 5·1 ÷ 10   (f) 1 ÷ 10   (g) 18 ÷ 100   (h) 0·8 ÷ 10

Souvenirs

Decimals: approximation and estimation
Heinemann Mathematics P7
Textbook pages 40 and 41

15

£7·88   £17·38

£14·99

£12·68

£25·25

1 Write each price to the nearest pound.

2 Find **mentally** the **approximate** cost of
   (a) 3 pens   (b) 4 books   (c) 8 T-shirts
   (d) a book and a pen   (e) a T-shirt and a ship-in-a-bottle
   (f) a ship-in-a-bottle and a cap   (g) a book and a T-shirt.

3 Find **mentally** the **approximate** amount left from £30 after buying
   (a) a ship-in-a-bottle   (b) a cap   (c) a T-shirt.

4 Calculate, **mentally**, **approximate** answers for
   (a) £100 − £69·52   (b) £23·15 + £16·19   (c) £50 − £19·58

These are the weights, in kilograms, of some large souvenirs.

         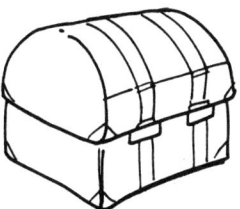

Bronze   **Vase**   **Statue**   **Chest**
39·1 kg   16·6 kg   23·3 kg   27·8 kg

5 Round each weight **to the nearest kilogram**.

6 For each of these pairs of souvenirs, find
   • the **approximate** total weight mentally   • the **exact** total using a calculator.
   (a) the bronze and the vase   (b) the statue and the chest
   (c) the statue and the vase   (d) the chest and the vase

7 For each of these pairs of souvenirs, find
   • the **approximate** difference in weight mentally   • the **exact** difference using a calculator.
   (a) the statue and the bronze   (b) the vase and the chest

8 Find **mentally, approximate** answers for
   (a) 16·8 + 47·95   (b) 50 − 7·19   (c) 21·72 − 5·8   (d) 31·65 + 18·37

Gifts

Decimals: approximation and estimation
Heinemann Mathematics P7
Workbook pages 7 and 8

16

1. Round these prices to the **nearest ten pounds**. (a) £131·81 (b) £65·20

2. Find **mentally** an **approximate** total for each bill.

   (a) *The Gift Box*
   £
   Jacket 87·87
   Jumper 41·95
   Total

   (b) *The Gift Box*
   £
   Necklace 123·26
   Ear-rings 58·65
   Total

   (c) *The Gift Box*
   £
   Shoes 62·45
   Bag 26·90
   Racquet 72·17
   Total

   Using a **calculator**, find the **exact** totals. Check your approximations.

3. (a) Round to the nearest £1 and find **mentally** the **approximate** total cost of these three gifts.

   £19·75   £26·95   £32·40

   (b) Which one of these displays do you think shows the exact total for **(a)**?

   £89·10   £77·90   £79·10   £81·40

   (c) Check your answer to **(b)** with a calculator.

4. Copy and complete, with an **exact** answer, any of these calculations which have an approximate answer of '**about 10**'.

   | 6·85 + 16·9 = | 46·8 − 37·1 = | 8 × 4·5 = |
   | 73·5 ÷ 7 = | 3·54 × 6 = | 1·95 × 5 = |

5. Use one of these numbers each time.

   | 41·91 | 3·61 | 81·7 | 6·95 | 52·7 | 65·7 |

   Copy and complete each statement below. Check with a calculator.

   (a) 4·3 × 19 = ☐

   (b) 100 − ☐ = 58·09

   (c) ☐ + 6·15 = 71·85

   (d) 48·65 ÷ 7 = ☐

Theatre outing

Decimals: calculator
Heinemann Mathematics P7
Textbook page 43

17

Ticket prices		
Stalls	Adults	£12·80
	Children	£ 6·35
Balcony	Adults	£18·50
	Children	£10·95

In each example, check your answer.

1 Find the total cost for each of these groups visiting the theatre at Port Minor.
  (a) 8 adults going to the stalls
  (b) 23 children going to the stalls
  (c) 35 adults going to the balcony
  (d) 19 children going to the balcony
  (e) 4 adults and 7 children going to the stalls
  (f) 6 adults and 18 children going to the balcony.

2 How much more would it cost a group of 5 adults and 9 children to go to the balcony than to the stalls?

3 A group of 12 people went to the stalls. The total cost was £102. How many adults and how many children were in the group?

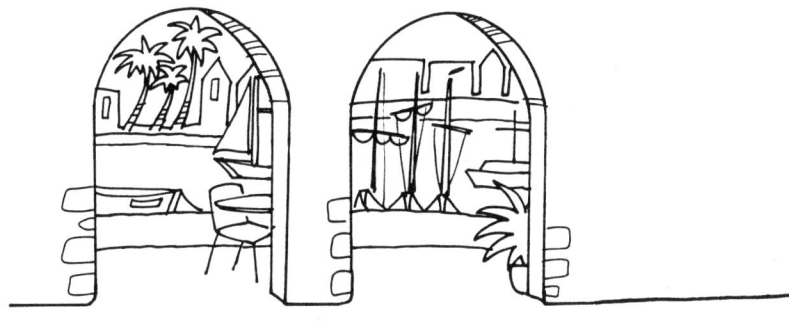

4 What is the greatest amount which can be saved by buying a season ticket for
  (a) the stalls
  (b) the balcony?

5 Vera bought a season ticket for the stalls and Tom bought one for the balcony. They each managed to attend only 9 shows. Did either of them save any money by buying a season ticket? Explain.

6 Janine spent £40·50 more than she needed to because she bought a balcony season ticket but missed some shows. How many shows did she manage to attend?

Special offer
Adult season tickets for **12 shows**.
Stalls £110
Balcony £170

© SPMG 1996. Restricted copyright cleared.

Heinemann Mathematics P7

Farm kits

Percentages: link with fractions, calculations based on 10%
Heinemann Mathematics P7
Textbook page 46 and 47

18

1. Kitbits Company makes *Tractor* kits.
   60% of the tractors have cabins.
   What **fraction** of the tractors have cabins?

2. Write as a fraction in simplest form.
   (a) 30% (b) 45% (c) 8% (d) 85% (e) 32% (f) 18%

3. There 80 pieces in the *Farm Animals* kit.
   10% of the pieces are cows, 25% are sheep,
   50% are chickens and the rest are pigs.
   How many of each type of animal are there?

4. Find **mentally**.
   (a) 50% of 30 (b) 10% of 120 (c) 25% of 28 (d) 1% of 400 (e) 50% of 180
   (f) 25% of 52 (g) 1% of 700   (h) 10% of 850 (i) 75% of 80   (j) 75% of 36

5. The table shows the number of
   Farm Building kits made in
   three months. In each month,
   - 50% were farmhouses
   - 25% were barns
   - 10% were stables.
   How many of each type of
   building were made in
   (a) June (b) July (c) August?

Months	June	July	August
Number of kits	480	1260	3040

6. In September, 2450 *Off-road Vehicle*
   kits were made. 10% were battery operated
   and 30% were radio controlled.
   How many were radio controlled?

7. Find
   (a) 20% of 250 (b) 30% of 460 (c) 40% of 330 (d) 70% of 210 (e) 60% of 190

8.
   Tractor kits
   Today's target
   180

   15% of the target had been reached
   by 10 am, 50% by 12 noon and 75% by 4pm.
   How many tractors had been made by
   (a) 10 am (b) 12 noon (c) 4 pm?

9. Find
   (a) 15% of 320 (b) 15% of 860 (c) 15% of 780 (d) 15% of 2000 (e) 15% of 5400

10. **Farm Vehicles**
    24 000

    75% of the vehicles were tractors.
    15% of the **tractors** had trailers.
    How many tractors had trailers?

© SPMG 1996. Restricted copyright cleared.

Heinemann Mathematics P7

Taking orders

Percentages: fractions as percentages
Heinemann Mathematics P7
Textbook page 49

19

1 Write the number of jigsaws ordered in each size as a **fraction** and as a **percentage** of each shop's **total order**.

(a)
Order for Toyworld	
size	number
small	13
medium	29
large	58
total	100

(b)
Order for Playtime	
size	number
small	35
medium	22
large	43
total	100

(c)
Order for Gamezone	
size	number
small	27
medium	11
large	62
total	100

2 Write the number of large *Buildakits* as a fraction and as a percentage of each total order.

Buildakit orders

	(a)	(b)	(c)	(d)	(e)	(f)	(g)	(h)
Large	12	10	37	4	17	13	3	29
Total	50	25	50	20	25	20	25	50

3 A Kitbits delivery van is carrying
- 6 crates of Constructakits
- 4 crates of Buildakits
and
- 10 crates of Electrokits.

Write each number of crates as a fraction and as a percentage of the **total** number of crates.

4 The delivery van made 24 deliveries on Tuesday, 6 of them in the morning. What percentage of deliveries were made in the morning?

5 Write each fraction as a percentage.

(a) $\frac{3}{12}$ (b) $\frac{7}{14}$ (c) $\frac{6}{60}$ (d) $\frac{18}{24}$ (e) $\frac{9}{36}$ (f) $\frac{45}{90}$ (g) $\frac{900}{1000}$

Another code competition

Percentages: fractions, decimals
Heinemann Mathematics P7
Textbook page 50

20

Kitbits Company sent out this Trial Card to those wishing to try their second Code Competition.

Kitbits Competition Trial Card

1. Change each fraction to (a) a decimal (b) a percentage.

   $\frac{1}{4}$ $\frac{3}{20}$ $\frac{29}{100}$ $\frac{41}{50}$ $\frac{7}{25}$

2. Change each decimal to (a) a fraction (b) a percentage.

   0·37   0·58   0·3   0·8   0·07

3. Change each percentage to (a) a decimal (b) a fraction.

   63%   20%   24%   6%   1%

Competition Code

4.

| $\frac{3}{4}$ → A | 18% → B | 40% → G | 5% → I |
| $\frac{1}{2}$ → K | 0·15 → N | 0·06 → S | 0·22 → T |

To enter the prize draw decode the message correctly.

| 0·4 | $\frac{5}{100}$ | 75% | $\frac{3}{20}$ | 22% | | 0·18 | 0·75 | $\frac{11}{50}$ | 0·05 | 50% | | 0·5 | $\frac{1}{20}$ | $\frac{22}{100}$ | 6% |

5. Of the people who decoded the message correctly in the competition, 0·34 were adults, $\frac{9}{25}$ were girls and the rest were boys.
   (a) What percentage of the correct messages were sent by boys?
   (b) Did more boys or more girls send correct messages?

6. The table shows the fraction of the correct messages sent from England, Scotland and Northern Ireland in each of four weeks.

Country	Week 1	Week 2	Week 3	Week 4
England	0·63	0·6	0·56	0·7
Scotland	$\frac{9}{50}$	$\frac{23}{100}$	$\frac{6}{25}$	$\frac{3}{20}$
Northern Ireland	19%			

(a) Copy and complete the table, writing **every** fraction as a percentage.
(b) In which weeks did more correct messages come from Scotland than Northern Ireland?

Plant experiments

Pattern: formulae using symbols
Heinemann Mathematics P7
Textbook pages 54 and 55

21

Plant experiments are carried out at Global Research Technology.

Weedout! Add 5 drops for each litre of water.

Weedclear Add one drop for each litre of water and then add 2 more drops.

1 For each of the weedkillers,
  (a) make a table like this →
  (b) write a rule in words for finding the number of drops
  (c) write a formula for **D** the number of drops, which uses **L** the number of litres of water.

Number of litres (L)	Number of drops (D)
1	→
2	→
3	
4	
5	
6	

2 For each table, write a formula for **D** using **L**.

(a)
L	D
1 →	7
2 →	14
3 →	21
4 →	28

(b)
L	D
5 →	3
6 →	4
7 →	5
8 →	6

(c)
L	D
4 →	1
8 →	2
12 →	3
16 →	4

(d)
L	D
2 →	9
3 →	10
4 →	11
5 →	12

Global Research Technology
Packet of Mystery seeds £4.
Trays £1 each.

3 (a) Make a table like this to show the cost of **one packet** of Mystery seeds and 1, 2, 3 . . . . 6 trays.
  (b) Write a formula for the cost **C**, using **T**.

  C = ☐

  (c) Use the formula to find the cost of **one** packet of Mystery seeds and
    • 10 trays • 12 trays • 20 trays.

Number of trays (T)	Cost in £ of seeds and trays (C)
1 →	5
2	
3	
4	
5	
6	

4 For each formula, find **K** when **N** = 15.
  (a) K = 4 × N   (b) K = N + 10   (c) K = N − 5   (d) K = N ÷ 3

Small creatures

Length: millimetres
Heinemann Mathematics P7
Textbook page 68

22

The length of this Dragonfly is
73 mm or **7 cm and 3 mm** or **7·3 cm**

Dragonfly

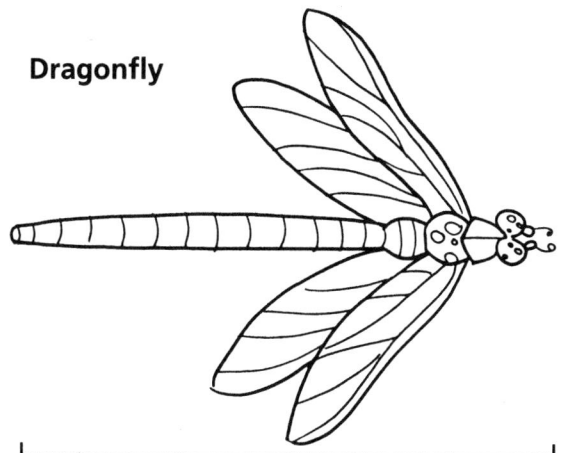

1 Measure then write the lengths of these creatures in the same three ways.

(a) **Great Pond Snail**

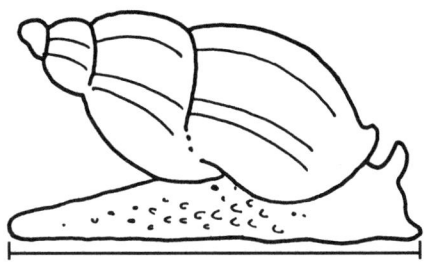

(b) **Grass Frog**

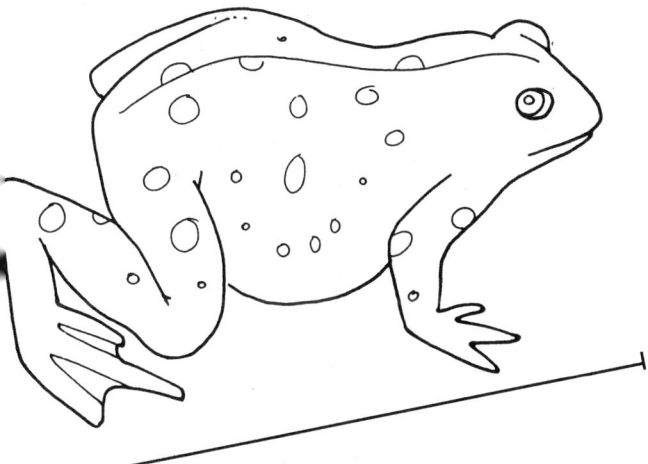

(c) **Square-tailed Worm**

(d) **Water Spider**

(e) **Dragonfly Nymph**

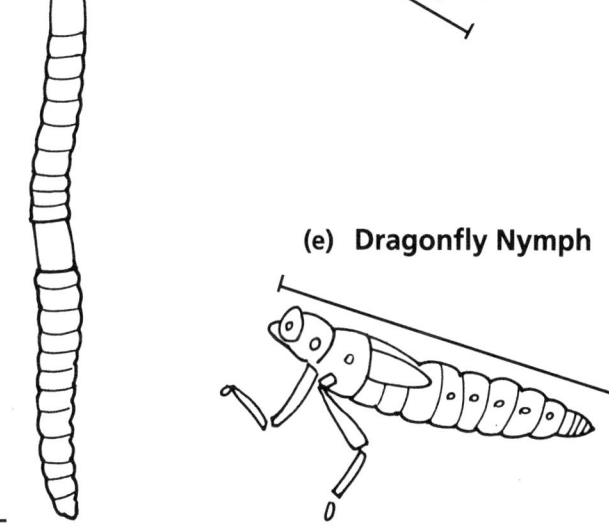

2 Write in millimetres.
(a) 6 cm 6 mm (b) 9 cm (c) $6\frac{1}{2}$ cm (d) 2·1 cm (e) 0·3 cm

3 Write in centimetres.
(a) 34 mm (b) 80 mm (c) 6 mm (d) 3 cm 1 mm

4 List these creatures in order, starting with the shortest.

Name	Length
Sludge Worm	5 cm 9 mm
Palmate Newt	9·0 cm
Raft Spider	19 mm
Pea Clam	0·9 cm
Whirligig Beetle Larva	1·8 cm

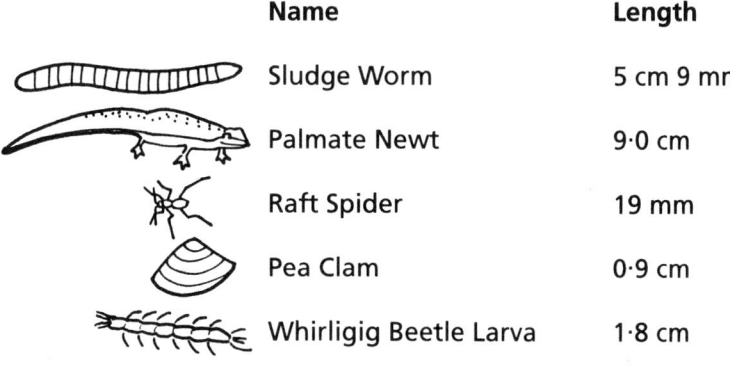

Name	Length: drawing to scale
	Heinemann Mathematics P7 Workbook page 15

Walled garden

1 (a) Use centimetre squared paper Draw rectangular areas for these garden plots.
Use a scale of **1 cm to 10 m**.

Fruit bushes: 80 m by 50 m	Rose bed: 85 m by 20 m
Lawn: 105 m by 80 m	Flower border: 120 m by 15 m

(b) Colour, label and cut out your drawings. Arrange them on the plan below leaving
  • paths between the areas
  • a rectangular area for greenhouses.
Stick your drawings in place.

(c) Draw a rectangular area for your greenhouses.

Calculate the true length ——— and breadth ——— of your greenhouse area.

Walled garden　　　　　　　　　　　　　　　　**Scale : 1 cm to 10 m**

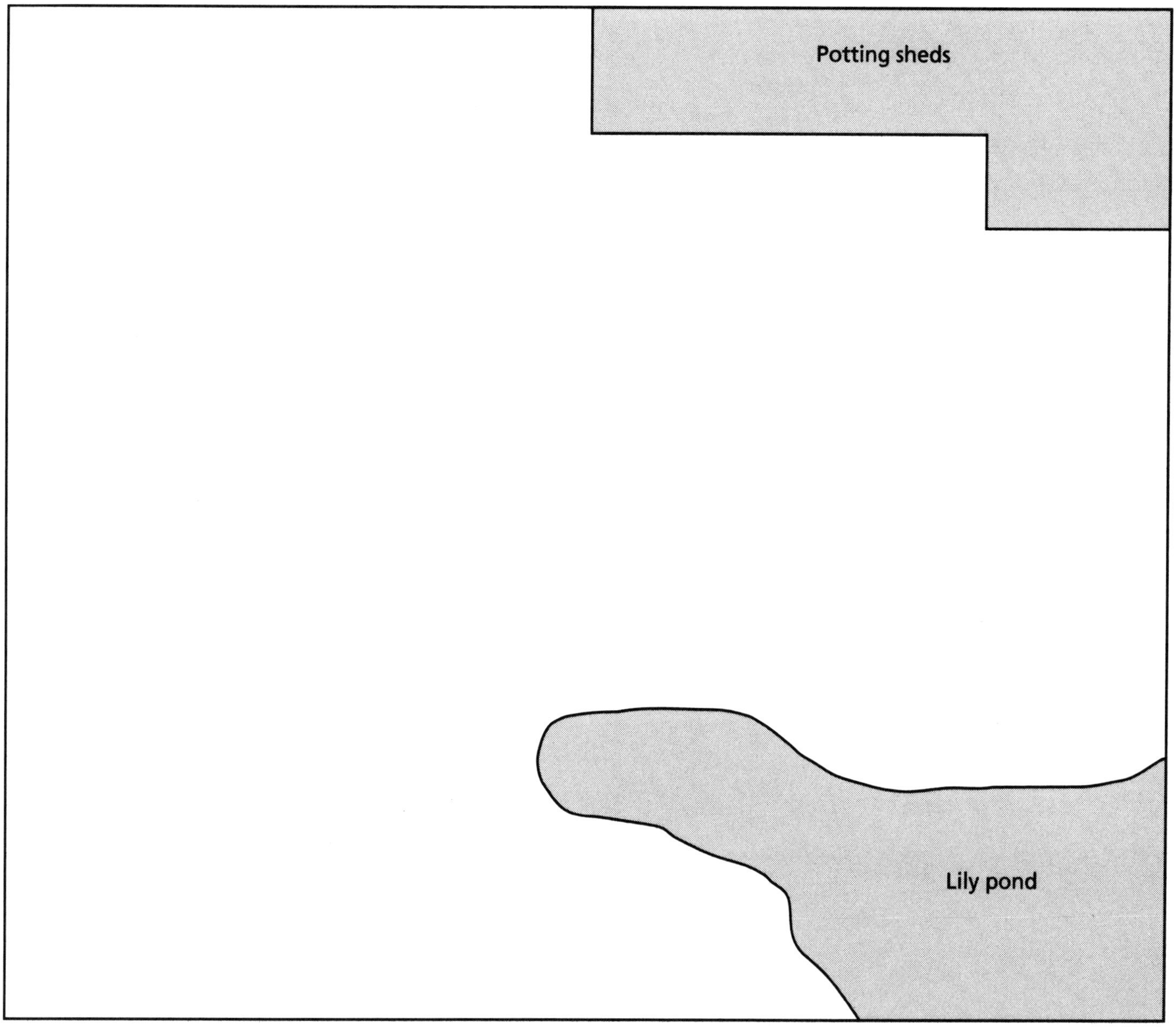

Potting sheds

Lily pond

© SPMG 1996. Restricted copyright cleared.

Label designs

Area: composite shapes
Heinemann Mathematics P7
Textbook page 76

24

1 Measure, then calculate the area of each label.

(a)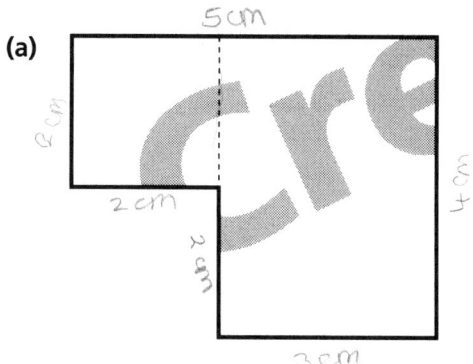

(b)

(c)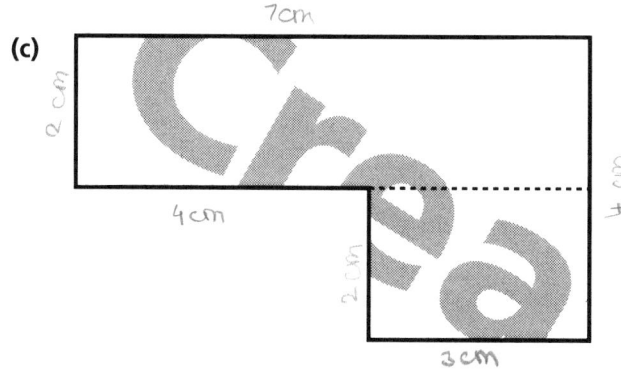

(d)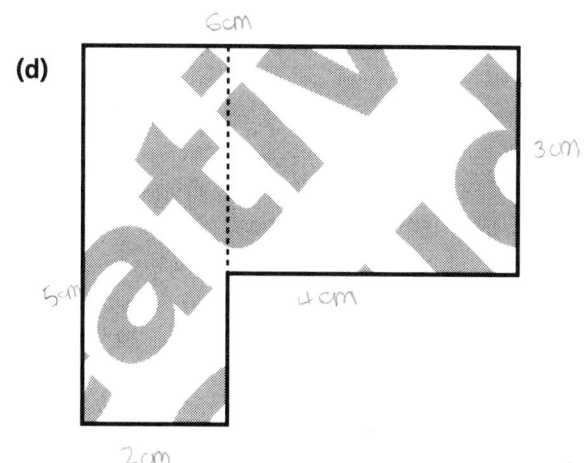

2 Sketch each label and calculate its area.

(a)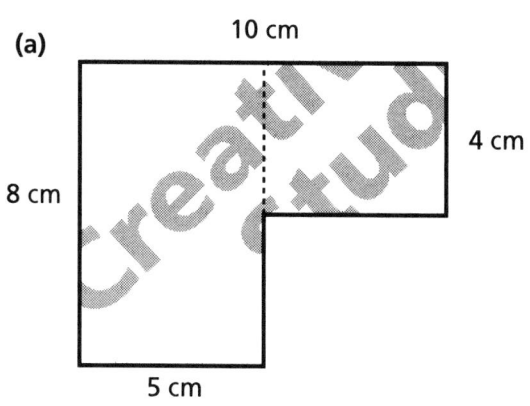

(b)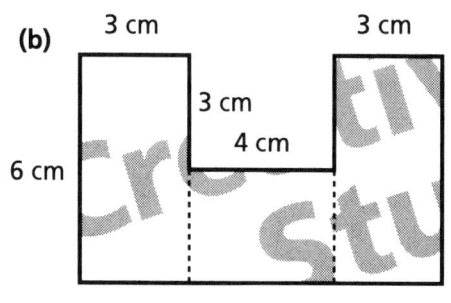

(c)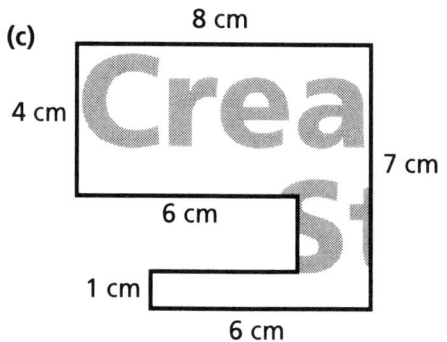

(d)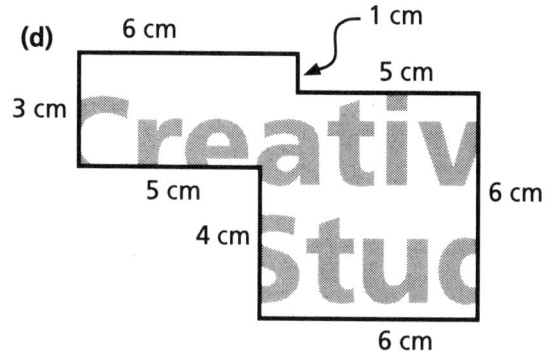

© SPMG 1996. Restricted copyright cleared.

Name	Area: right-angled triangles
	Heinemann Mathematics P7
	Workbook page 25, Textbook page 77

Lick 'n' stickers

Lick 'n' stickers are given away with breakfast cereals.

1 Draw the surrounding rectangle for each triangle. Find the area of each sticker.

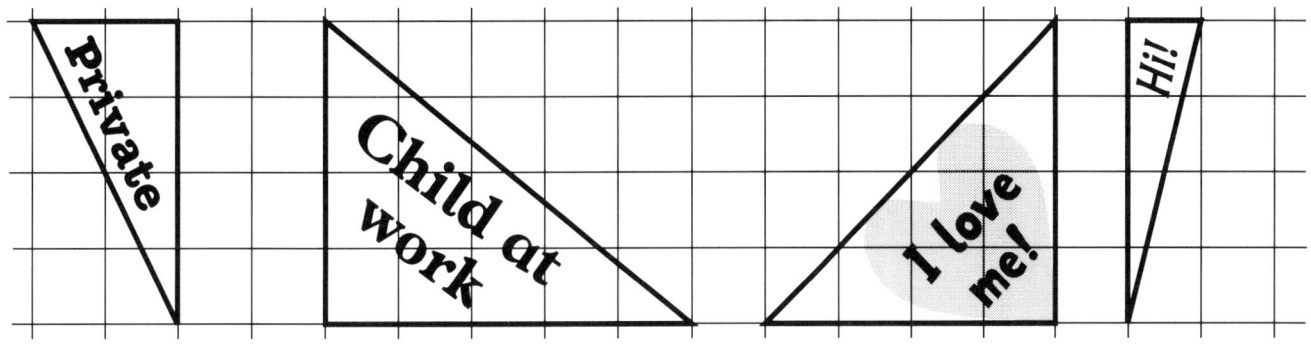

Area = ____ cm²   Area = _____   Area = _____   Area = _____

2 Measure, then calculate the area of each sticker.

Area = ____ cm²   Area = _____   Area = _____

3 Find the area of each of these right-angled triangles:

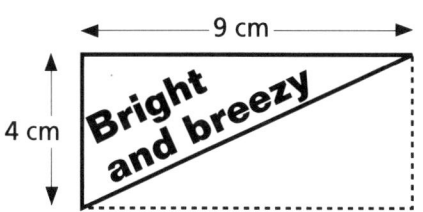

Area of rectangle = ____ cm²

Area of triangle = $\frac{1}{2}$ of ____ = ____ cm²

Area of rectangle = _____

Area of triangle = _____

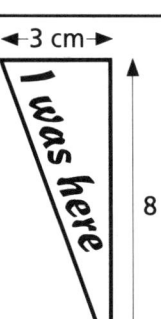

Area of rectangle = _____

Area of triangle = _____

Area of rectangle = _____

Area of triangle = _____

© SPMG 1996. Restricted copyright cleared.   Heinemann Mathematics P7

Name	Area: composite shapes	26
	Heinemann Mathematics P7 Workbook page 26	

Doodles

Doodles sells a range of artist's materials.

1 Divide each label into rectangles and right-angled triangles then find its area.

Area = _____ cm^2

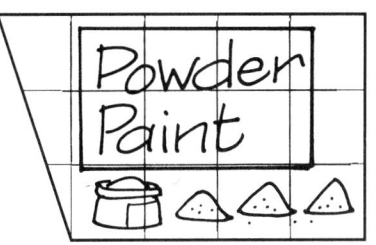

Area = _____

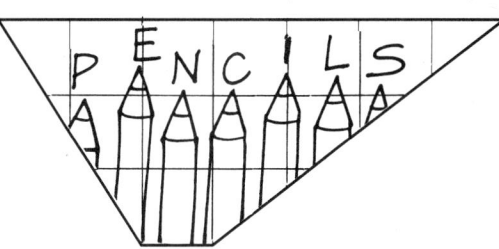

Area = _____

2 Measure, then calculate the area of each label.

Area = _____ cm^2

Area = _____

Area = _____

3 Calculate the area of each label.

8 cm 6 cm
5 cm

Area = _____ cm^2

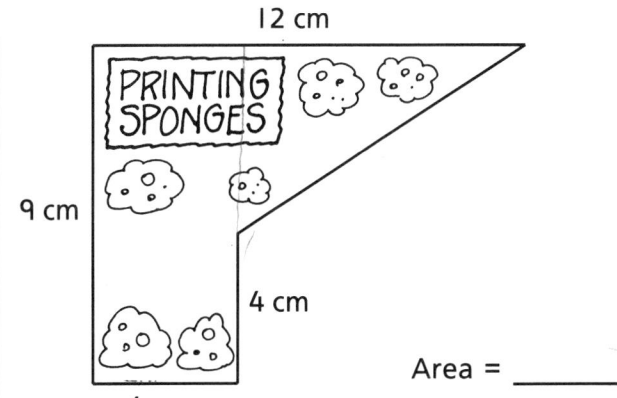

12 cm
9 cm
4 cm
4 cm

Area = _____

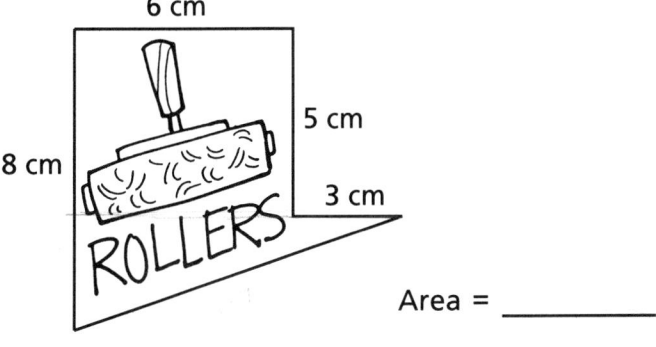

6 cm
8 cm 5 cm
3 cm

Area = _____

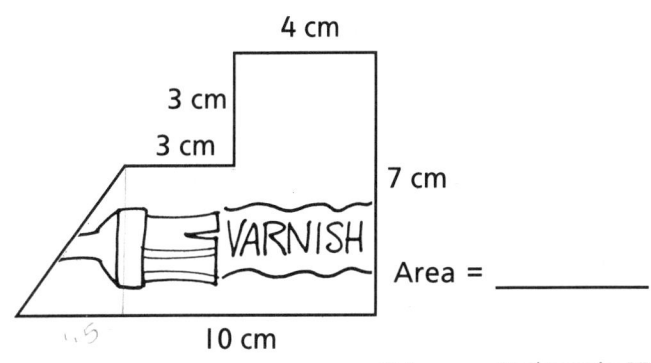

4 cm
3 cm
3 cm
7 cm
10 cm

Area = _____

© SPMG 1996. Restricted copyright cleared.

Running speeds

Speed: metres per second, kilometres per hour
Heinemann Mathematics P7
Textbook pages 85 and 86

27

1 Global Research Technology gathered this information for a project.
Find the speed of each animal in **metres per second**.

Greyhound
180 metres
in 12 seconds

Horse
840 metres
in 1 minute

Fox
116 metres
in 8 seconds

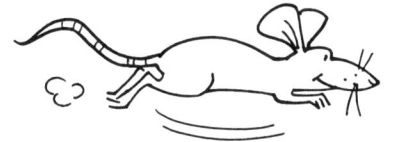

Rat
403 metres
in 65 seconds

2 The table shows winning times at GRT's Annual Family Sports.

(a) Find the speed of each winner in metres per second, **to the nearest whole number**.

(b) Who do you think would win a race between the person and the animal in question 1 that ran **about** the same distance? Explain.

Race	Winner	Time
100 m	Elton	11 seconds
200 m	Lesley	26 seconds
400 m	Jan	54 seconds
800 m	Wes	1 minute and 58 seconds

3 Each animal was taken home after the project was finished.

144 km
in 3 hours

196 km
in 5 hours

258 km
in 6 hours

93 km
in 2 hours

(a) Calculate the speed of each vehicle in **kilometres per hour**.

(b) How far would van **3** travel in 4 hours at this speed?

4 The table shows distances and times for journeys to Scotland. Find the speed of each vehicle in kilometres per hour, to **the nearest whole number**.

Vehicle	Distance	Time
1	355 km	8 hours
2	341 km	6 hours
3	520 km	9 hours
4	395 km	7 hours

Time: 24-hour clock, durations

Heinemann Mathematics P7
Textbook pages 88 and 89

28

Hotel Sublimo

07:45

The clock shows when Miguel, the hotel clerk, starts work.

1 Write each time from his day as a 24-hour time.

(a) phone bus company 8 am
(b) exchange currency 3 pm
(c) check-in new guests 10.30 am
(d) arrange day-trips 1.40 pm
(e) book taxis 3.15 pm
(f) meet tour guides 11.55 am
(g) finish work 4.06 pm
(h) lunch with manager 12 noon

2 Write each time as a 12-hour time. Use am or pm.
(a) 05.20 (b) 22.22 (c) 00.30 (d) 06.00 (e) 12.59
(f) 16.42 (g) 20.00 (h) 07.07 (i) 10.10 (j) 00.01

Yvonne, the film star, is a guest at the Hotel Sublimo. This is part of her schedule for one day.

July 25	
08.10	Wake-up call
09.05 – 09.40	Breakfast
10.25 – 11.05	Interview
11.10 – 12.15	Sunbathing
12.55 – 13.50	Lunch
14.00 – 14.55	Photo session
15.05	Start of coach trip
21.40	Coach returns

3 (a) How long after her wake-up call did Yvonne **start** breakfast?
(b) How long did she spend being interviewed?
(c) Which took more time, breakfast or lunch? How much more time?
(d) For how many **minutes** did she sunbathe?
(e) How much time did the coach trip take?
(f) Which activity took most time, apart from the coach trip?
(g) Yvonne went to bed at midnight. How long was this after the coach returned?

© SPMG 1996. Restricted copyright cleared.

Weekend in London

Time: 24-hour clock, counting on and counting back
Heinemann Mathematics P7
Workbook page 16, Textbook pages 90 and 91

29

1. One Friday, five friends travelled to London to spend a weekend together.

	Karen	Dawn	Ayesha	Naomi	Frances
Left home at	14.45	08.55	18.20	15.30	17.50
Journey-time	3 hours	7 hours	55 minutes	45 minutes	25 minutes

   (a) Find the arrival time for each person.
   (b) Who arrived first?

2. The friends all left their hotel at 09.45 on Saturday morning.
   They were away from the hotel for the following times:

   Dawn – 2 hours 10 minutes   **Karen** – 1 hours 40 minutes
   Ayesha and Naomi – $2\frac{1}{2}$ hours   **Frances** – 1 hour 55 minutes

   (a) When did each person return to the hotel?
   (b) They started lunch as soon as they had **all** returned to the hotel.
       It took 1 hour 35 minutes. When did they finish lunch?

3. This table shows where they went on Saturday evening.

	Karen and Ayesha	Naomi	Dawn and Frances
Where they went	to a party	to her Gran's	to the theatre
Time away from hotel	3 hours	1 hour 25 minutes	2 hours 50 minutes

   (a) They all returned to the hotel at 23.30. When did each person leave the hotel?
   (b) Karen and Ayesha left the party at 23.10 after being there for 1 hour 35 minutes.
       When did they arrive at the party?

4. Ayesha, Dawn and Naomi all arrived home at 16.30 on Sunday.
   Their journeys took the same time as in question 1.
   When did each of them leave London?

© SPMG 1996. Restricted copyright cleared.

Angles

You need a protractor.

1 For each angle
- write acute, obtuse or reflex
- measure its size in degrees.

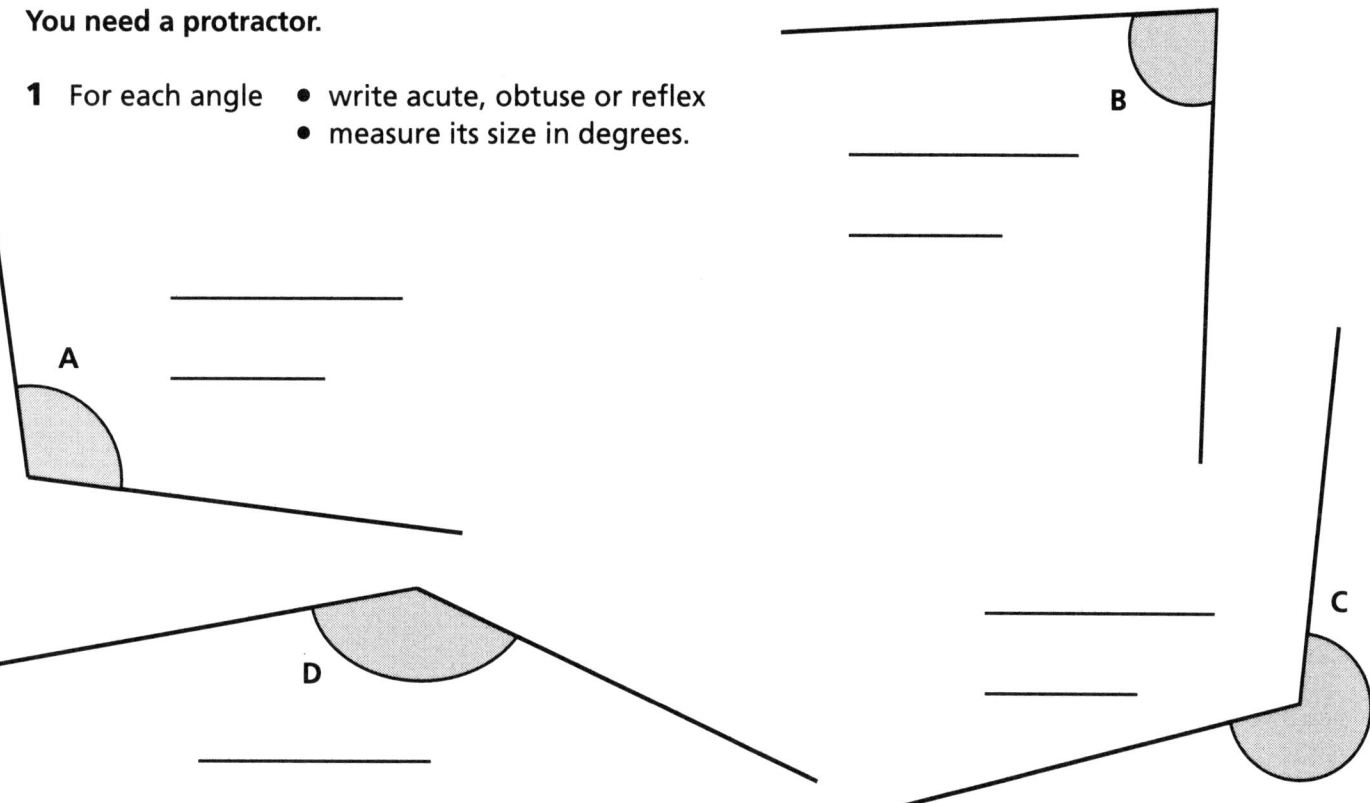

2 Measure and write the size of each marked angle.

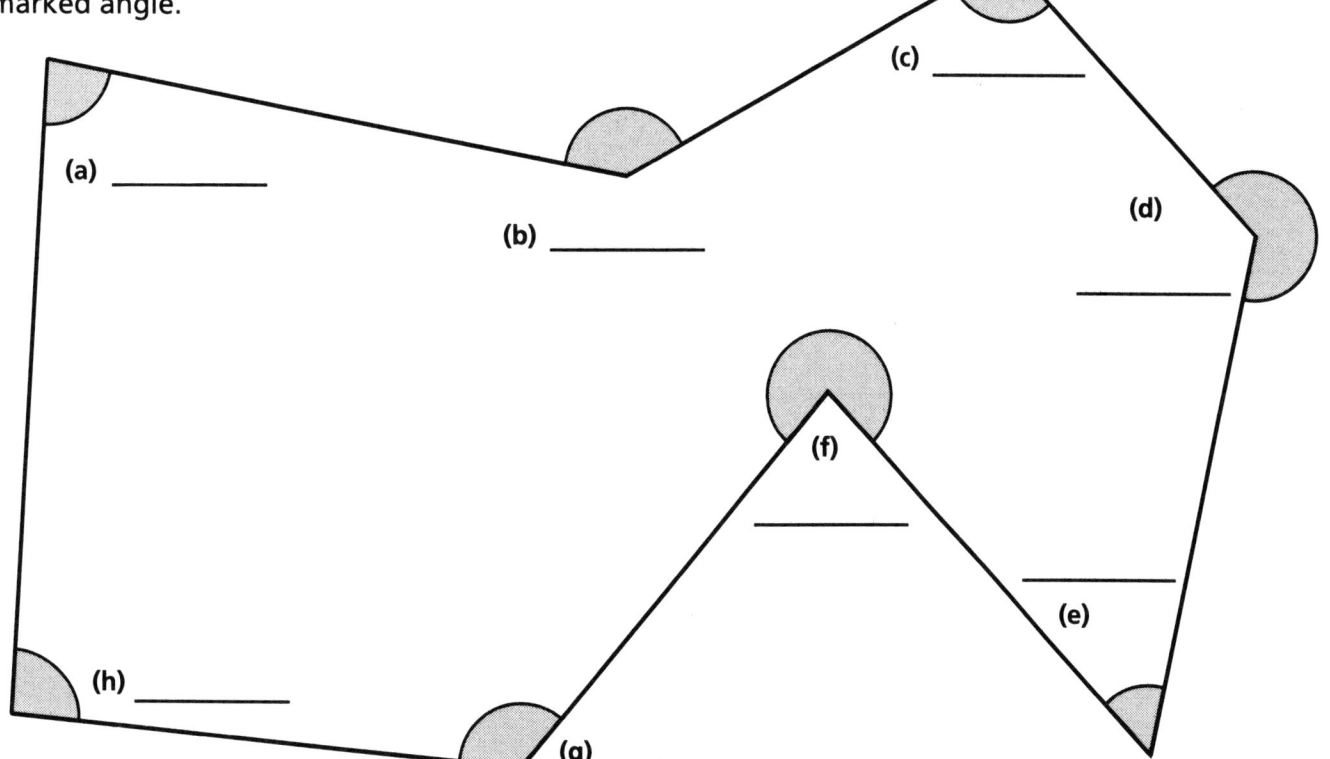

Shape talk

2D Shape: sides, angles
Heinemann Mathematics P7
Textbook pages 101 and 102

31

1 This shape folds along the line of symmetry as shown.

Copy and complete:
The shape has _____ equal sides.
It has _____ of equal angles.

2 Which three- or four-sided shape is each person talking about?

It has three equal sides and three equal angles.

It has no line of symmetry and fits its own outline in exactly two ways in one complete turn.

It has exactly two pairs of equal sides, two equal angles and one line of symmetry.

It has exactly two equal angles, two equal sides and one line of symmetry.

3 (a) Which four-sided shapes **could** each of these clues describe?

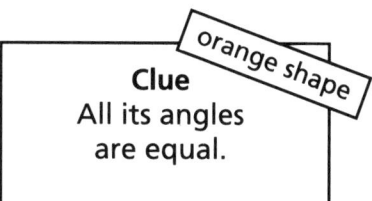

Clue — orange shape
All its angles are equal.

Clue — yellow shape
It fits its own outline in exactly two ways in one complete turn.

(b) Write a second clue for each so that there is **only one** possible
  • orange shape • yellow shape.

Sponsors for the cycle-cross

Handling data: class intervals
Heinemann Mathematics P7
Workbook page 34, Textbook page 114

32

1 The table shows the number of sponsors for each child who took part in the cycle-cross.

Number of sponsors									
11	13	18	4	26	20	32	28	47	56
12	3	7	20	28	33	11	25	27	34
14	19	26	32	30	24	26	22	36	48
6	10	18	24	12	30	19	26	31	14
8	14	22	30	36	17	21	18	26	12

(a) How many children were sponsored?

(b) What is the range of the number of sponsors?

2 (a) How many class intervals are shown on the graph?
  (b) How many children are there in the class interval
   • 13–24   • 49–60?
  (c) How many children had
   • less than 25 sponsors
   • more than 36 sponsors?

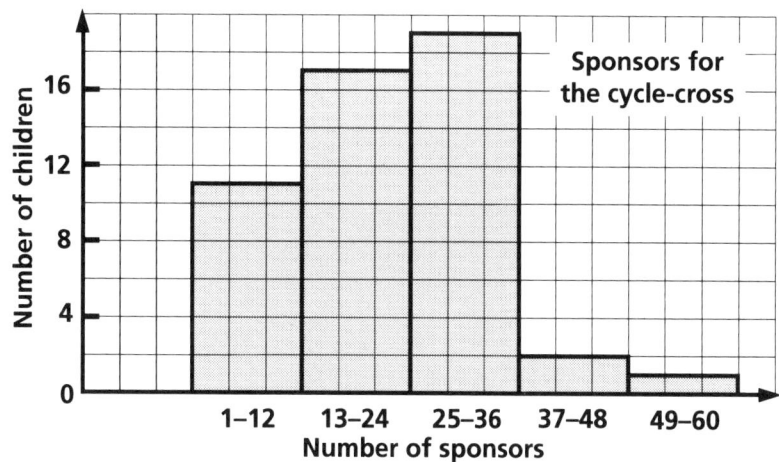

3 The graph shows the sponsorship money collected by **some** of the children.

How many children's sponsorship money is shown?

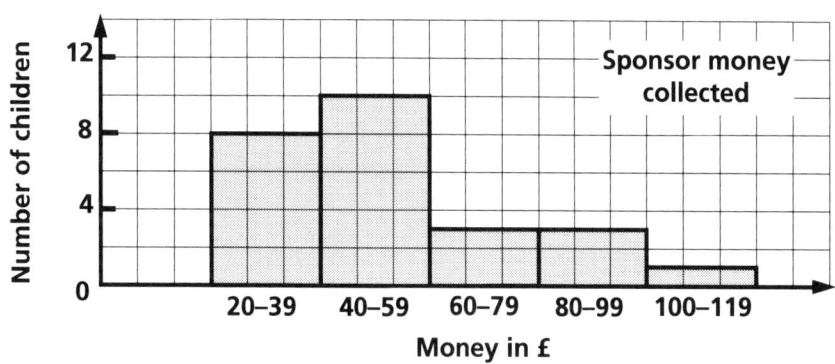

4 The sponsorship money collected by the other children is shown in this table.

Sponsorship money in £						
45	20	90	80	110	100	30
95	30	40	45	50	40	60
25	45	50	80	100	35	50
40	65	75	45			

Use the same class intervals as in the graph above to
(a) make a frequency table
(b) draw a graph
(c) find the number of these children with sponsorship money
  • less than £60
  • £60 or more.

Answers

1 Droids at work

1 (a) 81 rods in container A (b) 37 rods
44 rods in container B

2 (a) 41 (b) 23 (c) 62 (d) 17 (e) 72
(f) 70 (g) 17 (h) 61 (i) 29 (j) 97
(k) 27 (l) 69 (m) 91 (n) 37 (o) 80

3 gloves 120   helmets 190   lasers 210
drills 198   boots 235   visors 218

4 (a) 80 and 110 (b) 210 and 110
(c) 80 and 230

5 (a) 134 (b) 133 (c) 199 (d) 215 (e) 258
(f) 112 (g) 107 (h) 238 (i) 119 (j) 413
(k) 216 (l) 276 (m) 317 (n) 211 (o) 435

6 (a) 28 (b) 39 (c) 48 (d) 38
(e) 70 (f) 66 (g) 56 (h) 60

Orders of calculation depend on children's choice.

2 Zarco's command centre

1 fuel   4000 galactolitres
air   7000 galactolitres
cargo   6000 galactograms
distance   2000 galactometres

2 (a) 4000 (b) 8000 (c) 3000 (d) 9000
(e) 8000 (f) 13 000 (g) 21 000 (h) 18 000
(i) 34 000 (j) 62 000 (k) 28 000 (l) 43 000

3 Fuel   4200 galactolitres
Air   6800 galactolitres

4 (a) 2400 (b) 8400 (c) 2800 (d) 7100
(e) 15 300 (f) 32 300 (g) 19 600 (h) 66 700
(i) 41 400 or 41 500 (j) 70 000

5 (a) about 6000 Varum rods
(b) about 9000 Ambal rods
(c) about 6000 Rodon rods

6 (a) about 6000 (b) about 8000
(c) about 5000 (d) about 7000
(e) about 31 000 (f) about 17 000
(g) about 11 000 (h) about 20 000
(i) about 32 000

3 Work camps

1 (a) 250 workers (b) 1490 workers
(c) 2600 workers

2 (a) 430 (b) 950 (c) 1380 (d) 1040
(e) 6000

3 (a) 3600 credits (b) 12 700 credits
(c) 34 000 credits

4 (a) 6500 (b) 2000 (c) 40 700
(d) 82 000 (e) 24 300 (f) 70 000

5 (a) 58 000 phone units
(b) 102 000 phone units
(c) 480 000 phone units

6 (a) 72 000 (b) 89 000 (c) 205 000
(d) 362 000 (e) 490 000 (f) 273 000

7 (a) 108 energy packs (b) 144 energy packs

8 (a) 68 (b) 75 (c) 78
(d) 38 (e) 108 (f) 119

9 (a) 120 food packs (b) 200 food packs
(c) 320 food packs (d) 360 food packs

10 (a) 120 (b) 420 (c) 720 (d) 240
(e) 560 (f) 1200 (g) 3500 (h) 1600
(i) 3600 (j) 4000

11 (a) 800 (b) 1800 (c) 4900 (d) 4000
(e) 5400

12 (a) about 800 (b) about 300
(c) about 600 (d) about 800
(e) about 800 or about 1000

4 Lineum crystals

1 (a) 8 boxes (b) 25 boxes (c) 150 boxes

2 (a) 34 (b) 57 (c) 476 (d) 2200 (e) 1076

3 January 87 credits   March 154 credits
May 210 credits   July 300 credits
September 1076 credits

4 Lineum crystals – continued

4 (a) 68 (b) 90 (c) 392 (d) 903 (e) 3500

5 (a) 6 gg (b) 26 gg (c) 705 gg
   (d) 290 gg (e) 80 gg (f) 800 gg

6 (a) 530 (b) 15 (c) 76
   (d) 410 (e) 1010 (f) 9000
   (g) 600 (h) 30 000 (i) 110

7 40 crates

8 (a) 40 (b) 50 (c) 30 (d) 60 (e) 70
   (f) 40 (g) 90 (h) 70 (i) 60 (j) 80

5 Transporters

1 12 842 600

2 (a) 103 400 000 galactoseconds
   (b) 94 024 000 galactoseconds
   (c) 3 105 050 galactoseconds

3 (a) thirty-two million, four hundred and five thousand galactoseconds
   (b) one hundred and forty-three million, two hundred and forty thousand, seven hundred galactoseconds
   (c) seven million, forty-six thousand, three hundred and fifty galactoseconds
   (d) one hundred million, three hundred and seven thousand and sixty galactoseconds

4 Zarco 300 000 000, 1 000 000, 4000
   Nina 80 000 000, 90 000, 50
   Marco 90 000 000, 800 000, 3000

5 (a) Zarco
   (b) Zarco, Marco
   (c) Nina
   (d) Marco
   (e) Nina, Marco

6 Nina −10 000 000
   Marco +100 000 000
   Maria +10 000
   Joa −100 000

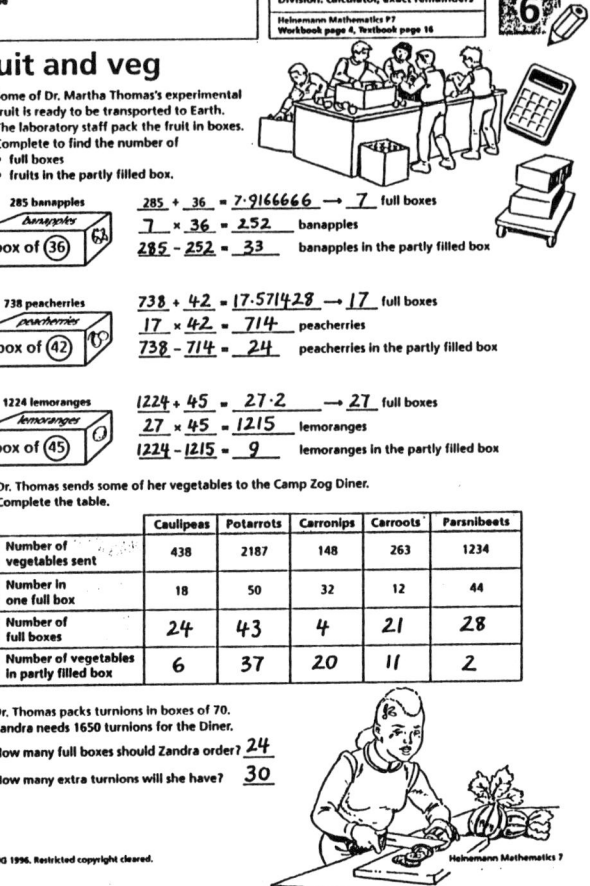

7 Droids on Planet Ag

1 (a) Multiplying the two unit digits 8 × 2 gives 16. The units digit in the answers must be 6.
   (b) 125 696

2 (a) 8250 (b) 28 476 (c) 280 021
   (d) 1212 (e) 56 088 (f) 4444

3 (a) 23 420 gg (b) 7230 gg
   (c) 31 200 gg (d) 35 000 gg

8 Mosaics

1. (a) $\frac{5}{6} = \frac{15}{18}$ (b) $\frac{5}{8} = \frac{10}{16}$

2. (a) $\frac{3}{5} = \frac{6}{10}$ (b) $\frac{1}{3} = \frac{5}{15}$ (c) $\frac{7}{8} = \frac{14}{16}$
   (d) $\frac{7}{10} = \frac{35}{50}$ (e) $\frac{1}{2} = \frac{6}{12}$ (f) $\frac{3}{4} = \frac{12}{16}$
   (g) $\frac{5}{6} = \frac{20}{24}$ (h) $\frac{9}{50} = \frac{18}{100}$

3. (a) $\frac{12}{20} = \frac{6}{10}$ (b) $\frac{16}{24} = \frac{4}{6}$

4. (a) $\frac{9}{12} = \frac{3}{4}$ (b) $\frac{8}{20} = \frac{2}{5}$ (c) $\frac{35}{50} = \frac{7}{10}$
   (d) $\frac{30}{42} = \frac{5}{7}$ (e) $\frac{27}{36} = \frac{3}{4}$ (f) $\frac{12}{32} = \frac{3}{8}$
   (g) $\frac{63}{81} = \frac{7}{9}$ (h) $\frac{14}{35} = \frac{2}{5}$

5. (a) $\frac{60}{90}$ ÷10 = $\frac{6}{9}$ ÷3 = $\frac{2}{3}$
   (b) $\frac{24}{60}$ ÷6 = $\frac{4}{10}$ ÷2 = $\frac{2}{5}$
   (c) $\frac{36}{48}$ ÷4 = $\frac{9}{12}$ ÷3 = $\frac{3}{4}$

6. (a) $\frac{1}{4}$ (b) $\frac{3}{4}$ (c) $\frac{3}{5}$ (d) $\frac{3}{5}$ (e) $\frac{2}{5}$
   (f) $\frac{2}{5}$ (g) $\frac{3}{8}$ (h) $\frac{1}{3}$ (i) $\frac{3}{4}$ (j) $\frac{4}{5}$
   (k) $\frac{7}{9}$ (l) $\frac{5}{6}$

9 Kitbits Shapes packs

1. small $\frac{1}{2}$, standard $\frac{2}{5}$, medium $\frac{1}{2}$, large $\frac{2}{5}$, extra large $\frac{2}{3}$

2. (a) circles $\frac{1}{12}$, squares $\frac{1}{2}$, rectangles $\frac{1}{4}$, triangles $\frac{1}{6}$
   (b) circles $\frac{1}{9}$, squares $\frac{2}{9}$, rectangles $\frac{1}{15}$, triangles $\frac{3}{5}$

3. (a) $2\frac{1}{4}, \frac{9}{4}$ (b) $1\frac{3}{5}, \frac{8}{5}$
   (c) $4\frac{2}{3}, \frac{14}{3}$ (d) $3\frac{5}{8}, \frac{29}{8}$

4. (a) $\frac{15}{8}$ (b) $\frac{18}{5}$ (c) $\frac{19}{8}$ (d) $\frac{22}{5}$ (e) $\frac{7}{3}$
   (f) $\frac{37}{10}$ (g) $\frac{17}{6}$

5. (a) $3\frac{1}{3}$ (b) $3\frac{3}{4}$ (c) $3\frac{2}{5}$ (d) $3\frac{5}{6}$
   (e) $2\frac{1}{2}$ (f) $2\frac{1}{3}$ (g) $3\frac{1}{2}$ (h) $2\frac{2}{3}$
   (i) 3 (j) $1\frac{1}{3}$ (k) $2\frac{5}{7}$ (l) 5
   (m) $5\frac{5}{7}$ (n) $6\frac{1}{3}$

10 Kitbits colourama

1. $1\frac{1}{5}$ kg

2. (a) $\frac{4}{5}$ (b) $\frac{1}{2}$ (c) $\frac{2}{3}$ (d) $1\frac{1}{10}$ (e) $1\frac{1}{4}$
   (f) $1\frac{1}{4}$

3. (a) $\frac{2}{5}$ (b) $\frac{3}{7}$ (c) $\frac{1}{4}$ (d) $\frac{2}{5}$ (e) $\frac{1}{3}$ (f) $\frac{3}{5}$

4. $1\frac{3}{4}$ l

5. (a) $2\frac{2}{3}$ (b) $3\frac{3}{4}$ (c) $2\frac{1}{3}$ (d) $1\frac{3}{5}$ (e) $2\frac{1}{2}$
   (f) $3\frac{2}{3}$

6. (a) $2\frac{1}{5}$ (b) $3\frac{1}{2}$ (c) $4\frac{2}{5}$ (d) $5\frac{4}{7}$
   (e) $3\frac{1}{2}$ (f) 2 (g) $3\frac{1}{2}$ (h) $3\frac{2}{5}$
   (i) $4\frac{3}{5}$ (j) $2\frac{1}{4}$ (k) $3\frac{2}{3}$ (l) $4\frac{1}{4}$

7. $2\frac{2}{5}$ kg

8. (a) $2\frac{3}{8}$ (b) $3\frac{2}{5}$ (c) $1\frac{3}{7}$ (d) $4\frac{2}{3}$ (e) $3\frac{2}{5}$
   (f) $2\frac{1}{4}$

9. (a) $2\frac{3}{5}$ (b) $1\frac{4}{7}$ (c) $3\frac{5}{6}$ (d) $1\frac{3}{4}$
   (e) $\frac{4}{5}$ (f) $2\frac{3}{4}$ (g) $\frac{3}{4}$ (h) $1\frac{2}{3}$
   (i) $3\frac{3}{5}$ (j) $1\frac{1}{4}$ (k) $\frac{4}{7}$ (l) $2\frac{3}{4}$

11 Orlando

1. (a) $4\frac{716}{1000}$ kg or 4716 g (b) $2\frac{310}{1000}$ kg or 2310 g
   (c) $15\frac{3}{1000}$ kg or 15 003 g (d) $\frac{97}{1000}$ kg or 97 g

2. (a) 5574 g (b) 14 010 g (c) 75 500 g
   (d) 250 g (e) 7000 g

3. (a) 3·07 kg (b) 0·444 kg (c) 2·003 kg
   (d) 3 kg (e) 0·059 kg

4. 20 kg, 2·202 kg, 2·2 kg, 2·02 kg, 2·002 kg

5. (a) 32·123 km (b) 110·09 km
   (a) 99·999 km (d) 42·5 km

6. (a) 6 units (b) 4 tenths (c) 9 thousandths
   (d) 5 tens (e) 1 hundred (f) 2 hundredths

12 All at sea

1 (a) 109·7 km (b) 96·6 km (c) 110·0 km
   (d) 102·3 km (e) 159·4 km

2 (a) 15·1 km (b) 16·8 km (c) 4·3 km
   (d) 7·4 km (e) 11·6 km (f) 9·1 km

3 (a) 117·30 seconds (b) 121·05 seconds
   (c) 122·72 seconds (d) 100·09 seconds
   (e) 91·68 seconds

4 (a) 9·28 seconds (b) 1·07 seconds
   (c) 1·28 seconds (d) 0·29 seconds
   (e) 0·68 seconds

5 Flo by 10·10 seconds and David by 13·82 seconds

6 (a) 44·01 (b) 42·20 (c) 7·16
   (d) 24·82 (e) 65·21 (f) 15·43

13 Team games

Game 1 Paul's team 741·7, Leon's team 728·7, Jan's team 674·2, Jan's team won.

Game 2 Kim's team 101·12, Ann's team 101·26, Jim's team 101·96, Kim's team won.

Game 3 Hsu-sing's team
$2·6 \times 10 = 26$
$5·18 \times 1000 = 5180$
Joe's team
$3·15 \times 10 = 31·5$
$2·4 \times 100 = 240$
$43·6 \times 1000 = 43\,600$
Niall's team
$6·14 \times 100 = 614$
Niall's team won.

14 Children's club

1 (a) 8·7 m (b) 5·9 m (c) 6·2 m

2 (a) 3·67 (b) 4·87 (c) 6·09 (d) 9·34
   (e) 2·43 (f) 3·46 (g) 3·15 (h) 6·34

3 (a) £6·80 (b) £11·25 (c) £7·50

4 (a) 18·37 (b) 11·24 (c) 10·26 (d) 14·72
   (e) 10·03 (f) 24·15 (g) 34·68 (h) 69·25

5 (a) 0·25 litres (b) 0·034 kg

6 (a) 6·4 (b) 20·5 (c) 0·38 (d) 1·63
   (e) 3·04 (f) 1·643 (g) 0·8 (h) 0·185

7 (a) 2·86 (b) 7·14 (c) 3·528 (d) 2·346
   (e) 0·654 (f) 0·089 (g) 0·07 (h) 0·006

8 (a) 1·23 (b) 1·984 (c) 6·271 (d) 0·843
   (e) 0·51 (f) 0·1 (g) 0·18 (h) 0·08

15 Souvenirs

1 T-shirt £8, ship-in-a-bottle £17, book £15, cap £13, pen £25

2 (a) £75 (b) £60 (c) £64 (d) £40
   (e) £25 (f) £30 (g) £23

3 (a) £13 (b) £17 (c) £22

4 (a) £30 (b) £39 (c) £30

5 Bronze 39 kg, Vase 17 kg, Statue 23 kg, Chest 28 kg

6 (a) 56 kg, 55·7 kg (b) 51 kg, 51·1 kg
   (c) 40 kg, 39·9 kg (b) 45 kg, 44·4 kg

7 (a) 16 kg, 15·8 kg (b) 11 kg, 11·2 kg

8 (a) 65 (b) 43 (c) 16 (d) 50

16 Gifts

1 (a) £130 (b) £70

2 (a) £130, £129·82 (b) £180, £181·91
   (c) £160, £161·52

3 (a) £79 (b) £79·10 (c) £79·10

4 $46·8 - 37·1 = 9·7$ $73·5 \div 7 = 10·5$
   $1·95 \times 5 = 9·75$

5 (a) $4·3 \times 19 = 81·7$ (b) $100 - 41·91 = 58·09$
   (c) $65·7 + 6·15 = 71·85$ (d) $48·65 \div 7 = 6·95$

17 Theatre outing

1. (a) £102·40 (b) £146·05 (c) £647·50
   (d) £208·05 (e) £95·65 (f) £308·10

2. £69·90

3. 4 adults and 8 children were in the group.

4. (a) £43·60 (b) £52

5. Vera saved £5·20.
   Tom could have paid £166·50 for 9 shows, so he did not save money by buying a season ticket at £170.

6. Janine attended 7 shows.

18 Farm kits

1. $\frac{3}{5}$

2. (a) $\frac{3}{10}$ (b) $\frac{9}{20}$ (c) $\frac{2}{25}$ (d) $\frac{17}{20}$ (e) $\frac{8}{25}$
   (f) $\frac{9}{50}$

3. 8 cows, 20 sheep, 40 chickens, 12 pigs

4. (a) 15 (b) 12 (c) 7 (d) 4 (e) 90
   (f) 13 (g) 7 (h) 85 (i) 60 (j) 27

5.
	(a) June	(b) July	(c) August
farm houses	240	630	1520
barns	120	315	760
stables	48	126	304

6. 735 were radio controlled

7. (a) 50 (b) 138 (c) 132 (d) 147 (e) 114

8. (a) 27 tractors (b) 90 tractors
   (c) 135 tractors

9. (a) 48 (b) 129 (c) 117 (d) 300 (e) 810

10. 2700 tractors had trailers.

19 Taking orders

1. (a) small $\frac{13}{100}$, 13% (b) small $\frac{35}{100}$, 35%
   medium $\frac{29}{100}$, 29% medium $\frac{22}{100}$, 22%
   large $\frac{58}{100}$, 58% large $\frac{43}{100}$, 43%
   (c) small $\frac{27}{100}$, 27%
   medium $\frac{11}{100}$, 11%
   large $\frac{62}{100}$, 62%

2. (a) $\frac{12}{50}$, 24% (b) $\frac{10}{25}$, 40% (c) $\frac{37}{50}$, 74%
   (d) $\frac{4}{20}$, 20% (e) $\frac{17}{25}$, 68% (f) $\frac{13}{20}$, 65%
   (g) $\frac{3}{25}$, 12% (h) $\frac{29}{50}$, 58%

3. $\frac{6}{20}$, 30% Constructakits $\frac{4}{20}$, 20% Buildakits
   $\frac{10}{20}$, 50% Electrokits

4. 25% of deliveries

5. (a) 25% (b) 50% (c) 10% (d) 75%
   (e) 25% (f) 50% (g) 90%

20 Another code competition

1. (a) 0·25   0·15   0·29   0·82   0·28
   (b) 25%   15%   29%   82%   28%

2. (a) $\frac{37}{100}$ $\frac{29}{50}$ $\frac{3}{10}$ $\frac{4}{5}$ $\frac{7}{100}$
   (b) 37%   58%   30%   80%   7%

3. (a) 0·63   0·2   0·24   0·06   0·01
   (b) $\frac{63}{100}$ $\frac{1}{5}$ $\frac{6}{25}$ $\frac{3}{50}$ $\frac{1}{100}$

4. GIANT BATIK KITS

5. (a) 30% (b) More girls sent correct messages.

6. (a)

Country	Week 1	Week 2	Week 3	Week 4
England	63%	60%	56%	70%
Scotland	18%	23%	24%	15%
Northern Ireland	19%	17%	20%	15%

(b) In Week 2 and Week 3.

21 Plant experiments

1

Weedout

(a)
Number of litres (L)	Number of drops (D)
1	5
2	10
3	15
4	20
5	25
6	30

(b) The number of drops is 5 times the number of litres.
(c) $D = 5 \times L$

Weedclear

(a)
Number of litres (L)	Number of drops (D)
1	3
2	4
3	5
4	6
5	7
6	8

(b) The number of drops is the number of litres plus 2.
(c) $D = L + 2$

2 (a) $D = 7 \times L$ (b) $D = L - 2$ (c) $D = L \div 4$ (d) $D = L + 7$

3 (a)
Number of Trays (T)	Cost in £ of seeds and trays (C)
1	5
2	6
3	7
4	8
5	9
6	10

(b) $C = T + 4$
(c) £14, £16, £24

4 (a) $K = 60$ (b) $K = 25$ (c) $K = 10$ (d) $K = 5$

22 Small creatures

1 (a) 56 mm or 5 cm and 6 mm or 5·6 cm
(b) 83 mm or 8 cm and 3 mm or 8·3 cm
(c) 72 mm or 7 cm and 2 mm or 7·2 cm
(d) 15 mm or 1 cm and 5 mm or 1·5 cm
(e) 48 mm or 4 cm and 8 mm or 4·8 cm

2 (a) 66 mm (b) 90 mm (c) 65 mm
(d) 21 mm (e) 3 mm

3 (a) 3·4 cm (b) 8 cm (c) 0·6 cm
(d) 3·1 cm

4 Pea Clam, Whirlygig Beetle Larva, Raft Spider, Sludge Worm, Palmate Newt.

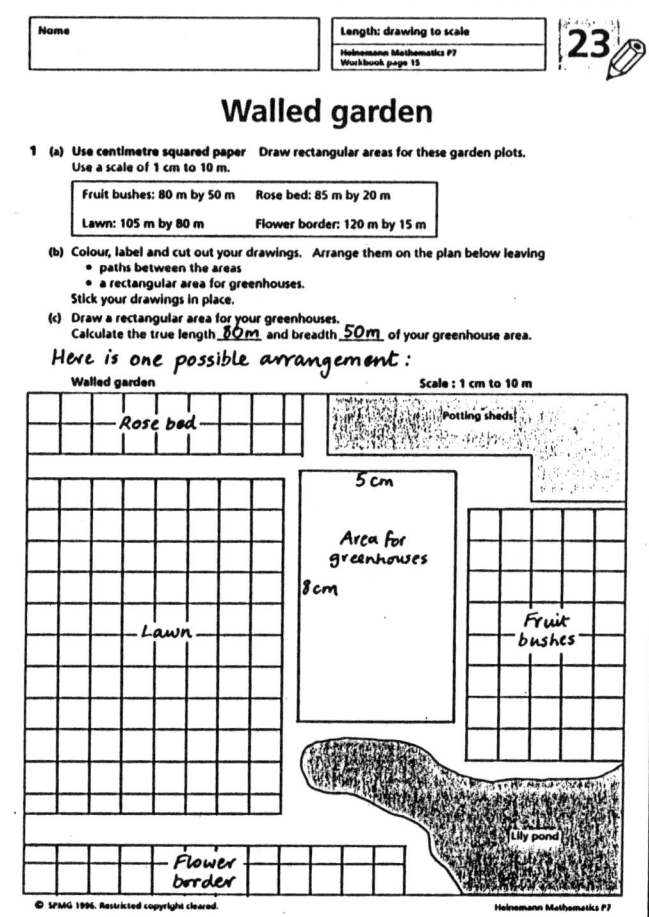

24 Label designs

1 (a) 16 cm² (b) 26 cm² (c) 20 cm²
(d) 22 cm²

2 (a) 60 cm² (b) 48 cm² (c) 42 cm²
(d) 52 cm²

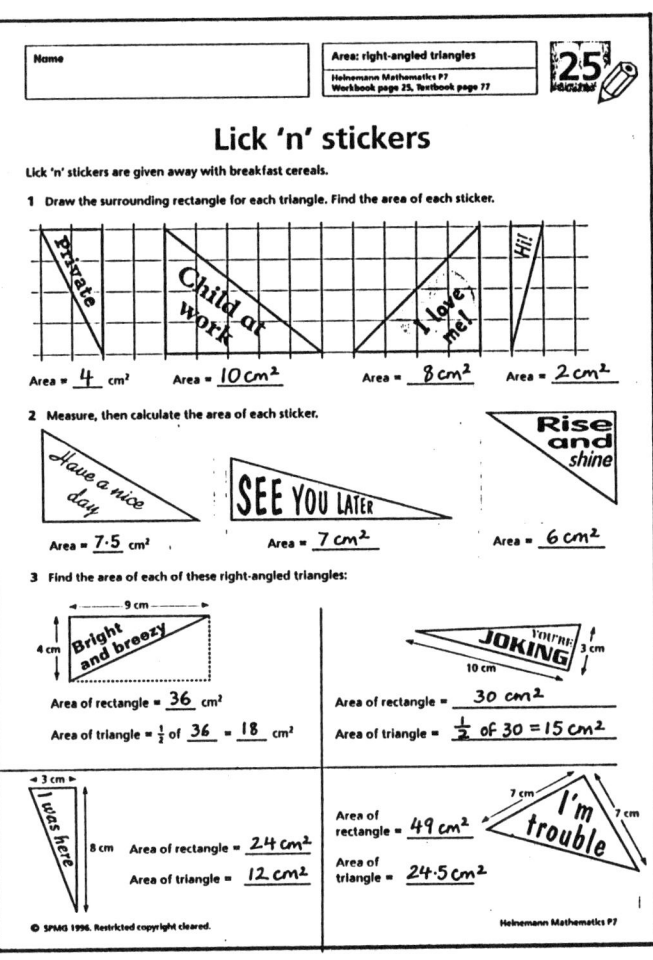

27 Running speeds

1 Greyhound, 15 metres per second
Horse, 14 metres per second
Fox, 14·5 metres per second
Rat, 6·2 metres per second

2 (a) Elton, 9 metres per second
Lesley, 8 metres per second
Jan, 7 metres per second
Wes, 7 metres per second
(b) The Fox would beat Elton.
The Greyhound would beat Lesley.
Jan would beat the Rat.
The Horse would beat Wes.

3 (a) GRT1   48 kilometres per hour
GRT2   39·2 kilometres per hour
GRT3   43 kilometres per hour
GRT4   46·5 kilometres per hour
(b) Van 3 would travel 172 kilometres in 4 hours.

4 Vehicle 1   44 kilometres per hour
Vehicle 2   57 kilometres per hour
Vehicle 3   58 kilometres per hour
Vehicle 4   56 kilometres per hour

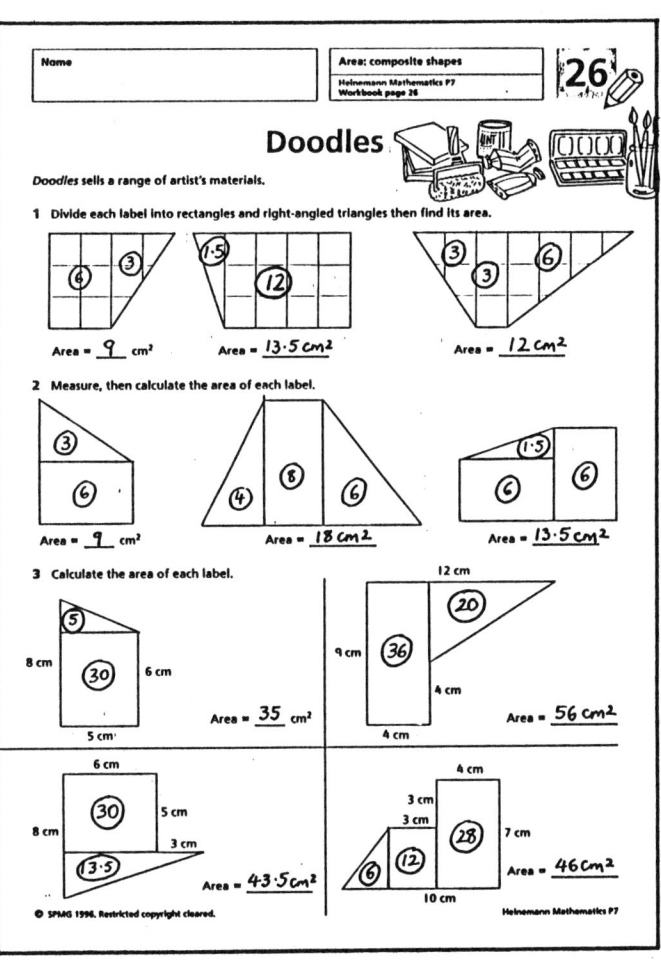

28 Hotel Sublimo

1 (a) 08.00   (b) 15.00   (c) 10.30   (d) 13.40
(e) 15.15   (f) 11.55   (g) 16.06   (h) 12.00

2 (a) 5.20 am   (b) 10.22 pm   (c) 12.30 am
(d) 6 am   (e) 12.59 pm   (f) 4.42 pm
(g) 8 pm   (h) 7.07 am   (i) 10.10 am
(j) 12.01 am

3 (a) 55 minutes   (b) 40 minutes
(c) lunch, 20 minutes more
(d) 65 minutes   (e) 6 hours 35 minutes
(f) sunbathing   (g) 2 hours 20 minutes

29 Weekend in London

1. (a) Karen 17.45, Dawn 15.55, Ayesha 19.15, Naomi 16.15, Frances 18.15
   (b) Dawn

2. (a) Dawn 11.55, Karen 11.25. Ayesha and Naomi 12.15, Frances 11.40
   (b) 13.50

3. (a) Karen and Ayesha 20.30, Naomi 22.05, Dawn and Frances 20.40
   (b) 21.35

4. Ayesha 15.35, Dawn 09.30, Naomi 15.45

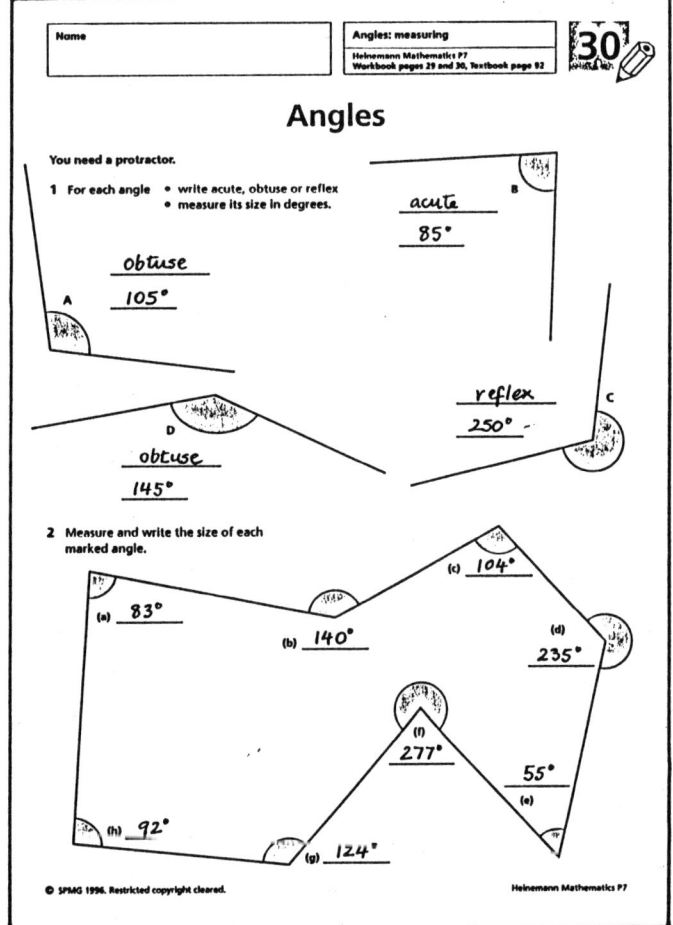

31 Shape talk

1. This shape has **two** equal sides. It has **two pairs** of equal angles.

2. equilateral triangle   parallelogram
   kite   isosceles triangle

3. (a) Orange shape: square or rectangle
   Yellow shape: rectangle, rhombus or parallelogram
   (b) Many different answers are possible.
   Orange shape: All its sides are equal (square).
   Yellow shape: All its angles are right angles (rectangle).

32 Sponsors for the cycle-cross

1. (a) 50 children   (b) 53

2. (a) 5 class intervals
   (b) 17 children in class interval 13–24
   1 child in class interval 49–60
   (c) less than 25 sponsors, 28 children
   more than 36 sponsors, 3 children

3. 25 children

4. (a)

Money in £	Tally marks	Frequency
20–39	|||||	5
40–59	||||| |||||	10
60–79	|||	3
80–99	||||	4
100–119	|||	3

(b)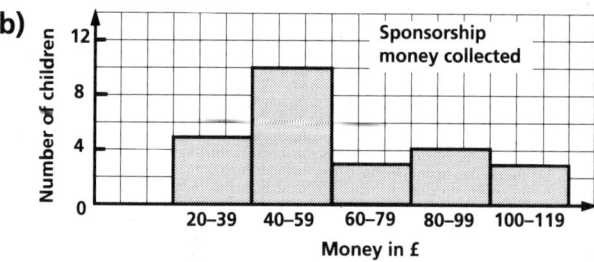

(c) less than £60, 15 children
£60 or more, 10 children

Teacher's Guide

For children working towards:

- Year 6 of the NNS *Framework for teaching mathematics* (England)
- Levels D and E of *Mathematics 5–14* (Scotland)
- Levels 4 and 5 of *Lines of Development* (Northern Ireland)

PROPERTY OF
COPSEWOOD
PRIMARY

Series editors   Peter Clarke
                      Len Frobisher

Writing team   Janine Blinko
                      Paula Coombes
                      Hilary Koll
                      Steve Mills
                      Jeanette Mumford

Heinemann Educational Publishers
Halley Court, Jordan Hill, Oxford, OX2 8EJ
a division of Harcourt Education Ltd
www.heinemann.co.uk

Heinemann is a registered trademark of Harcourt Education Ltd

© Harcourt Education Ltd 2003

This book is copyright and reproduction of the whole or part without the publisher's written permission is prohibited.

First published 2003

06 05 04 03
10, 9, 8, 7, 6, 5, 4, 3, 2, 1

ISBN 0 435 20723 7

Designed by Artistix, Thame, Oxon
Cover illustration by David Cockburn
Cover design by Paul Goodman
Printed in the UK by Page Bros, Norwich

Contents

Introduction	4
Spotlight 5 and the NNS *Framework*	7
Spotlight 5 and *Mathematics 5–14* (Scotland)	16
Teacher's Notes	22

Introduction

Maths Spotlight

Maths Spotlight aims to encourage mathematically able children from ages 5 to 11 to develop their understanding of mathematics at a suitably accelerated pace. An emphasis has been given to problem solving and investigational work, to motivate and extend children, whilst fostering a sense of enjoyment in thinking mathematically.

Curriculum information

Planning with *Maths Spotlight*

Maths Spotlight 5, intended for use with Year 5 (or P6) children, supports the maths content for Year 6 of the teaching programme in the *Framework for teaching mathematics* (England), Levels D and E of *Mathematics 5–14* (Scotland) and Levels 4 and 5 of *Lines of Development* (Northern Ireland). It consists of 4 interrelated components:

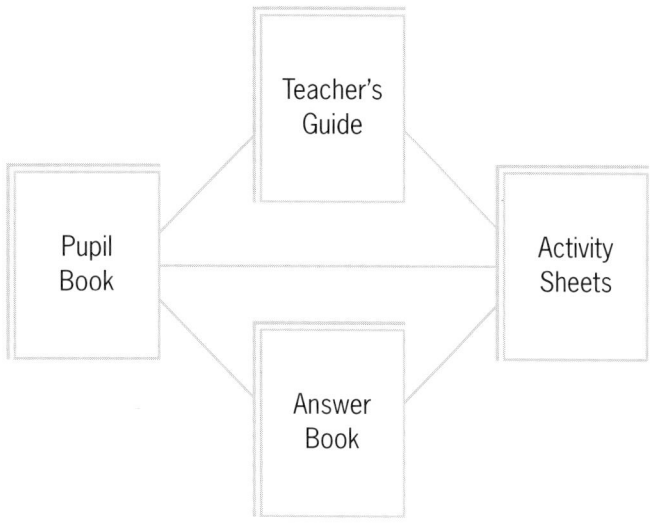

Although the Pupil Book pages, Activity Sheets and the notes in the Teacher's Guide broadly follow the order of the teaching programme in the *Framework*, teachers will be able to 'dip in' to the materials in accordance with their planning documents.

The majority of children in most primary classrooms are likely to be working on the same topic and broad objective(s) in most mathematics lessons. The planning charts on pages 7 to 20 therefore match the whole-class learning objective(s) for the majority of children in Year 5 (or P6), with the specific objective(s) for those working on *Maths Spotlight 5*. These charts will assist teachers to plan a programme of work for their mathematically able children that will run easily alongside their core scheme of work.

Providing challenge for the most able during the daily mathematics lesson

Maths Spotlight incorporates valuable learning opportunities for mathematically able children. These include:

- providing activities that require children to use and apply their knowledge to problem solving or investigations
- encouraging children to make connections between different aspects of mathematics
- promoting thinking skills such as hypothesising, predicting, reasoning
- encouraging initiative and self-direction.

Classroom organisation

Maths Spotlight is likely to be of most value during the central part of the daily mathematics lesson, when children are working independently, in pairs or as a group. Where children are being introduced to new concepts, it is recommended that teachers explain the key ideas in more detail. However, topics that extend children's knowledge or ask them to use and apply their existing skills in a problem-solving context require only a small amount of teacher input.

Children's material

Maths Spotlight 5 consists of a 92-page Pupil Book and 60 Activity Sheets, each designed to provide approximately 20 to 25 minutes of work. Most of the activities can be completed without a high level of teaching input. Any prerequisite skills are listed in the Teacher's Notes. Where it is important for Pupil Book pages and/or Activity Sheets on related topics to be completed in a specific order, this is stated in the Teacher's Notes.

Each Pupil Book page or Activity Sheet contains one or more of the following:

- Let's practise

    A short practice exercise is normally followed by activities that aim to develop deeper understanding.

- Let's play

    Paired or small group games allow children to use and apply their knowledge in an interesting and imaginative context. Most of the games use readily available classroom resources.

- Let's solve problems

    These activities provide opportunities for children to analyse, then solve problems and to reflect on alternative methods that could be used.

- Let's investigate

    Here children need to use and apply their mathematical knowledge in more open-ended situations. They are encouraged to approach their work in a systematic way and to take responsibility for recording it. Investigations may be done individually, in pairs or as a group.

The icon ? denotes a question that suggests a way of extending an investigation.

The icon 🖩 denotes a section where the use of a calculator is appropriate.

Teaching support

Each Pupil Book page and Activity Sheet is supported by Teacher's Notes. Where two pages of children's material are covered by one set of Teacher's Notes, then children should start with the page that is first to feature in the Notes.

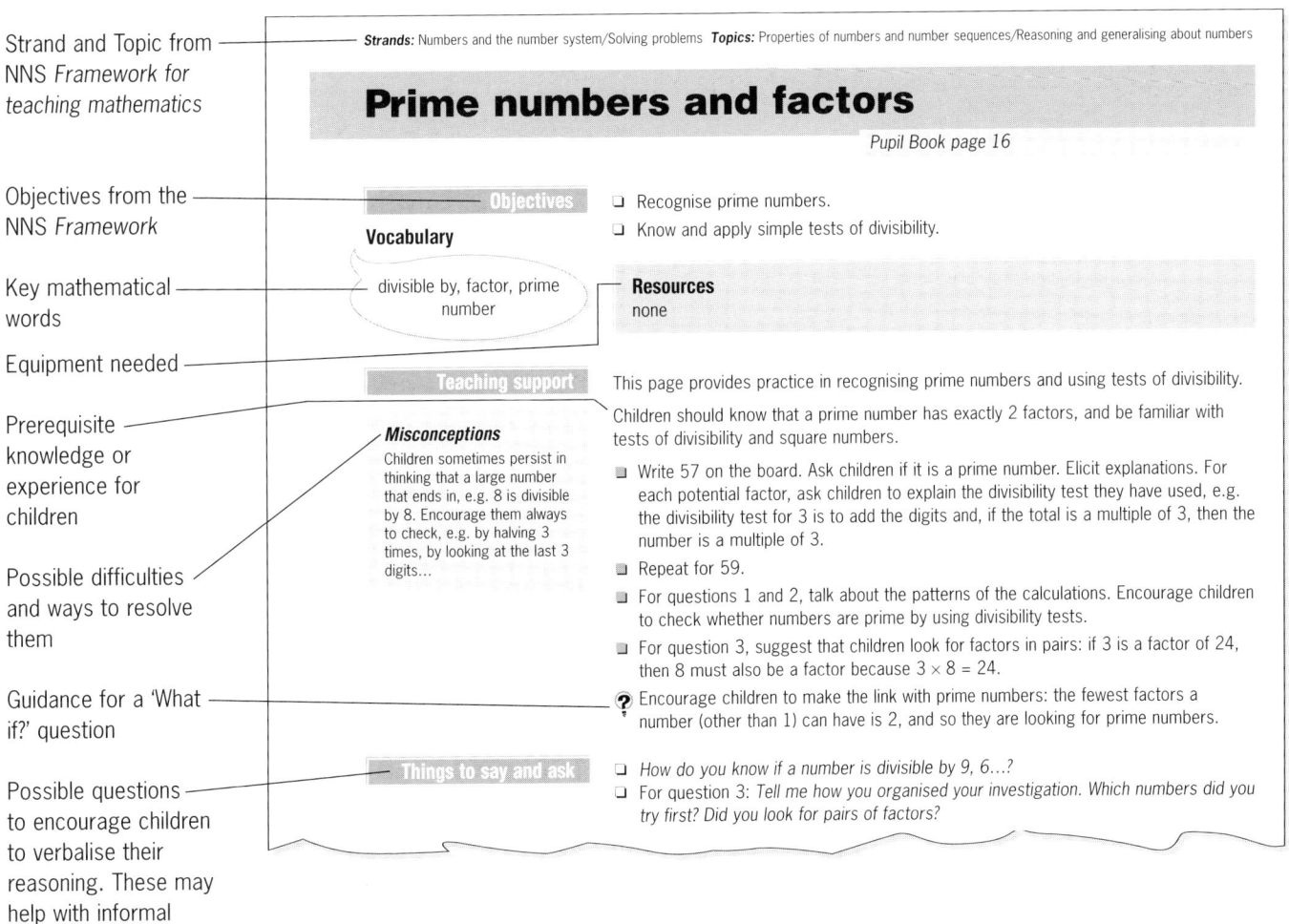

Strand and Topic from NNS *Framework for teaching mathematics*

Strands: Numbers and the number system/Solving problems **Topics:** Properties of numbers and number sequences/Reasoning and generalising about numbers

Prime numbers and factors

Pupil Book page 16

Objectives from the NNS *Framework*

Objectives
- Recognise prime numbers.
- Know and apply simple tests of divisibility.

Key mathematical words

Vocabulary
divisible by, factor, prime number

Resources
none

Equipment needed

Teaching support

This page provides practice in recognising prime numbers and using tests of divisibility.

Children should know that a prime number has exactly 2 factors, and be familiar with tests of divisibility and square numbers.

Prerequisite knowledge or experience for children

Misconceptions
Children sometimes persist in thinking that a large number that ends in, e.g. 8 is divisible by 8. Encourage them always to check, e.g. by halving 3 times, by looking at the last 3 digits...

- Write 57 on the board. Ask children if it is a prime number. Elicit explanations. For each potential factor, ask children to explain the divisibility test they have used, e.g. the divisibility test for 3 is to add the digits and, if the total is a multiple of 3, then the number is a multiple of 3.
- Repeat for 59.
- For questions 1 and 2, talk about the patterns of the calculations. Encourage children to check whether numbers are prime by using divisibility tests.
- For question 3, suggest that children look for factors in pairs: if 3 is a factor of 24, then 8 must also be a factor because $3 \times 8 = 24$.

Possible difficulties and ways to resolve them

Guidance for a 'What if?' question

? Encourage children to make the link with prime numbers: the fewest factors a number (other than 1) can have is 2, and so they are looking for prime numbers.

Things to say and ask
- *How do you know if a number is divisible by 9, 6...?*
- *For question 3: Tell me how you organised your investigation. Which numbers did you try first? Did you look for pairs of factors?*

Possible questions to encourage children to verbalise their reasoning. These may help with informal assessment.

Providing support for investigations and problem solving

Investigations and problems provide opportunities for children to think and reason for themselves, and to use and apply their mathematical knowledge and skills. Initially many children may find this a daunting task, as it contrasts with much of their other work in mathematics, where they learn and then practise what has been taught and can experience immediate 'success'. It is therefore important to give sufficient support and encouragement for children to be able to recognise that their thinking, reasoning and decision-making are valued aspects of their learning.

Points to bear in mind:

- make sure children understand the task
- give children time to explore the task and ways of tackling it
- discuss possible strategies and allow children to share ideas
- let children use strategies different from those discussed
- permit strategies that may appear to be inefficient or to be leading to a 'dead end'
- encourage the use of lists, tables and charts to organise data
- suggest that children look for patterns and relationships, and use them to make and test predictions
- encourage children to think of their own way of overcoming a difficulty
- suggest possible ways forward by saying, 'I wonder if …' or 'What about trying this…?'
- encourage children to persevere.

The investigations and problems in *Maths Spotlight* are presented in interesting, challenging and enjoyable ways, and are designed to promote positive attitudes towards mathematics.

Spotlight 5 and the NNS *Framework*

NNS *Framework* page	Objective for Year 5	Objective for Year 6	Teacher's Guide page	Pupil Book page	Activity Sheet number
NUMBERS AND THE NUMBER SYSTEM					
Place value, ordering and rounding					
3	Read and write whole numbers in figures and words, and know what each digit represents.		22		1
7	**Multiply and divide any positive integer up to 10 000 by 10 or 100 and understand the effect** (e.g. 9900 ÷ 10, 737 ÷ 10, 2060 ÷ 100).	**Multiply and divide decimals mentally by 10 or 100, and integers by 1000, and explain the effect.**	22, 23	1, 2	
9	Use the vocabulary of comparing and ordering numbers, including symbols such as <, >, ≤, ≥, =.		24	3, 4	
	Give one or more numbers lying between two given numbers.		24	3, 4	
	Order a set of integers less than 1 million.		24	3, 4	
11	Use the vocabulary of estimation and approximation. Make and justify estimates of large numbers, and estimate simple proportions such as one third, seven tenths.	Use the vocabulary of estimation and approximation.	25	5	
13	Round any integer up to 10 000 to the nearest 10, 100 or 1000.	Consolidate rounding an integer to the nearest 10, 100 or 1000.	25		2
15	**Order a given set of positive and negative integers** (e.g. on a number line, on a temperature scale).	Order a set of positive and negative integers.	26	6	
	Calculate a temperature rise or fall across 0°C.	Find the difference between a positive and a negative integer, or two negative integers, in a context such as temperature or the number line.	26, 27	6	3
Properties of numbers and number sequences					
17	Recognise and extend number sequences formed by counting from any number in steps of constant size, extending beyond zero when counting back. For example: – count on in steps of 25 to 1000, and then back; – count on or back in steps of 0·1, 0·2, 0·3...	Recognise and extend number sequences.	27–30, 33, 107	7, 8	3, 4, 5, 6, 11, 46
		Recognise and extend number sequences, such as the sequence of square numbers.	27, 30	7	6
		Recognise and extend number sequences, such as the sequence of triangular numbers 1, 3, 6, 10, 15...	28, 30	8	5, 6
		Count on in steps of 0·1, 0·2, 0·25, 0·5..., and then back.	29	9	
19	Make general statements about odd or even numbers, including the outcome of sums and differences.	Make general statements about odd or even numbers, including the outcome of products.	31		7

Numbers in the first column refer to the relevant page(s) of the Supplement of examples in the *Framework for teaching mathematics*. Objectives covered in *Maths Spotlight 5* are shown on a tinted background. Key objectives for the year are shown in bold.

Spotlight 5 and the NNS Framework

NNS Framework page	Objective for Year 5	Objective for Year 6	Teacher's Guide page	Pupil Book page	Activity Sheet number
19	Recognise multiples of 6, 7, 8, 9, up to the 10th multiple.	Recognise multiples up to 10×10.	32	10	
	Know and apply tests of divisibility by 2, 4, 5, 10 or 100.	Know and apply simple tests of divisibility.	33	11, 16	8
		Find simple common multiples.	34	12	9
21	Know squares of numbers to at least 10×10.	Recognise squares of numbers to at least 12×12.	35	13	10
		Recognise prime numbers to at least 20.	36, 38	14, 16	
	Find all the pairs of factors of any number up to 100.	Factorise numbers to 100 into prime factors.	36	15	
Fractions, decimals, percentages, ratio and proportion					
23	Use fraction notation, including mixed numbers, and the vocabulary numerator and denominator.		39	17	
	Change an improper fraction to a mixed number (e.g. change $\frac{13}{10}$ to $1\frac{3}{10}$).	Change a fraction such as $\frac{33}{8}$ to the equivalent mixed number $4\frac{1}{8}$, and vice versa.	39, 41	17	12
		Recognise relationships between fractions: for example, that $\frac{1}{10}$ is ten times $\frac{1}{100}$, and $\frac{1}{16}$ is half of $\frac{1}{8}$.	40	18	
	Recognise when two simple fractions are equivalent, including relating hundredths to tenths (e.g. $\frac{70}{100} = \frac{7}{10}$).	**Reduce a fraction to its simplest form by cancelling common factors** in the numerator and denominator.	40, 41	19	12
	Order a set of fractions such as 2, $2\frac{3}{4}$, $1\frac{3}{4}$, $2\frac{1}{2}$, $1\frac{1}{2}$, and position them on a number line.	Order fractions such as $\frac{2}{3}$, $\frac{3}{4}$ and $\frac{5}{6}$ by converting them to fractions with a common denominator, and position them on a number line.	42	20	13
25	**Relate fractions to division**, and use division to find simple fractions, including tenths and hundredths, of numbers and quantities (e.g. $\frac{3}{4}$ of 12, $\frac{1}{10}$ of 50, $\frac{1}{100}$ of £3).	**Use a fraction as an 'operator' to find fractions**, including tenths and hundredths, **of numbers or quantities** (e.g. $\frac{5}{8}$ of 32, $\frac{7}{10}$ of 40, $\frac{9}{100}$ of 400 centimetres).	43, 44	21	14
27	Solve simple problems using ideas of ratio and proportion ('one for every...' and 'one in every...').	**Solve simple problems involving ratio and proportion.**	44, 45	22	15
29	**Use decimal notation for tenths and hundredths.**	Use decimal notation for tenths and hundredths in calculations, and tenths, hundredths and thousandths when recording measurements.	46, 47	23	16, 17
	Know what each digit represents in a number with up to two decimal places.	Know what each digit represents in a number with up to three decimal places.	46, 47	23	16, 17
		Give a decimal fraction lying between two others (e.g. between 3·4 and 3·5).	47, 48	24	17
	Order a set of numbers or measurements with the same number of decimal places.	**Order a mixed set of numbers** or measurements **with up to three decimal places**.	46, 48	24	16

Spotlight 5 and the NNS Framework

NNS Framework page	Objective for Year 5	Objective for Year 6	Teacher's Guide page	Pupil Book page	Activity Sheet number
31	**Round a number with one or two decimal places to the nearest integer.**	Round a number with two decimal places to the nearest tenth or to the nearest whole number.	48	25	
	Relate fractions to their decimal representations: that is, recognise the equivalence between the decimal and fraction forms of one half, one quarter, three quarters… and tenths and hundredths (e.g. $\frac{7}{10} = 0.7$, $\frac{27}{100} = 0.27$).	Recognise the equivalence between the decimal and fraction forms of one half, one quarter, three quarters, one eighth… and tenths, hundredths and thousandths (e.g. $\frac{700}{1000} = \frac{70}{100} = \frac{7}{10} = 0.7$).	49, 50	26	18
		Begin to convert a fraction to a decimal using division.	50		18
33	Begin to understand percentage as the number of parts in every 100.	**Understand percentage as the number of parts in every 100.**	51, 52	27, 28	19
	Express one half, one quarter, three quarters, and tenths and hundredths, as percentages (e.g. know that $\frac{3}{4} = 75\%$).	Express simple fractions such as one half, one quarter, three quarters, one third, two thirds…, and tenths and hundredths, as percentages (e.g. know that $\frac{1}{3} = 33\frac{1}{3}\%$).	51, 52	27, 28, 29, 30	19, 20
	Find simple percentages of small whole-number quantities (e.g. 25% of £8).	**Find simple percentages of small whole-number quantities** (e.g. find 10% of £500, then 20%, 40% and 80% by doubling).	52, 53, 67	29, 30	20, 26
CALCULATIONS					
Rapid recall of addition and subtraction facts					
39	Derive quickly or continue to derive quickly: – decimals that total 1 (e.g. 0·2 + 0·8) or 10 (e.g. 6·2 + 3·8); – all two-digit pairs that total 100 (e.g. 43 + 57); – all pairs of multiples of 50 with a total of 1000 (e.g. 350 + 650).		54		21
Mental calculation strategies (+ and –)					
41	Find differences by counting up through next multiple of 10, 100 or 1000, e.g. **calculate mentally a difference such as 8006 – 2993.**	Consolidate all strategies from previous year, including: – find a difference by counting up – add or subtract the nearest multiple of 10, 100 or 1000, then adjust – use the relationship between addition and subtraction – add several numbers.	55–7	31, 32, 33	22
	Partition into H, T and U, adding the most significant digits first.				
	Identify near doubles, such as 1·5 + 1·6.				
	Add or subtract the nearest multiple of 10 or 100, then adjust.				
43	Develop further the relationship between addition and subtraction.				
	Add several numbers (e.g. four or five single digits, or multiples of 10 such as 40 + 50 + 80).				
45, 47	Use known number facts and place value for mental addition and subtraction (e.g. 470 + 380, 810 – 380, 7·4 + 9·8, 9·2 – 8·6).	Use known number facts and place value to consolidate mental addition/subtraction (e.g. 470 + 380, 810 – 380, 7·4 + 9·8, 9·2 – 8·6).	58	34	

Spotlight 5 and the NNS *Framework*

NNS *Framework* page	Objective for Year 5	Objective for Year 6	Teacher's Guide page	Pupil Book page	Activity Sheet number
Pencil and paper procedures (addition)					
49	Use informal pencil and paper methods to support, record or explain additions. **Extend written methods to:** – column addition of two integers less than 10 000; – addition of more than two integers less than 10 000; – addition of a pair of decimal fractions, both with one or both with two decimal places (e.g. £29·78 + £53·34).	Use informal pencil and paper methods to support, record or explain additions.	59, 60	35, 36	
		Extend written methods to column addition.	59, 60	35, 36	
		Extend written methods to column addition of numbers involving decimals.	61, 62	37	23
Pencil and paper procedures (subtraction)					
51	Use informal pencil and paper methods to support, record or explain subtractions. **Extend written methods to:** – column subtraction of two integers less than 10 000; – subtraction of a pair of decimal fractions, both with one or both with two decimal places.	Use informal pencil and paper methods to support, record or explain subtractions.	62, 63	38	24
		Extend written methods to column subtraction.	62, 63	38	24
		Extend written methods to column subtraction of numbers involving decimals.	64	39	
Understanding multiplication and division					
53, 55	Understand the effect of and relationships between the four operations, and the principles (not the names) of the arithmetic laws as they apply to multiplication.	Understand and use the relationships between the four operations, and the principles (not the names) of the arithmetic laws.	68	42	
	Begin to use brackets.	Use brackets.	68	43	
57	Begin to express a quotient as a fraction, or as a decimal when dividing a whole number by 2, 4, 5 or 10, or when dividing £·p.	Express a quotient as a fraction.	69		27
		Express a quotient as a decimal rounded to one decimal place.	70	44	
		Divide £·p by a two-digit number to give £·p.	70	45	
	Round up or down after division, depending on the context.	Round up or down after division, depending on the context.	71	46	
Rapid recall of multiplication and division facts					
59	**Know by heart all multiplication facts up to 10 × 10.**	Consolidate knowing by heart: multiplication facts up to 10 × 10.	72	47	
	Derive quickly or continue to derive quickly: – division facts corresponding to tables up to 10 × 10.	**Derive quickly:** – **division facts corresponding to tables up to 10 × 10.**	72		28
	Derive quickly or continue to derive quickly: – doubles of all whole numbers 1 to 100 (e.g. 78 × 2); – doubles of multiples of 10 to 1000 (e.g. 670 × 2); – doubles of multiples of 100 to 10 000 (e.g. 6500 × 2); – and the corresponding halves.	Derive quickly: – squares of multiples of 10 to 100 (e.g. 60 × 60); – doubles of two-digit numbers (e.g. 3·8 × 2, 0.76 × 2); – doubles of multiples of 10 to 1000 (e.g. 670 × 2); – doubles of multiples of 100 to 10 000 (e.g. 6500 × 2); – and the corresponding halves.	72, 73	47	29

NNS Framework page	Objective for Year 5	Objective for Year 6	Teacher's Guide page	Pupil Book page	Activity Sheet number
Mental calculation strategies (× and ÷)					
61	Use doubling or halving, starting from known facts. For example: – double/halve any two-digit number by doubling/halving the tens first; – double one number and halve the other; – to multiply by 25, multiply by 100 then divide by 4; – find the ×16 table facts by doubling the ×8 table; – find sixths by halving thirds.	Use related facts and doubling or halving. For example: – double or halve the most significant digit first; – to multiply by 25, multiply by 100 then divide by 4; – double one number and halve the other; – find the ×24 table by doubling the ×6 table twice.	73	48	
	Use factors (e.g. 8 × 12 = 8 × 4 × 3).	Use factors (e.g. 35 × 18 = 35 × 6 × 3).	74		30
63	Use closely related facts (e.g. multiply by 19 or 21 by multiplying by 20 and adjusting; develop the ×12 table from the ×10 and ×2 tables).	Use closely related facts: for example, – multiply by 49 or 51 by multiplying by 50 and adjusting; – develop the ×17 table by adding facts from the ×10 and ×7 tables.	75		31
	Partition (e.g. 47 × 6 = (40 × 6) + (7 × 6)).	Partition (e.g. 87 × 6 = (80 × 6) + (7 × 6); 3·4 × 3 = (3 × 3) + (0·4 × 3)).	76	49	
	Use the relationship between multiplication and division.	Use the relationship between multiplication and division.	76	50	
65	Use known facts and place value to multiply and divide mentally.	Use known number facts and place value to consolidate mental multiplication and division.	76, 77	50	32
Pencil and paper procedures (multiplication)					
67	Approximate first. Use informal pencil and paper methods to support, record or explain multiplications. **Extend written methods to:** **– short multiplication of HTU or U·t by U;** **– long multiplication of TU by TU.**	Approximate first. Use informal pencil and paper methods to support, record or explain multiplications.	78–81	51, 53	33, 34
		Extend written methods to multiplication of ThHTU × U (short multiplication).	78	51	
		Extend written methods to short multiplication of numbers involving decimals.	79		33
		Extend written methods to long multiplication of a three-digit by a two-digit integer.	80, 81	53	34
Pencil and paper procedures (division)					
69	Approximate first. Use informal pencil and paper methods to support, record or explain divisions. **Extend written methods to:** **– short division of HTU by U** (with integer remainder).	Approximate first. Use informal pencil and paper methods to support, record or explain divisions.	82–85	54, 55, 56	35, 36
		Extend written methods to short division of TU or HTU by U (mixed-number answer).	82	54	35
		Extend written methods to division of HTU by TU (long division, whole-number answer).	83, 84	55	36
		Extend written methods to short division of numbers involving decimals.	85	56	

Spotlight 5 and the NNS *Framework*

NNS *Framework* page	Objective for Year 5	Objective for Year 6	Teacher's Guide page	Pupil Book page	Activity Sheet number
Using a calculator					
71	Develop calculator skills and use a calculator effectively.	Develop calculator skills and use a calculator effectively.	23, 25, 46, 65, 86, 88, 99	5, 23, 40, 58, 68	2, 37
Checking results of calculations					
73	Check with the inverse operation when using a calculator.	Check with the inverse operation when using a calculator.	82, 86	54	35, 37
	Check the sum of several numbers by adding in the reverse order.	**Check the sum of several numbers by adding in the reverse order.**	84, 86	36, 37	
	Check with an equivalent calculation.	Check with an equivalent calculation.	54, 61, 62	38	21, 23
	Estimate by approximating (round to nearest 10 or 100), then check result.	Estimate by approximating (round to nearest 10, 100 or 1000), then check result.	65, 91	40, 60	
	Use knowledge of sums and differences of odd/even numbers.	Use knowledge of sums, differences and products of odd/even numbers.	66		25
		Use tests of divisibility.	87	57	
SOLVING PROBLEMS					
Making decisions					
75	Choose and use appropriate number operations to solve problems, and appropriate ways of calculating: mental, mental with jottings, written methods, calculator.	Choose and use appropriate number operations to solve problems, and appropriate ways of calculating: mental, mental with jottings, written methods, calculator.	55, 58, 60, 61, 63–67, 77, 79, 90, 91, 93	31, 34, 36, 37, 39, 40, 41, 45, 52, 59, 60, 62	23, 24, 25, 26, 32
Reasoning and generalising about numbers or shapes					
77	Explain methods and reasoning, orally and in writing.	Explain methods and reasoning, orally and in writing.	57, 63, 67, 70, 82, 84, 92, 106, 107	45	22, 24, 26, 35, 36, 39, 45, 46
79	Solve mathematical problems or puzzles, recognise and explain patterns and relationships, generalise and predict. Suggest extensions asking 'What if…?'	Solve mathematical problems or puzzles, recognise and explain patterns and relationships, generalise and predict. Suggest extensions asking 'What if…?'	27–30, 32, 38, 97, 104–7	3, 4, 7, 8, 10, 33, 73, 75	4, 5, 6, 11, 41, 44, 45, 46
81	Make and investigate a general statement about familiar numbers or shapes by finding examples that satisfy it.	Make and investigate a general statement about familiar numbers or shapes by finding examples that satisfy it.	31, 106, 108	74	7, 45
	Explain a generalised relationship (formula) in words.	Develop from explaining a generalised relationship in words to expressing it in a formula using letters as symbols (e.g. the cost of *n* articles at 15p each).	29, 98, 105	66	4, 44
Problems involving 'real life'					
83	**Use all four operations to solve simple word problems involving numbers and quantities** based on 'real life', using one or more steps, including finding simple percentages. **Explain methods and reasoning.**	**Identify and use appropriate operations (including combinations of operations) to solve word problems involving numbers and quantities** based on 'real life', using one or more steps, including calculating percentages. **Explain methods and reasoning.**	55, 60, 61, 63, 64, 66, 67, 71, 82, 84, 85	31, 36, 37, 39, 41, 46, 54, 56	24, 26, 36

NNS Framework page	Objective for Year 5	Objective for Year 6	Teacher's Guide page	Pupil Book page	Activity Sheet number
Problems involving money					
85	**Use all four operations to solve simple word problems involving numbers and quantities** based on money, using one or more steps, including making simple conversions of pounds to foreign currency and finding simple percentages. **Explain methods and reasoning**.	**Identify and use appropriate operations (including combinations of operations) to solve word problems involving numbers and quantities** based on money, using one or more steps, including converting pounds to foreign currency, or vice versa, and calculating percentages such as VAT. **Explain methods and reasoning**.	53, 66, 67, 70, 71, 79, 82	29, 30, 41, 45, 46, 52, 54	26, 36
Problems involving measures					
87, 89	**Use all four operations to solve simple word problems involving numbers and quantities** based on measures (**including time**), using one or more steps, including finding simple percentages. **Explain methods and reasoning**.	**Identify and use appropriate operations (including combinations of operations) to solve word problems involving numbers and quantities** based on measures (including time), using one or more steps, including calculating percentages. **Explain methods and reasoning**.	25, 43, 55, 58, 60, 64, 71, 85, 90, 93, 94, 96, 100	5, 21, 31, 34, 37, 39, 46, 56, 59, 62, 63, 65, 69	42
MEASURES					
Length, mass and capacity					
91	Use, read and write standard metric units (km, m, cm, mm, kg, g, l, ml), including their abbreviations, and relationships between them.	Use, read and write standard metric units (km, m, cm, mm, kg, g, l, ml, cl), including their abbreviations, and relationships between them.	88, 90, 91, 94	58, 59, 60, 63	
	Convert larger to smaller units (e.g. km to m, m to cm or mm, kg to g, l to ml).	Convert smaller to larger units (e.g. m to km, cm or mm to m, g to kg, ml to l) and vice versa.	88, 91, 94	58, 60, 63	
	Know imperial units (mile, pint, gallon).	Know imperial units (mile, pint, gallon, lb, oz).	89, 91–3, 95, 96	61, 62, 64, 65	38, 39, 40
		Know rough equivalents of lb and kg, oz and g, miles and km, litres and pints or gallons.	89, 91–3, 95, 96	61, 62, 64, 65	38, 39, 40
93	Suggest suitable units and measuring equipment to estimate or measure length, mass or capacity.	Suggest suitable units and measuring equipment to estimate or measure length, mass or capacity.	88, 91, 92, 96	58, 60	39, 40
95	Measure and draw lines to the nearest millimetre.		90	59	
	Record estimates and readings from scales to a suitable degree of accuracy.	Record estimates and readings from scales to a suitable degree of accuracy.	90–2, 94–6	59, 61, 63, 64, 65	39, 40
Area and perimeter					
97	**Understand area measured in square centimetres (cm²).**	**Calculate the perimeter and area of simple compound shapes that can be split into rectangles.**	97–9	66, 67, 68	41
	Understand and use the formula in words 'length × breadth' for the area of a rectangle.				
	Understand, measure and calculate perimeters of rectangles and regular polygons.				

Spotlight 5 and the NNS Framework

NNS Framework page	Objective for Year 5	Objective for Year 6	Teacher's Guide page	Pupil Book page	Activity Sheet number
Time					
99	Use units of time.		101	70	
101	Read the time on a 24-hour digital clock and use 24-hour clock notation, such as 19:53.		100, 101	69, 70	42
	Use timetables.	Appreciate different times around the world.	100	69	42
SHAPE AND SPACE					
Properties of 3-D and 2-D shapes					
103		Describe and visualise properties of solid shapes such as parallel or perpendicular faces or edges.	102	71	
	Recognise properties of rectangles.	Classify quadrilaterals, using criteria such as parallel sides, equal angles, equal sides…	103, 104	72, 73	43
	Classify triangles (isosceles, equilateral, scalene), using criteria such as equal sides, equal angles, lines of symmetry.				
105	Make shapes with increasing accuracy.	Make shapes with increasing accuracy.	103–105	72, 73	43, 44
	Visualise 3-D shapes from 2-D drawings and identify different nets for an open cube.	Visualise 3-D shapes from 2-D drawings and identify different nets for a closed cube.	108, 109	74, 75	
Reflective symmetry, reflection and translation					
107	Recognise reflective symmetry in regular polygons: for example, know that a square has four axes of symmetry and an equilateral triangle has three.		110	76	
	Complete symmetrical patterns with two lines of symmetry at right angles (using squared paper or pegboard).		111		47
	Recognise where a shape will be after reflection in a mirror line parallel to one side (sides not all parallel or perpendicular to the mirror line).	Recognise where a shape will be after reflection: – in a mirror line touching the shape at a point (sides of shape not necessarily parallel or perpendicular to the mirror line).	110, 111, 113	76, 77	47
		Recognise where a shape will be after reflection: – in two mirror lines at right angles (sides of shape all parallel or perpendicular to the mirror line).	113	77	
	Recognise where a shape will be after a translation.	Recognise where a shape will be after two translations.	113		48
Position and direction					
109	Recognise positions and directions: – read and plot coordinates in the first quadrant.	**Read and plot coordinates in all four quadrants.**	27, 114–116	78, 79	3, 49,
	Recognise perpendicular and parallel lines.		116		49

Spotlight 5 and the NNS *Framework*

NNS *Framework* page	Objective for Year 5	Objective for Year 6	Teacher's Guide page	Pupil Book page	Activity Sheet number
Angle and rotation					
111	Understand and use angle measure in degrees.		117	80	
	Identify, estimate and order acute and obtuse angles.	Recognise and estimate angles.	117, 120	80	51
	Use a protractor to measure and draw acute and obtuse angles to the nearest 5°.	**Use a protractor to measure** and draw **acute and obtuse angles to the nearest degree**.	117, 118, 120	80, 81	51
	Calculate angles in a straight line.	Check that the sum of the angles of a triangle is 180°: for example, by measuring or paper folding.	118	81	
		Calculate angles in a triangle or around a point.	118, 120	81	51
		Recognise where a shape will be after a rotation through 90° about one of its vertices.	121		52
HANDLING DATA					
Probability					
113	Discuss the chance or likelihood of particular events.	Use the language associated with probability to discuss events, including those with equally likely outcomes.	121–126	82, 83, 84, 85, 86	53, 54, 55
Organising and interpreting data					
115, 117	Solve a problem by representing and interpreting data in tables, charts, graphs and diagrams, including those generated by a computer, for example: – bar line charts, vertical axis labelled in 2s, 5s, 10s, 20s or 100s, first where intermediate points have no meaning (e.g. scores on a dice rolled 50 times), then where they may have meaning (e.g. room temperature over time).	**Solve a problem by** representing, **extracting and interpreting data in tables, graphs, charts** and diagrams, including those generated by a computer, for example: – line graphs (e.g. for distance/time, for a multiplication table, a conversion graph, a graph of pairs of numbers adding to 8); – frequency tables and bar charts with grouped discrete data (e.g. test marks 0–5, 6–10, 11–15…).	127–131	87, 88, 89, 90	56, 57, 58
117	Find the mode of a set of data.	Find the mode and range of a set of data.	132	91	59
		Begin to find the median and mean of a set of data.	133	92	60

Spotlight 5 and *Mathematics 5–14* (Scotland)

Target for Level D	Target for Level E	Teacher's Guide page	Pupil Book page	Activity Sheet number
NUMBER, MONEY AND MEASUREMENT				
Range and type of numbers				
Work with: – whole numbers up to 100 000 – whole numbers up to a million		22, 24, 25, 31	3, 4, 5	1, 7
– fractions (all previous plus twentieths, fiftieths, hundredths) and equivalences among these and decimals	**Work with:** – negative numbers – all widely used fractions and equivalences among these and decimals	26, 27 39, 40, 41, 42, 43, 44, 49, 50	6 17, 18, 19, 20, 21, 26	3 12, 13, 14, 18
	– decimals to 3 places	46, 47, 48	23, 24	16, 17
– percentages, decimals to 2 places and equivalences among these in money and measurement		51, 52, 53, 67	27, 28, 29, 30	19, 20, 26
Money				
Use all UK coins/notes to £20 worth or more, including exchange	**Use relationships between currencies** to do simple calculations	80	52	
Add and subtract				
	Add and subtract: – mentally for 2 digit numbers including decimals	54		21
Add and subtract: – mentally for 2 digit whole numbers, beyond in some cases, involving multiples of 10 or 100		57	33	
– without a calculator for 4 digits with at most 2 decimal places (easy examples only)	– without a calculator for 4 digits with at most 2 decimal places	55, 56, 57, 58, 59, 60, 61, 62, 63, 64, 66	31, 32, 34, 35, 36, 37, 38, 39	22, 23, 24, 25
– with a calculator for 4 digits with at most 2 decimal places	– with a calculator for any number of digits with at most 3 decimal places in applications in number, measurement and money – positive and negative numbers in applications such as rise in temperature	65, 66, 86	40, 41	37
Multiply and divide				
Multiply and divide: – mentally for whole numbers by single digits: easy examples only	**Multiply and divide:**	32, 33, 34, 38, 68, 72, 73, 76	10, 11, 12, 16, 42, 43, 47, 48, 49	8, 9, 28, 35

Objectives covered in *Maths Spotlight 5* are shown on a tinted background.

Spotlight 5 and *Mathematics 5–14* (Scotland)

Target for Level D	Target for Level E	Teacher's Guide page	Pupil Book page	Activity Sheet number
– mentally for 4 digit numbers including decimals by 10 or 100		22, 23	1, 2	
– without a calculator for 4 digits with at most 2 decimal places by a single digit	– mentally for any whole number by a multiple of 10 or 100	73, 76	50	29
– with a calculator for 4 digits with at most 2 decimal places	– mentally for any numbers including decimals by 10, 100 or 1000	70, 86	45	37
	– without a calculator for 4 digits with at most 2 decimal places by a single digit – with a calculator for any pair of numbers but at most 3 decimal places in the answer	78, 79, 83, 85	51, 55, 56	33
Round numbers				
Round any number to the nearest appropriate whole number, ten or hundred		25, 71	46	2
	Round any number to one decimal place	48, 70	25, 44	
Fractions, percentages and ratio				
Work with fractions and percentages: – find simple fractions of quantities involving at most 4 digits (easy examples only)	**Work with fractions and percentages:** – mentally find widely used fractions and percentages of whole number quantities – with a calculator find a fraction of a percentage of a quantity – without a calculator as previously defined	43, 44, 52, 53, 67, 69	21, 29, 30	14, 20, 26, 27
	Find ratios between quantities; **Use simple unitary ratio**	44, 45	22	15
Patterns and sequences				
Continue and describe more complex sequences:	**Continue and describe sequences:** – involving square and triangular numbers – find specified items in sequences	29, 30, 38, 107 27, 28, 30, 35	9 7, 8	4, 5, 11, 46 6, 10
	– prime numbers	36, 38	14, 15, 16	
Functions and equations				
Recognise and explain simple relationships: – between two sets of numbers or objects	**Use a "function machine" in reverse for inverse operations** **Solve simple equations and inequations** **Use notation** to describe general relationships between 2 sets of numbers **Use and devise simple rules**			

Spotlight 4 and *Mathematics 5–14* (Scotland)

Target for Level D	Target for Level E	Teacher's Guide page	Pupil Book page	Activity Sheet number
Measure and estimate				
Measure in standard units: – length: small lengths in millimetres and large lengths in metres – weight: extended range of articles – volume: accuracy extended to small containers in millilitres – area: right angled triangles on cm squared grids – temperature **Estimate** small weights, areas and volumes in standard units **Recognise** when kilometres are appropriate **Select appropriate measuring devices** and units for weight **Be aware of common imperial units** in practical applications	**Measure and draw using standard units:** – accuracy and device as appropriate to the application **Estimate measurements:** – areas in square metres – small lengths in millimetres – larger lengths in metres **Work with square kilometre, hectare, tonne** **Read scales** on measuring devices **Realise that volume can be conserved** when shape changes	88, 90 91, 93 94, 95, 96 90 89 96 89, 91, 92, 93, 95, 96	58, 59 60, 62 63, 64, 65 59 61, 62, 64, 65	 38 40 38, 39, 40
Time				
Work with time: – use 24-hour times and equate with 12-hour times – calculate duration in hours/minutes, mentally if possible – time activities in seconds with a stopwatch – calculate speeds	**Time activities** with a digital stopwatch in seconds, tenths, hundredths	100, 101	69, 70	42
Perimeter, formulae and scales				
Calculate perimeter of simple straight shapes by adding lengths	**Calculate using rules:** – areas of rectangles and squares – volumes of cuboids and cubes **Use scales** to interpret or draw maps etc to make models	97, 98 98, 99	66 67, 68	41
SHAPE, POSITION and MOVEMENT				
Range of shapes				
Collect, discuss, make and use 3D and 2D shapes: – discuss 3D and 2D shapes referring to faces, edges, vertices, diagonals, sides, angles – recognise pentagon, hexagon – identify and name equilateral and isosceles triangles – extend shape vocabulary to radius, diameter, circumference – create or copy a tiling using a shape template – make 3D models, including using nets; cube and cuboid only – use the rigidity property of triangles in model-making	**Use properties of 2D and 3D shapes:** – discuss the side, angle, diagonal properties of quadrilaterals: square, rectangle, rhombus, parallelogram, kite, trapezium – define and classify quadrilaterals – relate diameter and circumference – make 3D models, including using nets; triangular prism, pyramid, tetrahedron **Draw triangles:** – given 3 sides, 2 sides and included angle, 2 angles and 1 side – to scale in applications	102 103, 106 104 108, 109	71 72 73 74, 75	 43, 45

Target for Level D	Target for Level E	Teacher's Guide page	Pupil Book page	Activity Sheet number
Position and movement				
Discuss position and movement: – give directions for a route or journey – use an 8 point compass rose – use a coordinate system to locate a point on a grid – create patterns by rotating a shape	**Discuss position and movement:** – use bearings and distances to produce accurate scale drawings of routes – use coordinates in all 4 quadrants to plot position – calculate distances along grid lines	27, 114, 115, 116	78, 79	3, 49
Symmetry				
Work with symmetry: – identify and draw lines of symmetry up to 4 – create symmetrical shapes	**Work with symmetry:** – determine whether or not shapes have rotational symmetry – move a tile of a shape to translate, reflect or rotate it	110 111, 113, 121	76 77	 47, 48, 52
Angle				
Angles: – draw, copy and measure angles accurately within 5 degrees – use standard notation to express bearings	**Angles:** – use "reflex" to describe angles – use the fact that vertically opposite angles are equal – use the properties of angles formed by a line crossing parallel lines – know the sum of the angles of a triangle is 2 right angles	117, 118, 120 117 117 118, 120	80, 81 80 80 81	51 51
INFORMATION HANDLING				
Collect				
By selecting sources of information for tasks, including a questionnaire which allows several responses to each question	**By selecting sources of information** for tasks, including – practical experiments – surveys using questionnaires – sampling using a simple strategy	131	90	58
Organise				
By using diagrams or tables **By using a database or spreadsheet table** with up to three fields defined by pupils	**By designing and using diagrams and tables** **By designing and using a database or** spreadsheet with fields defined by pupils With the aid where appropriate of a computer package	129		57
Display				
	By constructing straight line and curved graphs for continuous data where there is a relationship such as direct proportion	127, 128	87	56
By constructing graphs and pie charts: – involving simple fractions or decimals – involving continuous data which has been grouped	**By constructing pie charts of data** expressed in percentages With the aid, where appropriate of a computer package	131 129, 130, 132	90 89	58 57, 59

Spotlight 4 and *Mathematics 5–14* (Scotland)

Target for Level D	Target for Level E	Teacher's Guide page	Pupil Book page	Activity Sheet number
Interpret				
From a range of display and databases by retrieving information subject to one condition		127, 128, 130, 131, 132, 133	87, 88, 89, 90, 91, 92	59
	From an extended range of displays and databases, retrieving information subject to more than one condition With the aid where appropriate of a computer package, involving the use of logical operators **By describing the main features of a graph** so as to show an awareness of the significance of the information **By calculating the average (mean)** to compare sets of data	134		60

Strand: Numbers and the number system **Topic:** Place value, ordering and rounding

Understanding place value

Activity Sheet 1

Objective

- Read and write whole numbers in figures and words, and know what each digit represents.

Vocabulary

million, hundred thousand, ten thousand, thousands, hundreds, tens, units, ones, partition

Resources

none

Teaching support

The key idea is that the pattern of H T U headings is repeated for large numbers as HTh TTh Th and HM TM M. This sheet explores understanding of large numbers, their digits and the relationships between such numbers.

Children should be confident working with numbers to 10 000.

- Write a 7-digit number, e.g. 4 612 739. Elicit that the first group of 3 digits from the right tells you how many hundreds, tens and units there are, and that the next group how many hundreds, tens and units of thousands. Discuss how the pattern continues in the same way for hundreds, tens and units of millions for numbers with more digits.
- For question 2, draw attention to the fact that the separate scores are multiples of 10, 100, 1000 and so on. This will assist the children when tackling question 3.
- For question 5, children may begin by looking at numbers up to 100. However, useful patterns emerge for numbers 101 to 200, which can be extrapolated for 201 to 300, 301 to 400…
- Encourage children to use a systematic approach and to record results carefully as they investigate. It is probably easier to find and eliminate numbers with 3 and 2 zeros first.

Misconceptions

To avoid misreading of place value, encourage children to group digits in 3s from the right when writing numbers greater than or equal to ten thousand, e.g. 3856694 becomes 3 856 694.

Things to say and ask

- *Point to the largest number on the sheet. How would we say it in words?*
- *What is the value of this digit?*
- *What is the smallest number?*

Multiplying by 10, 100 and 1000

Pupil Book page 1

Objective

- Multiply decimals mentally by 10 or 100, and integers by 1000, and explain the effect.

Vocabulary

million, hundred thousand, ten thousand, thousands, hundreds, tens, units, ones, tenths, multiply, zero, placeholder

Resources

2 dice (per pair)
set of 0–9 digit cards (optional)
decimal point card (optional)

Strand: Numbers and the number system **Topic:** Place value, ordering and rounding

Teaching support

Misconceptions

Avoid telling children to 'add a zero' when multiplying by 10 or to 'add 2 zeros' when multiplying by 100. This does not work with decimals, e.g. 7·3 × 10 does not equal 7·30, and confuses multiplying with adding. Children should be encouraged to see an extra zero as filling a gap, or holding the place, when digits move.

The key idea is that when you multiply a number by 10/100/1000, the digits move one/two/three places to the left. Children practise multiplying whole numbers by 10/100/1000 and decimals by 10/100.

- Show children a whole number, e.g. 35, and ask them to demonstrate how the digits move when the number is multiplied by 10 or 100. Extend to 1000.
- Now show 3·5 and talk about 'tenths'. Demonstrate how the digits move in the same way when multiplying by 10/100 but the decimal point stays fixed.
- When children are writing the answers to question 4 in words, encourage them to notice that when multiplying whole numbers up to 1000 by 1000 the answer is just the number followed by the word 'thousand', e.g. 379 × 1000 becomes three hundred and seventy-nine thousand. Remind them that a thousand thousands is the same as one million.

Things to say and ask

- How many thousands/hundreds/tens/units/tenths are in the number?
- What happens when we multiply this decimal by 10?
- Can you explain what happens to the digits when we multiply by 1000?

Dividing by 10, 100 and 1000

Pupil Book page 2

Objective

- Divide decimals mentally by 10 or 100, and integers by 1000, and explain the effect.

Vocabulary

million, hundred thousand, ten thousand, thousands, hundreds, tens, units, ones, tenths, divide, zero, placeholder, inverse

Resources

2 dice (per pair)
set of 0–9 digit cards (optional)
decimal point card (optional)

Teaching support

Misconceptions

Avoid telling children to 'cross off a 0' when dividing by 10. Where numbers do not end in zero this 'rule' is meaningless. Stress the movement of digits to the right while the decimal point and column headings remain fixed.

The key idea is that when you divide a number by 10/100/1000, the digits move one/two/three places to the right. Children practise dividing whole numbers by 10/100/1000 and decimals by 10/100.

- Show children a multiple of 10, e.g. 350, and ask them to demonstrate how the digits move when the number is divided by 10. Discuss what happens when you divide by 10 again and introduce the decimal point and tenths column. Demonstrate how the digits move when dividing, leaving the decimal point fixed. Extend to dividing by 1000.
- Repeat, starting from a decimal number, e.g. 68·9, and divide by 10 and then 100. Demonstrate how the digits move, leaving the decimal point fixed.
- Discuss how, when a number such as three hundred and forty-seven thousand is divided by 1000, the answer is just three hundred and forty-seven without the word 'thousand'. Encourage children to suggest other whole numbers for which this is true. Remind children that a thousand thousands are one million.
- Emphasise the link between multiplication and division.

Things to say and ask

- How many thousands/hundreds/tens/units/tenths are in this number?
- What happens when we divide this decimal by 10?
- Can you explain what happens to the digits when we divide by 1000? What is the effect?

Strands: Numbers and the number system/Solving problems **Topics:** Place value, ordering and rounding/Reasoning about numbers

Comparing and ordering

Pupil Book pages 3 and 4

Objectives

Vocabulary

<, >, ≤, ≥, =, greater/less than or equal to, compare, order, strategy

- Use the vocabulary of comparing and ordering numbers, including symbols such as <, >, ≤, ≥, =.
- Order a set of integers less than 1 million.
- Give one or more numbers lying between two given numbers.
- Solve mathematical problems or puzzles.

Resources
none

Teaching support

These pages provide opportunities for solving puzzles involving comparison and ordering. Page 3 focuses on large numbers while page 4 introduces calculations and missing operation puzzles. Children should already be familiar with the 'greater than/less than' signs but may need to be introduced to the 'greater/less than or equal to' signs ≤ and ≥.

Pupil Book page 3

- Write: 10 < 11 < 12. Ask children to say whether the statement is true or false. Repeat for 10 < 14 < 19. Rub out the middle number and ask children to suggest other numbers to fill the gap to make a true statement. Together find the set of whole numbers that completes the true statement (11, 12, 13, 14, 15, 16, 17 and 18).
- Change the signs to ≤, i.e. 10 ≤ ☐ ≤ 19. Explain that the sign is read as 'less than or equal to'. *Can anyone tell me the set of whole numbers that completes the statement now?* (10, 11, ..., 18, 19)
- Introduce the 'greater than or equals to' sign in a similar way, using large numbers, e.g. 900 010 ≥ ☐ ≥ 879 010.
- For question 4, encourage children to investigate totals and differences by comparing the most significant digits in turn.
- Encourage children to focus on the more significant digits first. *How many different ways are there of arranging the first three digits of the six-digit number?* (4) *Once you have selected the first three digits, how many ways are there of arranging the remaining three?* (6).

Pupil Book page 4

- For question 5, it is important that children realise that they should concentrate on the hundreds as the most significant digits. There are many possible answers, so you may like to ask individuals to focus on all the ways of making, e.g. 1 ☐ ☐ < 5 ☐ ☐.
- Children should quickly realise that there is a > statement corresponding to every < statement.

Things to say and ask

- Give me a number that is more than 395 250 but less than 395 280.
- A number is less than or equal to 400 009 and greater than or equal to 399 996. What could it be?
- How can we write this question using the ≤, ≥ signs?

Strands: Numbers and the number system/Calculations *Topics:* Place value, ordering and rounding/Using a calculator

Estimating and approximating

Pupil Book page 5

Objectives

- Use the vocabulary of estimation and approximation.
- Develop calculator skills and use a calculator effectively.

Vocabulary

estimate, approximate, round

Resources

calculator (per child)

Teaching support

Misconceptions

Children often believe that an estimate is worthless unless it produces the actual number or is very close to it. This can lead them to calculate first and then give an 'estimate' by adjusting slightly. The idea that an estimate simply provides a sensible idea of the exact answer should be encouraged.

This page gives practice in estimating and rounding to gain an approximate answer before using a calculator to find the exact answer. It also includes opportunities for children to make estimates of real-life situations, e.g. how many 1p coins will make a line 1 km long.

Children should have experience of using a calculator to perform simple operations.

- Revise rounding to an appropriate number, e.g. to the nearest 10, 100 or 1000. Some children may need to revise multiplying multiples of 10, 100 or 1000, e.g. $60 \times 40 = 6 \times 4 \times 10 \times 10 = 24 \times 100 = 2400$.
- For question 3, children should work in pairs to encourage discussion of estimates.
- Discuss how some estimates can be made by counting or measuring part of the whole first and then multiplying, e.g. if you know approximately how many meals you eat each day you can estimate the number of meals in a week, month, year, lifetime…

Things to say and ask

- *How did you round these two numbers?*
- *Can you do some measuring first to help you make a better estimate?*
- *How did you decide on that estimate?*

Rounding

Activity Sheet 2

Objectives

- Consolidate rounding an integer to the nearest 10, 100 or 1000.
- Develop calculator skills and use a calculator effectively.

Vocabulary

approximate, round to the nearest ten/hundred/thousand/million

Resources

calculator (per child)

Strand: Numbers and the number system **Topic:** Place value, ordering and rounding

Teaching support

The key idea is that there are occasions when rounding is more useful than giving an 'exact' number, e.g. 'Man wins £2 945 094 lottery' would more appropriately be reported with the amount rounded to the nearest million rather than to the nearest 10. The sheet first gives practice in rounding to 1000 and then to 100 for finding approximate answers.

Children should have experience of using a calculator to perform simple operations.

- In question 3, children are asked to find several numbers that round to a given number. Discuss how numbers above and below round to it. Elicit that when rounding to the nearest 10 the range of numbers will be 10, i.e. from the '5' below to the '4' above. Remind children that a number with 5 in the units place rounds up to the next multiple of 10. Similarly, when rounding to the nearest 100 the range of numbers will be 100, i.e. from the '50' below to the '49' above. Remind children that a number ending in 50 rounds up to the next multiple of 100...

- For question 4, discuss some examples such as those given on page 13 of section 6 of the NNS *Framework for teaching mathematics*.

Things to say and ask

- How can we use approximation to help us with calculating?
- If a number rounds to 27 390 to the nearest 10, what could the number be?
- How did you work that out?

Positive and negative numbers (1)

Pupil Book page 6

Objectives

- Order a set of positive and negative integers.
- Find the difference between a positive and a negative integer, or two negative integers, in a context such as temperature or the number line.

Vocabulary

positive, negative, integer, above/below zero, difference between

Resources

number lines (positive and negative numbers)
up to 10 counters in 2 colours (per pair)

Teaching support

Misconceptions

Children may need to be reminded to use the word 'negative' when referring to numbers, as in negative one, negative two... and the word 'minus' when referring to temperature, e.g. minus 6°.

This page extends the range of negative numbers and gives practice in ordering sets of positive and negative numbers. Children begin to find sums and differences. They should have sight of a number line ($^-50$ to $^+50$) or draw their own as needed.

Children should be confident in ordering single-digit negative numbers in a context such as temperature or the number line.

- Introduce children to the convention of using a superscript minus sign for negative numbers. Establish that this is to avoid possible confusion with the sign for subtraction.

- Ensure through questioning that children realise that, e.g. $^-11$ is less than $^-9$ although 11 is greater than 9.

- For question 2, encourage children to use a number line. They should aim to move towards the right on the number line to reach the answer 12, e.g. to start on a negative number such as $^-1$ and to count on 13 up to 12. This gives the addition fact $^-1 + 13 = 12$. Encourage children to work systematically to find a pattern.

- Remind children that numbers can be added in any order to give the same answer, e.g. if $^-5 + 17 = 12$, then $17 + ^-5 = 12$.

- Again children should use a number line and it may be helpful to work in pairs. Elicit that the subtraction equation finds the difference, so we are looking for a difference of 12. On a number line the 2 numbers will be 12 units apart.

Strand: Numbers and the number system *Topics:* Place value, ordering and rounding/Properties of numbers and number sequences

Things to say and ask
- Which numbers lie between negative 14 and negative 9?
- Give me a negative number greater than negative 5.
- Can you count back in threes from 7?

Positive and negative numbers (2)

Activity Sheet 3

Objectives
- Recognise and extend number sequences.
- Read and plot coordinates in all four quadrants.
- Find the difference between a positive and a negative integer, or two negative integers, in a context such as temperature or the number line.

Vocabulary

positive, negative, integer, above/below zero, difference between, adjacent, sequence

Resources
number lines (positive and negative numbers) (optional)

This page gives practice in continuing sequences with negative numbers, finding positive and negative numbers with a given difference and exploring negative numbers on a coordinate grid.

Teaching support

Misconceptions
Children may need to be reminded to use the word 'negative' when referring to numbers, as in negative one, negative two ... and the word 'minus' when referring to temperature, as in minus 6°.

- When continuing sequences, remind children to find the differences between adjacent terms, e.g. for the sequence 35, 26, 17, 8... the difference between terms is 9, so it is continued by counting back in 9s to $^-1$, then $^-10$...
- Introduce a coordinate grid with four quadrants and remind children about coordinate pairs in the first quadrant where the positive first number tells you how many across. Explain that 'across' can be moving from the origin to the right (in a positive direction) or moving to the left (in a negative direction). Repeat for the second coordinate and investigate points in each quadrant.
- Children will find this easier if you encourage them to look for and use patterns on number lines. When choosing a new pair, encourage them to relate it to one they have already investigated.

Things to say and ask
- How many do you need to subtract each time to continue this sequence?
- Can you point to the coordinates ($^-1$, $^-3$) ($^-3$, $^-1$), (1, $^-3$) ($^-1$, 3) (3, $^-1$)...

Whole number sequences (1)

Pupil Book page 7

Objectives
- Recognise and extend number sequences such as the sequence of square numbers.
- Recognise and explain patterns and relationships.

Vocabulary

sequence, predict

Resources
coloured counters

Strands: Numbers and the number system/Solving problems *Topics:* Properties of numbers and number sequences/Reasoning and generalising about numbers

Teaching support

Misconceptions
Look out for children who interpret 4^2 as 4×2 instead of 4×4.

The key idea is for children to build and then recognise the sequence of square numbers.

- Discuss a sequence that grows by adding the same number each time, e.g. 3, 6, 9, 12… and ask a volunteer to represent it with counters.

- Explain to children that there are some sequences that often appear in mathematics, e.g. square numbers. Invite children to discuss and explain why square numbers are so called, and ask volunteers to represent them with counters. Discuss the difference between successive square numbers: 3, 5, 7… Show children how to write square numbers as $1 \times 1 = 1^2$, $2 \times 2 = 2^2$ … and introduce page 7.
- Discuss the links between questions 1 and 2. Elicit that $2^2 - 1^2$ is just the difference between the first and second square numbers.

Things to say and ask

- Can you predict the next square number without making it with the counters?
- Can you describe the sequence of differences?

Whole number sequences (2)

Pupil Book page 8

Objectives

- Recognise and extend number sequences such as the sequence of triangular numbers 1, 3, 6, 10, 15.
- Recognise and explain patterns and relationships.

Vocabulary

sequence, predict

Resources
100 coloured counters (per pair)
calculator (per pair)

Teaching support

The key idea in this activity is for the children to build and then recognise the sequence of triangular numbers.

Children should be familiar with square numbers.

- Discuss a sequence that grows by adding the same number each time, e.g. 2, 5, 8… and ask a volunteer to represent it with counters.
- In question 3, the key to solving the problem is to be systematic in making and recording the pairs of counters. Children may need support in developing a system for this, such as matching every colour with blue, and then every colour (except for blue) with red…
- After children have worked on page 8, reflect with them on the emergence of triangular numbers in the results of the investigation.

Things to say and ask

- Can you predict the next triangular number without making it with counters?
- What do you think will be the next number in your table?

Strands: Numbers and the number system/Solving problems **Topics:** Properties of numbers and number sequences/Reasoning and generalising about numbers

Whole-number sequences (3)

Activity Sheet 4

Objectives

- Recognise and extend number sequences.
- Solve mathematical problems or puzzles, recognise and explain patterns and relationships, generalise and predict.
- Explain a generalised relationship in words.

Vocabulary

sequence, predict

Resources
none

Teaching support

This sheet practises recognising patterns that emerge in some sequences, and considering why they differ from sequence to sequence.

Children should have had plenty of experience of recognising and extending sequences that increase or decrease in steps of equal size. They should also have had some experience of making a general statement to explain the outcomes of simple investigations.

- Children work individually or in pairs.
- Rehearse the activity by demonstrating the example given in question 1. Show the children how to represent the last digit on a similar diagram drawn on the board. Continue the diagram until it matches the one on the activity sheet, and discuss where the next line will go. Explain that the sheet starts with this example and then moves on to other examples.

Things to say and ask

- What pattern do you think 'add 1' each time would make?
- What pattern do you think 'subtract 4' each time would make?

Decimal number sequences

Pupil Book page 9

Objectives

- Recognise and extend number sequences such as counting on in steps of 0·1, 0·2, 0·25, 0·5…, and then back.
- Recognise and explain patterns and relationships.

Vocabulary

sequence, predict

Resources
paper circle (per pair)
paper clip (per pair)
pencil (per pair)
number line marked in steps of 0·1

Strands: Numbers and the number system/Solving problems **Topics:** Properties of numbers and number sequences/Reasoning and generalising about numbers

Teaching support

Misconceptions

If children find counting in decimal steps too challenging, encourage them to use a number line and to draw on the steps they are taking as they count.

The key idea is that we can create decimal number sequences by counting on or back in steps of less than 1.

Children should be comfortable using decimal numbers and have had experience of continuing sequences with steps of 0·1 and 0·5 starting from a whole number.

- Begin with group oral practice in counting in steps of, e.g. 0·2, 0·5, 0·25, 0·6…
- Give some volunteers an opportunity to help you demonstrate how some of these sequences can be illustrated on the number line. In particular, show them how to draw steps of 0·25 by estimating the mid-point between two marked tenths.

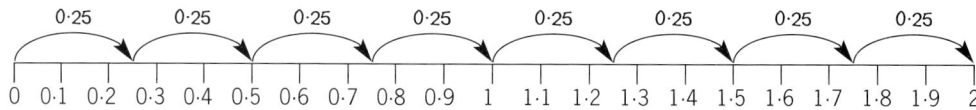

- Introduce the game. Later ask children to share the advantages and disadvantages of their recording strategies.

Things to say and ask

- *Before you count, try to predict where you will end up.*
- *Can you count back in steps of 0·1 from 5? Now try steps of 0·2 from 3·9.*

Shape number patterns

Activity Sheets 5 and 6

Objectives

Vocabulary

sequence, relationship, rule, predict

- Recognise and extend number sequences, such as the sequence of square numbers, or the sequence of triangular numbers 1, 3, 6, 10, 15…
- Recognise and explain patterns and relationships, generalise and predict.

Resources
For Activity Sheet 5:
    coloured pencils (optional)
    cm squared paper (optional)

Teaching support

Misconceptions

If children are having difficulty spotting patterns, encourage them to use a coloured pencil to mark the numbers they are looking for, e.g. when looking for patterns in even numbers, colour all the even numbers.

The key idea is for children to build and then recognise the structure of patterns such as Pascal's triangle and sequences of triangular, pentagonal and hexagonal numbers. They observe and describe some of the fascinating number patterns generated.

Children should have plenty of experience in recognising and describing sequences and patterns in numbers.

- Start by playing 'Guess my sequence'. Write a sequence on the board, e.g. 1·2, 1·7, 2·2, 2·7, 3·2, 3·7, 4·2… Ask pairs to discuss and decide the rule for the sequence, e.g. 'add 0·5 each time' or 'goes up in 0·5s.' Give children an opportunity to generate sequences for this game.

Strands: Numbers and the number system/Solving problems **Topics:** Properties of numbers and number sequences/Reasoning and generalising about numbers

Activity Sheet 5

- Introduce Activity Sheet 5. Give children an opportunity to share their findings from questions 1 and 2. Some children may wish to extend the triangle further to find out how the patterns develop.

- Show children how to orientate squared paper to use it to record their triangles:

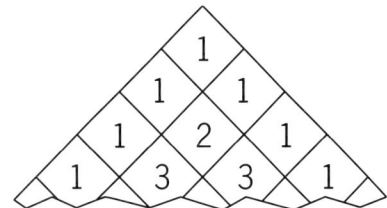

Encourage children to realise that the first few rows of the triangle will be unchanged because all the numbers are less than 5. Then two copies of Pascal's triangle begin to appear.

Activity Sheet 6

- Introduce Activity Sheet 6. Ask pairs to discuss the patterns in question 3 before sharing with the whole group.

Things to say and ask

Activity Sheet 5:
- How do you think this pattern would grow if you extended the triangle?
- What other multiples could you try?

Activity Sheet 6:
- Can you predict the next triangular/square/pentagonal/hexagonal number? Explain how you know.

Investigating odd and even numbers

Activity Sheet 7

Objectives

- Make general statements about odd or even numbers, including the outcome of products.
- Make and investigate a general statement about familiar numbers by finding examples that satisfy it.

Vocabulary

rule, predict, sum, difference between, product

Resources

none

Strands: Numbers and the number system/Solving problems **Topics:** Properties of numbers and number sequences/Reasoning and generalising about numbers

Teaching support

Misconceptions
Children may think that because odd + odd and odd − odd are even, odd × odd must also be even.

The key idea is that we can investigate whether general statements are true or not by finding examples that match or not.

Children should be familiar with the outcomes of the sums and differences of odd and even numbers.

- Write some incorrect calculations for children to check, e.g. 432 + 261 = 694 and 954 − 278 = 675. Ask them to describe ways of checking whether the answers are right or wrong. Elicit looking at the 'rules' for sums and differences.
- Ask children to work in pairs with Activity Sheet 7 to find out if there are any rules for the **products** of odd and even numbers.
- When they have completed the sheet, give them an opportunity to compare their answers and explanations with other pairs. Explaining the outcomes of the multiplications is the most difficult part of this activity. Remind children that multiplication is a quick way of calculating repeated additions. Encourage them to consider why the sums and differences of odd and even numbers have the outcomes they do and then apply this to multiplication, e.g. any even number multiplied by any number will have an even answer because even numbers are being added.
- Encourage children to realise that the extension is the same as question 3 because whether you add 1 to a number or take 1 from it, you will end up with either an odd number both times or an even number both times.

Things to say and ask

- *What do you think will happen when you try out some numbers?*
- *How are these outcomes different from the outcomes for sums and differences?*

Investigating multiples up to 10 × 10

Pupil Book page 10

Objectives

Vocabulary

multiple of, relationship

- Recognise multiples up to 10 × 10.
- Solve mathematical problems or puzzles, recognise and explain patterns and relationships.

Resources
none

Teaching support

Misconceptions
Children sometimes feel it is 'better' to start with the bigger numbers in an investigation. Encourage them to at least begin with easier numbers to avoid mistakes.

This page gives practice in looking for relationships and patterns in the multiplication square to 10 × 10.

- Ask children to look at the multiplication square and describe any patterns they spot, e.g. square numbers are on the diagonal; some rows have only even numbers, but there are no rows with only odd numbers… Encourage careful use of mathematical language.
- When they have completed the page, give them an opportunity to share the outcomes of the investigations with the rest of the group.
- Children will find that the difference between the sums of the diagonals is 4 for a 3 × 3 square and 10 for a 4 × 4 square. Ask children to try to work out why this is so. Is it true for any multiplication square?

Things to say and ask

- *What do you think will happen when you try larger squares?*
- *Why do you think there is always the same difference between the numbers?*

Strand: Numbers and the number system *Topic:* Properties of numbers and number sequences

Looking at divisibility

Activity Sheet 8 Pupil Book page 11

Objective
- Know and apply simple tests of divisibility.

Vocabulary
divisible by, divisibility, factor

Resources
coloured pencils

Teaching support

Misconceptions
Children sometimes persist in thinking that a large number that ends in, e.g. 8 is divisible by 8. Encourage them always to check, e.g. by halving 3 times, by looking at the last 3 digits…

The key idea is that there are some tests that are useful in determining whether one number is a factor of/divisible by another. Children explore divisibility on Activity Sheet 8, using tests they have already met and developing new ones. Pupil Book page 11 guides them formally through the tests and gives an opportunity to apply them to large numbers.

Children should be familiar with some simple tests for divisibility.

Activity Sheet 8

- Introduce the activities by reminding children of the divisibility tests they are already familiar with (2, 3, 4, 5, 10 and 100). Record these for reference.
- In question 3, children try to come up with some tests for divisibility by 6, 8 and 9. Encourage them to relate tests for 6 to tests for 2 and 3, tests for 8 to the test for 2 and tests for 9 to the test for 3.
- Encourage children to form the converse of the tests, e.g. if the sum of the digits is not a multiple of 9 then the number is not divisible by 9.

Pupil Book page 11

- Talk about the children's findings from Activity Sheet 8 and elicit/teach the children the following divisibility tests:

    6 The number must be even. Add the digits of the number. If the answer is a multiple of 3, then the number is a multiple of 6, e.g. 516 → 5 + 1 + 6 = 12. 12 is a multiple of 3, therefore 516 is a multiple of 6.

    9 Add the digits of the number. If the answer is a multiple of 9, then the number is a multiple of 9, e.g. 6165 → 6 + 1 + 6 + 5 = 18. 18 is a multiple of 9, therefore 6165 is a multiple of 9.

    8 Look at the last 3 digits of the number. If they are a multiple of 8, then the number is a multiple of 8, e.g. 5304 → 304 is a multiple of 8, so 5304 is also a multiple of 8. This works because 1000 is a multiple of 8, so any number of thousands will also be a multiple of 8.

- For question 3 and its extension, encourage children to use the tests of divisibility.

Things to say and ask

Activity Sheet 8:
- *If a number is odd, is it divisible by 2/4/6/8/10…?*

Pupil Book page 11:
- *Which tests do you know without using the checklists?*

Strand: Numbers and the number system **Topic:** Properties of numbers and number sequences

Lowest common multiples

Pupil Book page 12

Objective
- Find simple common multiples.

Vocabulary

common multiple, product

Resources
none

Teaching support

Misconceptions

The most difficult lowest common multiples to find are those that are neither one of the numbers themselves, nor the product of the 2 numbers. Suggest that children develop strategies to check that they have the lowest common multiple, e.g. halve the product and test to see if the answer is still divisible by both numbers. Dividing by 3 is another good test.

The key idea in this activity is for children to be able to find common multiples and the lowest common multiple of 2 numbers. They need to realise that it is not always the product of the 2 numbers that is the lowest multiple common to both numbers, e.g. the lowest common multiple of 4 and 6 is not 24 (4 × 6), but 12.

Children should be familiar with the multiplication square to 10×10.

- Ask children to suggest 4 numbers that are multiples of both 3 and 5. Write up the suggestions and then ask them to identify the smallest. Encourage them to identify the lowest number possible that is a multiple of both 3 and 5. Explain that 15 is the 'lowest common multiple' of 3 and 5.
- Repeat for 3 and 9 (LCM 9), and 4 and 6 (LCM 12).
- For question 4, do an example together before children try it in pairs:
  I am a multiple of 10 and 6.
  My digits add up to 3.
  Who am I?   (30)

Things to say and ask
- *Which are the easiest lowest common multiples to find?*
- *Explain how you worked out the lowest common multiple for your numbers.*

Common multiples of 2 or 3 numbers

Activity Sheet 9

Objective
- Find simple common multiples.

Vocabulary

multiple of, lowest common multiple, product

Resources
calculator (per child)
scissors (per child)

Strand: Numbers and the number system *Topic:* Properties of numbers and number sequences

Teaching support

This sheet gives practice in finding common multiples, including lowest common multiples, of 2 and then 3 numbers.

Children should understand the term 'lowest common multiple', and have had some practice in finding lowest common multiples.

- Discuss the term 'lowest common multiple' and how to find one. The lowest common multiple could be one of the numbers themselves or the product of the 2 numbers. If it is neither of these, try one half or one third of the product. Children should check that any common multiple they find using these methods is in fact the lowest common multiple.
- Look at the activity sheet together and ask children why they think it will be helpful to use a calculator. Elicit that a number that is a multiple of 7 will be divisible by 7 (i.e. the quotient will have no digits after the decimal point).
- For the game children may choose to use a calculator in their search for the lowest common multiples but should find the differences between them mentally.
- When children have completed the sheet, discuss for which pairs of numbers it was easiest to find the lowest common multiple and which were the most difficult. Encourage children to explain their strategies.
- Suggest that children try 3 of the smaller numbers first. Encourage them to use an efficient strategy, e.g. finding the lowest common multiple of 2 of the numbers and seeing whether it is also divisible by the third number.

Things to say and ask

- Which are the easiest lowest common multiples to find?
- Explain how you worked out the lowest common multiple for your numbers.

Recognising and using square numbers

Pupil Book page 13 Activity Sheet 10

Objective

- Recognise squares of numbers to at least 12×12.

Vocabulary

square number

Resources
For the Pupil Book:
  2 dice and a calculator (per pair)
For the Activity Sheet:
  calculator (per child)

Strand: Numbers and the number system   **Topic:** Properties of numbers and number sequences

Teaching support

Misconceptions

Pupil Book page 13: For question 1, support children by pointing out that when you square numbers such as 70/700/7000 the answer will end with 2/4/6 zeros (twice as many as in the original number) and showing them why.

The focus of this unit is on recognising and using square numbers to at least 12×12.

Children should understand the nature of square numbers and have had previous opportunities to identify some and use notation, e.g. 5^2.

Pupil Book page 13

- Discuss why square numbers are special, e.g. because they make a square array in a visual representation. It is interesting for children to know that these numbers occur frequently in mathematics. They are also useful products to learn because nearby products can be calculated from them, e.g. if you know that $12 \times 12 = 144$, you can easily find 11×12 or 13×12.
- Write $13 \times 13 = 169$. *Who can tell me the value of 130^2?* (169 000)
- When children have completed question 1, ask them to identify examples of the way that knowing square numbers can support the calculation of nearby or similar products.
- In question 2, children should have found that all the odd numbers except 1 can be written as the difference between 2 square numbers. Can they explain why? Can they find a similar pattern in the numbers that can be written as the sum of 2 squares?

Activity Sheet 10

- Discuss where it is appropriate to use calculators on this sheet.

Things to say and ask

Pupil Book page 13:
- *Why have you chosen this number?*
- *Predict whether you can write 39 as the difference between two square numbers.*

Activity Sheet 10:
- *Who can tell me the value of 15^2? and 14×15? ...*

Prime numbers and prime factors

Pupil Book pages 14 and 15

Objectives

- Recognise prime numbers to at least 20.
- Factorise numbers to 100 into prime factors.

Vocabulary

divisible by, factor, prime number, factorise, prime factor

Resources

For Pupil Book page 14:
  2 cm squared paper

For Pupil Book page 15:
  none

Strand: Numbers and the number system *Topic:* Properties of numbers and number sequences

Teaching support

The key idea is to introduce prime numbers and then go on to factorise a number into its prime factors.

Children should have a good understanding and knowledge of multiplication facts and be able to find factors of any number to 100. They should be able to use factors to find products mentally.

Pupil Book page 14

- Introduce children to 'prime numbers'. It may be appropriate to demonstrate how some numbers can be illustrated with rectangles, e.g. 12 has 6 factors (1, 2, 3, 4, 6, 12) and can be represented by:

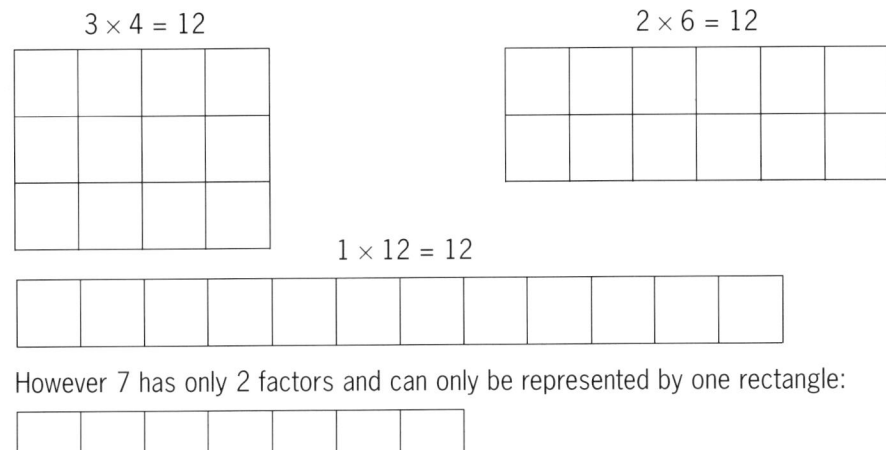

However 7 has only 2 factors and can only be represented by one rectangle:

So 7 is a prime number.

- Rehearse question 2 with volunteers to 'test' some numbers between 1 and 50.
- In question 3, where the grid has 6 columns, children will have noticed that the prime numbers occur in 2 columns: prime numbers are never even and so will not appear in the 'even' columns. There is a similar pattern for a grid with 8 columns. For grids with odd numbers of columns the vertical arrangement of prime numbers shifts to diagonal lines.

Pupil Book page 15

- Explain that any number can be made by multiplying together 2 or more prime numbers. These are called its 'prime factors'. *We say that we factorise a number when we write it as a product of its prime factors.*
- Together look at the prime factor tree in question 1. Ask for volunteers to demonstrate the procedure for factorising a number by drawing a factor tree for, e.g. 12. Suggest children draw a ring around each prime factor.
- Encourage children to check that they have a complete set of prime factors by multiplying them together to ensure they get the number they began with.

Things to say and ask

Pupil Book page 14:
❏ *Which tests of divisibility did you use to check for factors?*

Pupil Book page 15:
❏ *For which numbers can you find the prime factors without drawing a factor tree?*
❏ *Is there only one possible tree for each number?*

Strands: Numbers and the number system/Solving problems **Topics:** Properties of numbers and number sequences/Reasoning and generalising about numbers

Prime numbers and factors

Pupil Book page 16

Objectives

- Recognise prime numbers.
- Know and apply simple tests of divisibility.

Vocabulary

divisible by, factor, prime number

Resources
none

Teaching support

This page provides practice in recognising prime numbers and using tests of divisibility.

Children should know that a prime number has exactly 2 factors, and be familiar with tests of divisibility and square numbers.

Misconceptions

Children sometimes persist in thinking that a large number that ends in, e.g. 8 is divisible by 8. Encourage them always to check, e.g. by halving 3 times, by looking at the last 3 digits…

- Write 57 on the board. Ask children if it is a prime number. Elicit explanations. For each potential factor, ask children to explain the divisibility test they have used, e.g. the divisibility test for 3 is to add the digits and, if the total is a multiple of 3, then the number is a multiple of 3.
- Repeat for 59.
- For questions 1 and 2, talk about the patterns of the calculations. Encourage children to check whether numbers are prime by using divisibility tests.
- For question 3, suggest that children look for factors in pairs: if 3 is a factor of 24, then 8 must also be a factor because 3 × 8 = 24.
- Encourage children to make the link with prime numbers: the fewest factors a number (other than 1) can have is 2, and so they are looking for prime numbers.

Things to say and ask

- How do you know if a number is divisible by 9, 6…?
- For question 3: *Tell me how you organised your investigation. Which numbers did you try first? Did you look for pairs of factors?*

Looking for patterns

Activity Sheet 11

Objectives

- Solve mathematical problems or puzzles, recognise and explain patterns and relationships, generalise and predict.
- Recognise and extend number sequences.

Vocabulary

relationship, pattern, rule, predict

Resources
calculator (per child)

Strand: Numbers and the number system *Topic:* Fractions

Teaching support

Misconceptions

Ensure that the children try enough examples in question 2 so that the pattern in the answers emerges sufficiently to allow a prediction.

This sheet is about investigating patterns in the answers to a sequence of calculations, then predicting and testing.

Children will need to have had plenty of experience of recognising and continuing sequences.

- Introduce the sheet by asking children to think about multiplication tables. *Are there any that are easier to remember because they make an easy pattern?* Among their suggestions may be the 5-times table, which forms a pattern in which the units digit alternates between 5 and 0 and the tens digit increases by 1 every other number.
- Explain that the sheet is about looking for patterns in the answers to multiplications that are not in tables.
- Not all calculations of this nature produce an obvious pattern, so children are asked to experiment with different numbers.

Things to say and ask

- *How many multiplications do you think you should do before you look for a pattern?*
- *Which numbers made the best patterns?*

Improper fractions and mixed numbers

Pupil Book page 17

Objectives

Vocabulary

improper fraction, mixed number, numerator, denominator, prime number

- Use fraction notation, including mixed numbers, and the vocabulary numerator and denominator.
- Change a fraction such as $\frac{33}{8}$ to the equivalent mixed number $4\frac{1}{8}$, and vice versa.

Resources

two 1–6 dice and one 7–12 dice (per child)

counters (per child)

Teaching support

Misconceptions

Children need to be confident and accurate with mental calculations of multiplication and division facts. If they are still relying on a 'tables square', 'Beat the clock'-type games will help them gain confidence and speed.

The key idea is that improper fractions can be written as mixed numbers and vice versa.

Children need to have a good understanding of multiplication and division, place value and equivalence and some experience of converting improper fractions to mixed numbers. They should have been introduced to prime numbers.

- Look at the page together. Remind children that they need to use multiplication and division, and also link the work to division with remainders, e.g. *What is 21 divided by 4?* Elicit that $21 \div 4 = 5$ r 1 and that this can also be written as $\frac{21}{4} = 5\frac{1}{4}$.
- Pose further questions using the above vocabulary. Remind children how to convert an improper fraction to a mixed number, e.g. divide the numerator by the denominator and then express the remainder as a fraction. To convert a mixed number into an improper fraction, multiply the whole number by the denominator to find the number of fractional parts in the whole number and then include/add on the extra fractional parts.
- In question 2, encourage children to work systematically to find ways of using 3 primes to make a whole number. They should be able to make 2, 4, 6, 8, 10 and 12.

Things to say and ask

- *When I multiply three by a denominator, I get twenty-one. What is the denominator?*
- *When I divide the numerator sixty by a denominator, I get six remainder six. What is the denominator?*

Strand: Numbers and the number system **Topic:** Fractions

Related fractions

Pupil Book page 18

Objective

- Recognise relationships between fractions: for example, that $\frac{1}{10}$ is ten times $\frac{1}{100}$, and that $\frac{1}{16}$ is half of $\frac{1}{8}$.

Vocabulary

improper fraction, mixed number, equivalent

Resources

paper squares or circles (per child)

Teaching support

This page is about recognising how fractions can be related to each other in terms of size.

Children should have a sound understanding of simple fractions and equivalence, place value, multiplication and division.

Misconceptions
If the children have difficulty with question 2, they will need to do more practical activities such as paper folding.

- Before working on the page, do some practical paper folding. Use paper squares or circles and ask children to fold their shape in half with you, then in half again 3 more times before opening it out. Ask questions, e.g. *How many equal sections have you made?* (16) Fold your opened paper in half. *How many equal sections can you see now?* Ask children to make their own statements comparing the different fractions, e.g. $\frac{1}{2}$ of $\frac{1}{8} = \frac{1}{16}$. Continue like this to help children appreciate the relationships.
- When they have finished the page, challenge them to look at the unit fractions only and see if they can see a mathematical link between their statements and the denominators, e.g. $\frac{1}{4}$ is twice the size of $\frac{1}{8}$; $\frac{1}{8}$ is half of $\frac{1}{4}$; $4 \times 2 = 8$ and $8 \div 2 = 4$.

Things to say and ask

- Explain why $\frac{1}{2}$ of $\frac{1}{3}$ is $\frac{1}{6}$.
- How can you find half of three quarters?

Reducing fractions

Pupil Book page 19

Objective

- Reduce a fraction to its simplest form by cancelling common factors in the numerator and denominator.

Vocabulary

numerator, denominator, equivalent, reduced to, cancel

Resources

fraction chart/flip cards (optional)

Strand: Numbers and the number system **Topic:** Fractions

Teaching support

Misconceptions

If children find it difficult to see connections between numerators and denominators, practise counting exercises, e.g. start at 12 and count on in multiples of 3; start at 12, count on in multiples of 4 and stop at the number that is just before 100; start at 56 and count backwards in multiples of 4...

The key idea is to find the simplest form of a fraction by dividing both the numerator and denominator by the same number until you can't divide exactly any more.

Children should have a sound understanding of simple fractions and equivalence, place value, multiplication and division, and knowledge of factors and multiples.

- Ask questions, e.g. *Would you rather have one half or three fifths of your favourite pizza? Which is larger, one tenth or eleven hundredths?* Refer to the fraction wall on Pupil Book page 18 or have fraction flip cards available for the children.

- Remind children that equivalent fractions are the same size. Demonstrate the position of some simple equivalent fractions on a fraction number line and write, e.g. $\frac{1}{2} = \frac{2}{4} = \frac{3}{6} = \frac{4}{8} = \frac{5}{10} = \frac{50}{100}$. Elicit that it is easy to find an equivalent fraction by multiplying the numerator and the denominator by the same number.

- Discuss how it is often easier to work with fractions if they are in their simplest form. Encourage children to see that we can use division (the inverse operation to multiplication) to reduce the fractions (also known as cancelling), e.g. $\frac{15}{30} = \frac{15 \div 3}{30 \div 3} = \frac{5}{10} = \frac{5 \div 5}{10 \div 5} = \frac{1}{2}$. *Can anyone see a quicker way to get to $\frac{1}{2}$? Can we divide again?* Stress that the fraction is in its simplest form when it is impossible to find a number (other than 1) by which the numerator and denominator are both divisible.

- When children are confident, relate the division to finding a common factor.

- Suggest that children use unit fractions to start with and then look for equivalents, e.g. $\frac{1}{3} = \frac{2}{6} = \frac{4}{12}$. Encourage them to use multiples and factors to find possible equivalents efficiently.

Things to say and ask

- What number can I use to reduce $\frac{8}{16}$ to $\frac{1}{2}$?
- Tell me a common factor for 12 and 16. So how can you reduce $\frac{12}{16}$?

Changing and reducing fractions

Activity Sheet 12

Objectives

Vocabulary

proper/improper fraction, mixed number, numerator, denominator, equivalent, reduced to, cancel

- Change a fraction such as $\frac{33}{8}$ to the equivalent mixed number $4\frac{1}{8}$, and vice versa.
- Reduce a fraction to its simplest form by cancelling common factors in the numerator and denominator.

Resources

set of 1–10 number cards (per child)
multiples-of-10 cards (per child)

Teaching support

Misconceptions

If children become anxious about how to proceed, always return to a practical activity such as paper folding to give meaning to the notation again.

This sheet gives practice in cancelling proper fractions and extends this to improper fractions.

Children need to have completed Pupil Book pages 17 and 19.

- Introduce the sheet by reminding children how to change improper fractions into mixed numbers, and how to reduce fractions to their simplest form by cancelling. Practise together, e.g. $\frac{75}{50} = \frac{3}{2} = 1\frac{1}{2}$, $\frac{\square\square}{4} = 2\frac{1}{2}$ ... *Do I divide the numerator by the denominator or vice versa to change an improper fraction into a mixed number?*

- For 'Let's play', demonstrate how the digit and number cards can look like a fraction by placing one above the other. Ask questions, e.g. *What number can you divide both 6 and 30 by?* to remind children that they need to find a common factor when cancelling.

- This changes 'Let's play' into an exercise in cancelling improper fractions and expressing them as mixed numbers.

Strand: Numbers and the number system **Topic:** Fractions

Things to say and ask
- If both the numerator and denominator are even in an improper fraction, which number will always be a common factor?
- If I have thirty quarters of pizza, how many pizzas do I have altogether?

Ordering fractions (1)

Pupil Book page 20

Objective
- Order fractions such as $\frac{2}{3}$, $\frac{3}{4}$ and $\frac{5}{6}$ by converting them to fractions with a common denominator, and position them on a number line.

Vocabulary

numerator, denominator, common denominator, equivalent, convert

Resources
fraction board/flip cards (optional)

Teaching support

The key idea is that it is usually easier to order fractions if they have a common denominator.

Children should have a sound understanding of simple fractions and equivalence, place value, multiplication and division, and knowledge of factors and multiples.

Misconceptions
Children often find it difficult to remember to multiply the numerator as well as the denominator when converting fractions to ones with common denominators. Suggest that they use lists of equivalent fractions until they are confident.

- Refer to the fraction wall on Pupil Book page 20 or have fraction flip cards available to illustrate the relative sizes of different fractions. It may help to have a fraction board as well so that the pieces can be picked up and placed on top of each other. It is very important that children have practical experiences before they are introduced to finding common denominators.
- Identify some equivalent fractions on the fraction chart. Remind children that equivalent fractions are the same size and that they all occupy the same point on a fraction number line.
- Challenge children to suggest a way of finding the bigger of two fractions without using the fraction chart, e.g. $\frac{3}{5}$ and $\frac{2}{3}$. Elicit that it is useful to list the set of equivalent fractions for each one until two with a common denominator are reached, e.g. $\frac{3}{5}, \frac{6}{10}, \frac{9}{15}, \frac{12}{20}$... and $\frac{2}{3}, \frac{4}{6}, \frac{6}{9}, \frac{9}{12}, \frac{10}{15}$...; $\frac{10}{15}$ is bigger than $\frac{9}{15}$ and so $\frac{2}{3}$ is bigger than $\frac{3}{5}$.
- Discuss whether anyone can spot a quicker way to find the pair with a common denominator by using multiples. Encourage children to realise that we make the equivalent fractions by multiplying both the numerator and denominator by the same number. So we need to find a multiple that is common to both.

Things to say and ask
- What is the lowest common denominator you can use when changing/converting sixths and quarters?

Ordering fractions (2)

Activity Sheet 13

Objective
- Order fractions such as $\frac{2}{3}$, $\frac{3}{4}$ and $\frac{5}{6}$ by converting them to fractions with a common denominator, and position them on a number line.

Vocabulary

numerator, denominator, equivalent, proper/improper fraction, position

Resources
4 dice (per pair)

Strand: Numbers and the number system *Topic:* Fractions

Teaching support

Misconceptions

Children often find it difficult to remember to multiply the numerator as well as the denominator when converting fractions to ones with common denominators. Suggest that they use lists of equivalent fractions until they are confident.

This sheet gives practice in finding fractions with a common denominator through a game.

Children should have a sound understanding of simple fractions and equivalence, place value, multiplication and division, and knowledge of factors and multiples. They need to have completed Pupil Book page 20.

- Remind children that in a proper fraction the numerator is always less than the denominator.
- Introduce the game by demonstrating throws of the dice, recording the fractions and converting them into twelfths. *How do I change $\frac{3}{4}$ into twelfths? What is the first thing I need to do? What number do I need to multiply the numerator by?*

Things to say and ask

- *Why can't you change/convert a fraction with a denominator of five into twelfths?*

Fractions and division (1)

Pupil Book page 21

Objective

- Use a fraction as an 'operator' to find fractions, including tenths and hundredths, of numbers or quantities (e.g. $\frac{5}{8}$ of 32, $\frac{7}{10}$ of 40, $\frac{9}{100}$ of 400 centimetres).

Vocabulary

numerator, denominator, divide, divided by

Resources

cubes (optional)

Teaching support

The key idea is to relate fractions to division by finding fractions of quantities.

Children should have a sound understanding of simple fractions and equivalence, place value, multiplication and division as inverse operations, and knowledge of factors and multiples.

Misconceptions

When finding non-unitary fractions of quantities children may become confused over which number to multiply by the numerator. Encourage them to record the stages logically, giving them a framework to work in, and allow them to use cubes until they are confident.

- Children need to develop their skills of mental imagery to help them calculate. Encourage them to visualise a representation of the whole number in their head, which they can then split into the number of equal parts given by the denominator. They need to divide to find how many in each part, and then understand that the numerator tells them how many parts to take, e.g. $\frac{3}{4}$ of 12 could be seen as 12 cubes divided into 4 parts/groups of 3 and then 3 groups collected to make a total of 9. Repeat for a few similar questions, using cubes if necessary, so that children become confident.
- For questions 3–5, encourage children to give answers in their simplest form.

Things to say and ask

- *Find $\frac{1}{10}$ of 2 m, $\frac{3}{10}$ of 2 m; $\frac{1}{3}$ of 60p, $\frac{2}{3}$ of 60p.*
- *What fraction of £1 is 65p?*
- *What fraction of 1 m is 120 cm?*

43

Strand: Numbers and the number system **Topics:** Fractions/Ratio and proportion

Fractions and division (2)

Activity Sheet 14

Objective

- Use a fraction as an 'operator' to find fractions, including tenths and hundredths, of numbers or quantities (e.g. $\frac{5}{8}$ of 32, $\frac{7}{10}$ of 40, $\frac{9}{100}$ of 400 centimetres).

Vocabulary

numerator, denominator, divide, divided by

Resources

counters in 2 colours (per pair)

cubes (optional)

Teaching support

Misconceptions

When finding non-unitary fractions of quantities children may become confused over which number to multiply by the numerator. Encourage them to record the stages logically, giving them a framework to work in, and allow them to use cubes until they are confident.

This sheet provides practice in finding fractions of numbers and quantities.

Children should have a sound understanding of simple fractions and equivalence, place value, multiplication and division as inverse operations, and knowledge of factors and multiples. They need to be able to 'see' fractions in an abstract way and to have completed Pupil Book page 21.

- Begin by asking questions such as: *How many halves in $2\frac{1}{2}/6\frac{1}{2}$? ... thirds in $4\frac{1}{3}/5\frac{2}{3}$?*
- Remind children of the mental method of finding fractions of quantities suggested for Pupil Book page 21. If necessary, demonstrate with cubes.

Things to say and ask

- What number is multiplied by the numerator to find $\frac{3}{4}$ of 16?

Ratio and proportion (1)

Pupil Book page 22

Objective

- Solve simple problems using ideas of ratio and proportion.

Vocabulary

in every, for every, proportion, ratio

Resources

counters

red and blue pencils (per child)

Strand: Numbers and the number system *Topic:* Ratio and proportion

Teaching support

Misconceptions
The most common error is to mix up the 2 terms. Children need to remember through practical counting-out activities that ratio is a part-to-part (for every) comparison and proportion is a part-to-whole (in every) comparison.

The key idea is that ratio is a part-to-part comparison and proportion is a part-to-whole comparison.

Children should have experienced practical work involving colouring or making patterns following instructions using the terms 'for every' and 'in every'. They need to have a good understanding of multiplication and division and should be beginning to acquire the ability to 'see' fractions in an abstract way.

- The correct use of the vocabulary is the key to success with ratio and proportion.
- Begin by supporting activities practically with counters or similar, and talk through problems, e.g. *There are 12 fish in a tank, 3 are red and 9 are yellow.* Keep numbers simple and ask children to make statements, e.g. *For every red fish there are 3 yellow fish. One in every 4 fish is red. The fraction of red/yellow fish is $\frac{1}{4} / \frac{3}{4}$.*
- Use children themselves for practical demonstrations, e.g. choose 2 boys and 6 girls to stand up and ask others to make statements using the phrases 'for every' and 'in every'.
- Encourage children to invent their own problems using the phrases 'for/to every' and 'in every'.

Things to say and ask

- *The proportion of red squares is one quarter of a complete pattern of red and blue squares. How many red/blue squares are there if there are 24 squares altogether?*

Ratio and proportion (2)

Activity Sheet 15

Objective

- Solve simple problems using ideas of ratio and proportion.

Vocabulary

for/to every, ratio, in every, proportion

Resources
yellow and blue coloured pencils plus other colours of choice (per child)
isometric paper (optional)

Teaching support

Misconceptions
The most common error is to mix up the 2 terms. Children need to remember through practical counting-out activities that ratio is a part-to-part (for every) comparison and proportion is a part-to-whole (in every) comparison.

The key idea is that ratio is a part-to-part comparison and proportion is a part-to-whole comparison.

Children should have experienced practical work involving colouring or making patterns following instructions using the terms 'for every' and 'in every'. They need to have a good understanding of multiplication and division and should be beginning to acquire the ability to 'see' fractions in an abstract way.

- The correct use of the vocabulary is the key to success with ratio and proportion. The sheet has a variety of examples for children to practise following instructions using the language of ratio and proportion.
- When they have successfully completed the pattern in question 2, challenge children to write themselves similar rules using the language of ratio and proportion for a design on isometric paper.

Things to say and ask

- For question 1: *How many blue squares will you colour along the line?*

Strands: Numbers and the number system/Calculations *Topics:* Fractions and decimals/Using a calculator

Using decimals (1)

Pupil Book page 23

Objectives

- Use decimal notation for tenths and hundredths in calculations, and tenths, hundredths and thousandths when recording measurements.
- Know what each digit represents in a number with up to three decimal places.
- Develop calculator skills and use a calculator effectively.

Vocabulary

decimal fraction, decimal, decimal point, decimal place, thousandth

Resources

4 dice (per child)
calculator (per child)

Teaching support

This page is about decimal place value to 3 decimal places.

Children should be familiar with working with decimals to 2 decimal places. They need a good understanding of multiplication and division, particularly the effects of multiplying and dividing by 10 and 100.

- Together make a decimal place value chart of U · t h th and discuss the significance of the columns, e.g. that tenths are 10 times smaller than units, hundredths are 10 times smaller than tenths and 100 times smaller than units… Elicit that thousandths are 10 times smaller than hundredths… Ask questions, e.g. *What is the value of the 7 in 3·714, 5·473, 12·017? Which is the smaller number, 0·07 or 0·007?*
- For question 1, encourage children to describe the red digits in as many different ways as they can.
- The game makes use of calculators in order to help children understand the physical effects of multiplying and dividing decimal numbers by powers of 10. It also allows them to investigate the effect of adding or subtracting tenths, hundredths or thousandths. Remind children that it is the digits in numbers that move about the decimal point and that the point itself is fixed.

Things to say and ask

- *The decimal point is fixed. Which way do the digits move when any number is multiplied by 100?*
- *When the number 4·06 is divided by 100, how many decimal places will there be?*

Using decimals (2)

Activity Sheet 16

Objectives

- Use decimal notation for tenths and hundredths in calculations, and tenths, hundredths and thousandths when recording measurements.
- Know what each digit represents in a number with up to three decimal places.
- Order a mixed set of numbers or measurements with up to three decimal places.

Vocabulary

decimal fraction, decimal, decimal point, decimal place, thousandth

Resources

4 dice (per pair)

Strand: Numbers and the number system *Topic:* Fractions and decimals

Teaching support

This sheet provides further practice in using and understanding decimal place value to 3 decimal places.

Children should be familiar with working with decimals to 2 decimal places. They need a good understanding of multiplication and division, particularly the effects of multiplying and dividing by 10 and 100.

- Draw an unlabelled decimal number line marked in tenths and hundredths. Ask children to decide on its range and key numbers. Mark a starting number and ask children to read it.
- Position other numbers: *Give me a larger/smaller number. Give me a number close to 3·4...*

Things to say and ask

- Which number is closest to 1·235: 1·256 or 1·146? How do you know?

Using decimals (3)

Activity Sheet 17

Objectives

- Use decimal notation for tenths and hundredths in calculations, and tenths, hundredths and thousandths when recording measurements.
- Know what each digit represents in a number with up to three decimal places.
- Give a decimal fraction lying between two others (e.g. between 3·4 and 3·5).

Vocabulary

decimal fraction, decimal, decimal point, decimal place, thousandth

Resources
none

Teaching support

This sheet provides practice in using and understanding decimal place value to 3 decimal places through a game.

Children should be familiar with working with decimals to 2 decimal places. They need a good understanding of multiplication and division, particularly the effects of multiplying and dividing by 10 and 100.

- This is a challenging version of 'Mastermind' because 4 digits are used. If children have difficulty, demonstrate a game with them using your own secret number with units and tenths only. Then suggest that they start by using just units, tenths and hundredths.
- Challenge children to give a decimal number lying between 2 guesses if one was too small and one was too large.

Things to say and ask

- *Give me a number that lies between 4·2 and 4·3 with two/three decimal places.*

Strand: Numbers and the number system **Topic:** Fractions and decimals

Ordering decimals

Pupil Book page 24

Objectives

Vocabulary

decimal, decimal point, decimal place, thousandth

- Give a decimal fraction lying between two others (e.g. between 3·4 and 3·5).
- Order a mixed set of numbers or measurements with up to three decimal places.

Resources

unlabelled decimal number line (optional)

Teaching support

Misconceptions

When counting in decimal fractions, a common error is to say 'zero point twenty-five' instead of 'zero point two five'. All digits to the right of the decimal point are referred to by their names when read aloud to avoid place value confusion, except when reading amounts of money, when the digits to the right of the decimal point refer to pence and are read as such.

The key idea is to understand the significance of digits in decimal numbers with up to 3 decimal places and to practise ordering them.

Children should have been introduced to decimals to 3 decimal places and have experience in ordering numbers with 2 decimal places.

- Together make a decimal place value chart of U · t h th and discuss the significance of the columns, e.g. that tenths are 10 times smaller than units, hundredths are 10 times smaller than tenths and 100 times smaller than units… Elicit that thousandths are 10 times smaller than hundredths… Ask questions, e.g. *What is the value of the 7 in 3·714, 5·473, 12·017? Which is the smaller number, 0·07 or 0·007?* If any children say that 0·07 is smaller because it has fewer digits, look at a number line and position numbers with 1, then 2, then 3 decimal places.
- Practise counting to continue sequences, e.g. 2·4, 2·6, 2·8, …; 5·11, 5·14, 5·17, …
- Compare numbers, looking at the most significant digits, e.g. order 3·15, 4·07, 3·22, 3·17, 3·09. Look at the units first (4 is the biggest, with the rest 3), then the tenths where the units are equal (·2 in 3·22 is the biggest and 3·09 the smallest), then the hundredths where the tenths are equal (·07 in 3·17 is the biggest).
- In questions 4, 5 and 6, encourage children to use a place value chart, e.g. H T U · t h th as they order and find numbers between.

Things to say and ask

- *How many times smaller than one unit is one thousandth?*
- *Give me a number between 3·14 and 3·15.*

Rounding decimals

Pupil Book page 25

Objective

Vocabulary

decimal, decimal point, decimal place, thousandth

- Round a number with two decimal places to the nearest tenth or nearest whole number.

Resources

calculator (per child)

decimal place value cards (optional)

Strand: Numbers and the number system *Topic:* Fractions and decimals

Teaching support

Misconceptions

If children are insecure with hundredths and thousandths, practise identifying the names and value of the places with decimal place value cards.

The key idea is to round up if the last digit is 5 or above; if below, round down to the digit to the left.

Children should have been introduced to decimals to 3 decimal places and be confident in rounding decimals with 1 decimal place to the nearest whole number.

- Ask children to round decimals with 1 decimal place to the nearest whole number, e.g. 13·6, 28·3, 34·5, 15·8... Elicit the rule for rounding: that if the last digit is 5 or more, round up; if less than 5, round down to the digit to the left. Remind them that this rule is applied to the last digit on the right in a number, whatever the size of the number.
- Practise rounding numbers with 2 decimal places to the nearest tenth/to 1 decimal place and to the nearest whole number.
- For question 5, give children the starting point of 1 ÷ 4 and encourage them to continue logically, e.g. 2 ÷ 4, 3 ÷ 4, etc... (only recording those answers with exactly 2 decimal places). *Why isn't there any point in starting with 1 ÷ 2?* (because 0·5 has only 1 decimal place) Point out that they are actually converting fractions into their decimal equivalents in this investigation and refer to improper fractions and mixed numbers. Before they go too far, ask children to look for patterns and make predictions.
- Children should soon begin to notice that the divisors giving 2 decimal places are 4 and 8. Encourage them to work out which 2-digit numbers each applies to. (Odd numbers for 4 and even numbers for 8, excluding multiples of 4.)

Things to say and ask

- In a number that has two/three decimal places, what are the names of the decimal places?
- Tell me three numbers that round to 1·1 to one decimal place.

Fractions and equivalent decimals (1)

Pupil Book page 26

Objective

- Recognise the equivalence between the decimal and fraction forms of one half, one quarter, three quarters, one eighth...and tenths, hundredths and thousandths.

Vocabulary

decimal fraction, decimal, decimal point, decimal place, equivalent, thousandth

Resources

place value chart
decimal place value cards (toptional)

Teaching support

Misconceptions

If children are insecure with hundredths and thousandths, practise identifying the names and value of the places with decimal place value cards.

The key idea is that we can write fractions as decimal fractions and vice versa.

Children should have been introduced to decimals to 3 decimal places and be familiar with finding equivalences for decimals with 2 decimal places.

- Ask children to give examples of equivalences that they know, e.g. $\frac{1}{2} = 0.5$, $\frac{1}{4} = 0.25$, $\frac{3}{4} = 0.75$, $\frac{1}{100} = 0.01$. Split children into 2 groups, with group 1 stating a fraction in tenths, hundredths or thousandths for group 2 to give the equivalent decimal, then vice versa. Use a place value chart (U · t h th) for reference.
- For questions 1 and 2, talk about putting the final fraction into its simplest form when converting from a decimal. Practise some examples with mixed numbers, e.g. $3.05 = 3\frac{5}{100} = 3\frac{1}{20}$

Strand: Numbers and the number system **Topic:** Fractions and decimals

Things to say and ask

- What is the equivalent decimal fraction to $\frac{2}{10}$, $\frac{1}{5}$; $\frac{45}{100}$, $\frac{9}{20}$; $\frac{63}{1000}$?
- What is the equivalent fraction to 0·23, 3·08, 2·009, 0·378?

Fractions and equivalent decimals (2)

Activity Sheet 18

Objectives

- Recognise the equivalence between the decimal and fraction forms of one half, one quarter, three quarters, one eighth...and tenths, hundredths and thousandths.
- Begin to convert a fraction to a decimal using division.

Vocabulary

decimal fraction, decimal point, decimal place, equivalent

Resources

calculator (per pair)

scissors (per pair)

fraction chart or board (optional)

Teaching support

Misconceptions

If the children find it difficult to approximate to find the relative sizes of some of the fractions, they could use a fraction chart or board for some support.

The key idea is that we can write fractions as decimal fractions and vice versa. Children should have experience of converting a fraction to a decimal by dividing on a calculator.

Children should have been introduced to decimals to 3 decimal places and be familiar with finding equivalences for decimals with 2 decimal places.

- Ask children to give examples of equivalences that they know, e.g. $\frac{1}{2} = 0\cdot5$, $\frac{1}{4} = 0\cdot25$, $\frac{3}{4} = 0\cdot75$, $\frac{1}{100} = 0\cdot01$. Split children into 2 groups, with group 1 stating a fraction in tenths, hundredths or thousandths for group 2 to give the equivalent decimal, then vice versa. Use a place value chart (U · t h th) for reference.
- When introducing the game, ask both players to look carefully at all the cards before they cut them out to spot the decimal equivalents they know already. To compare the rest, point out that it may help to see whether a multiple of the denominator is equal to 10 or 100 or 1000. *How can you work out the approximate size of, e.g. $\frac{13}{40}$?* Encourage children to use strategies such as rounding the numerator up or down to make a fraction they can cancel and then recognise, e.g. $\frac{13}{40}$ is approximately (a little larger than) $\frac{10}{40}$ or $\frac{1}{4}$.
- Remind children that another way of thinking of a fraction is as a division. So an easy way to find a decimal equivalent is to divide using a calculator, e.g. $\frac{3}{4} = 3 \div 4 = 0\cdot75$, and that is how the calculation is entered on the calculator:

Things to say and ask

- What is an equivalent fraction to six twelfths? So what is an equivalent decimal fraction?

Strand: Numbers and the number system **Topic:** Fractions, decimals and percentages

Fractions, decimals and percentages

Pupil Book pages 27 and 28

Objectives

- Understand percentage as the number of parts in every 100.
- Express simple fractions such as one half, one quarter, three quarters, one third, two thirds...and tenths and hundredths, as percentages (e.g. know that $\frac{1}{3} = 33\frac{1}{3}\%$).

Vocabulary

percentage, per cent, % 'in every hundred', numerator

Resources

For Pupil Book page 27:
    1–100 number square (optional)

For Pupil Book page 28:
    two 1–9 dice and a calculator (per child)

Teaching support

The key idea is that we can write equivalent fractions, decimal fractions and percentages.

Children should be familiar with decimals and basic percentages. They need to understand how to multiply and divide the numerators and denominators of fractions to find equivalent fractions. They also need to understand the effects of multiplying decimals by 100.

Misconceptions

If children are insecure with percentages, work with a 100 square to show how 0·25 is 25 hundredths or 25% or $\frac{1}{4}$ of the square.

Pupil Book page 27

- Ask children to give examples of percentages and equivalent fractions that they know, e.g. 25% is $\frac{1}{4}$, 50% is $\frac{1}{2}$, 75% is $\frac{3}{4}$. Ask if they can give an approximation of $\frac{1}{3}$ and $\frac{2}{3}$. Encourage them to think of how many thirds there are in one whole and link that to dividing 100 by 3 to find one third. Discuss what might happen to the remainder (write it as a fraction).

- Remind children that 'per cent' means 'in every hundred' and link 'in every/out of' to proportion. Elicit that percentages are special fractions that always have a denominator of 100.

- For question 3, encourage children to cancel the fractions to terms that will be helpful in converting to decimal fractions, e.g. 8 out of 20 = $\frac{4}{10}$ = $\frac{40}{100}$ = 40%. Alternatively, they may be able to find the equivalent 'hundredths' fraction by multiplying the numerator and denominator directly, e.g. $\frac{8}{20} = \frac{8 \times 5}{20 \times 5} = \frac{40}{100}$. Other strategies are approximating or remembering the equivalent percentages.

Pupil Book page 28

- In the game, children use calculators to convert fractions into decimals. The decimals can then be converted into percentages by multiplying by 100 and by realising that, e.g. 0·14 is 14 hundredths which is equivalent to 14%.

Things to say and ask

- What is 75% as a fraction?
- What is 0.53 as a percentage?

Strand: Numbers and the number system **Topic:** Fractions, decimals and percentages

Fractions and equivalent percentages

Activity Sheet 19

Objectives

- Understand percentage as the number of parts in every 100.
- Express simple fractions such as one half, one quarter, three quarters, one third, two thirds...and tenths and hundredths, as percentages (e.g. know that $\frac{1}{3} = 33\frac{1}{3}\%$).

Vocabulary

percentage, per cent, %

Resources
calculator (per pair)
scissors (per pair)
stopwatch (optional)

Teaching support

Misconceptions
If children find it difficult to record their work logically at this stage, they may find it helpful to work in stages in a grid.

This sheet practises comparing fractions and percentages.

Children should be familiar with decimals and basic percentages. They need to understand how to multiply and divide the numerators and denominators of fractions to find equivalent fractions, and the effects of multiplying decimals by 100. They should have completed Pupil Book pages 27 and 28.

- Children use calculators to convert fractions into decimals. The decimals can then be converted into percentages by multiplying by 100 and by realising that, e.g. 0·14 is 14 hundredths which is equivalent to 14%.
- As children become more confident with the game, you could introduce a 'beat the clock' challenge, either personally or between players.

Things to say and ask

- What fractions are equivalent to 60%?
- What is $\frac{8}{25}$ as a percentage?

Finding percentages

Activity Sheet 20

Objectives

- Express simple fractions such as one half, one quarter, three quarters, one third, two thirds...and tenths and hundredths, as percentages (e.g. know that $\frac{1}{3} = 33\frac{1}{3}\%$).
- Find simple percentages of small whole-number quantities (e.g. find 10% of £500, then 20%, 40% and 80% by doubling).

Vocabulary

percentage, per cent, %

Resources
counters in 2 colours (per pair)

Strand: Numbers and the number system *Topic:* Fractions, decimals and percentages

Teaching support

The key idea is to find percentages of small whole-number quantities without a calculator.

Children should be familiar with decimals and basic percentages. They need to understand how to multiply and divide the numerators and denominators of fractions to find equivalent fractions, and the effects of multiplying decimals by 100. They should have completed Pupil Book pages 27 and 28 and Activity Sheet 19.

- Practise finding percentages of quantities, e.g. 43% of 1 m, 60% of 1 litre…
- In the game encourage children to convert the percentage into a fraction and then find the fraction of the number chosen. Remind them that doubling and halving strategies may be useful, e.g. to find one quarter of 300, halve, then halve again; to find 20%, 40% or 80%, divide by 10 to find 10%, then double that to get 20% and double again to get 40% …
- Stress that it is not always useful to convert percentages into their equivalent fraction in lowest terms.

Things to say and ask

- What fractions are equivalent to 30%?
- How would you find 30% of 30?

Fractions and percentages

Pupil Book pages 29 and 30

Objective

- Express simple fractions such as one half, one quarter, three quarters, one third, two thirds …, and tenths and hundredths as percentages (e.g. know that $\frac{1}{3} = 33\frac{1}{3}\%$).
- Find simple percentages of small whole-number quantities (e.g. find 10% of £500, then 20%, 40% and 80% by doubling).
- Identify and use appropriate operations (including combinations of operations) to solve word problems involving numbers and quantities based on money.

Vocabulary

percentage, per cent, %, discount, profit, loss

Resources

For Pupil Book page 29:
  none
For Pupil Book page 30:
  a dice and a counter (per child)

Strands: Numbers and the number system/Calculations **Topics:** Fractions, decimals and percentages/Mental calculation strategies (+ and −)

Teaching support

Misconceptions
If children find it difficult to record their work logically at this stage, they may find it helpful to work in stages in a grid.

These pages practise finding percentages of numbers, amounts and quantities. Children are also introduced to the ideas of discount, profit and loss.

Children should be familiar with decimals and basic percentages. They need to understand how to multiply and divide the numerators and denominators of fractions to find equivalent fractions, and the effects of multiplying decimals by 100. They should have completed the previous work on fractions, decimals and percentages.

Pupil Book page 29

- Ask children to give examples of percentages that they know. Talk about shops having 'sales', when 'discount' is nearly always given in percentages.
- For question 1, link the work to previous work on cancelling.
- Link questions 2, 3 and 4 to previous work on 'using a fraction as an operator'. Check that children are confident in using known equivalent fractions and finding tenths of measurements. Ask children to calculate mentally but show them how to record their answers logically.
- Remind them that doubling and halving strategies may be useful, e.g. to find one quarter of 300, halve, then halve again; to find 20%, 40% or 80%, divide by 10 to find 10%, then double that to get 20% and double again to get 40%.

Pupil Book page 30

- Discuss the concepts of making a profit or a loss and making or losing money.
- For question 1, encourage children to write answers only. Remind them of key mental strategies of halving/doubling and multiplying/dividing by 10.
- Read through the rules of the game together.

Things to say and ask

Pupil Book page 29:
- If a jacket costing £30 has a discount of 20%, will you pay more or less than £30 for it?

Pupil Book page 30:
- If you have made a 'profit', have you gained or lost money?

Recall of addition and subtraction facts

Activity Sheet 21

Objectives

Vocabulary

add, subtract, multiply, divide

- Derive quickly or continue to derive quickly, decimals that total 1 or 10, all 2-digit pairs that total 100, all pairs of multiples of 50 with a total of 1000.
- Check with an equivalent calculation.

Resources
none

Strands: Calculations/Solving problems **Topics:** Mental calculation strategies (+ and –)/Making decisions/Problems about 'real life'

Teaching support

This sheet provides opportunities for children to practise quick recall and derivation of number facts, including totals of whole numbers and decimals. Children should be confident with multiplication and division of numbers, including decimals, by 10 and 100.

Misconceptions
The most common error when adding decimal numbers to make 10 is that the numbers in fact add to 11, e.g. 6·5 + 4·5. Occasionally children also write an extra zero to the right of the answer, e.g. changing 35 + 65 = 100 to 350 + 650 = 10 000. This shows a confusion of addition with multiplication, e.g. 3 × 4 = 12 becomes 30 × 40 = 1200. Point out that a 3-digit number plus a 3-digit number cannot make a 5-digit number.

- Remind children of the importance of using known facts to derive quickly new unknown facts. Revise relationships between facts based on multiplying or dividing by 10, 100 or 1000. Write 36 + ___ = 100 and ask children to say the missing number. Now place a zero to the right of each number, making the fact 360 + 640 = 1000. Elicit that each number in the question has been multiplied by 10 and that the answer is also 10 times larger. Return to the original fact and ask children to divide each number by 10 to give the fact 3·6 + 6·4 = 10. Point out that 10·0 is the same as 10.

- Provide other examples with the total 100, e.g. 44 + 56 = 100, and ask children to suggest as many different facts as they can that can be derived from this fact, e.g. 4·4 + 5·6 = 10. Suggest that they also give related subtraction questions, e.g. 100 – 56 = 44 and 10 – 4·4 = 5·6…

- For the investigation in question 4, children should discover that columns start and finish on the same number. Encourage them to explain why this happens by describing relationships between 10, 100 and 1000, e.g. (10 – 5·3) × 100 is the same as (1000 – 530) and (10 – 5·3) × 10 is the same as (100 – 53).

Things to say and ask

- How did you find the total?
- Did you use a different fact to help you?
- How many times larger are the numbers in this question than in this question?

Using appropriate operations

Pupil Book page 31

Objectives

- Consolidate all strategies from the previous year, including finding a difference by counting up.
- Choose and use appropriate number operations to solve problems, and appropriate ways of calculating.
- Identify and use appropriate operations to solve word problems involving numbers based on 'real life', using one or more steps.

Vocabulary
addition, subtraction

Resources
none

Strand: Calculations **Topic:** Mental calculation strategies (+ and −)

Teaching support

The key idea is to identify the correct operation and solve a problem using mental or written methods as appropriate. Some problems are presented in a real-life context. The strategies and approaches vary between questions to ensure children can use a strategy without repeated practice of it first.

- Discuss different ways of calculating, e.g. recall, mental methods (including using jottings), informal written methods, formal written methods and using a calculator. Ask children to suggest when particular methods are most appropriate, e.g. when adding 2 small numbers, recall or mental methods are appropriate, or when subtracting 4 digits, written methods might be necessary. Stress, however, that this varies between questions, e.g. 7000 − 3785 is probably best done mentally (by counting up from the smaller number), whereas 3512 − 1645 might be better solved using a written method. Explain that the page includes both types of question.
- Remind children to make an approximation before any calculation to gain a feel for the size of the answer and to check answers using an appropriate strategy, e.g. using the inverse operation.

Things to say and ask

- Approximately what will the answer be?
- Which do you think is the most appropriate method for solving this calculation?
- How can you check your answer to this?

Mental methods of addition and subtraction (1)

Pupil Book page 32

Objective

- Consolidate all strategies from previous year, including add or subtract the nearest multiple of 10, 100 or 1000, then adjust.

Vocabulary

add, subtract, difference, strategy, decimal, adjust

Resources
none

Teaching support

The key idea is to use the most efficient mental method to add or subtract. Children are given practice in adding and subtracting near multiples of 10, 100, 1000 and related calculations involving decimals, e.g. adding or subtracting 0·9, 1·1, 1·9, 2·1, 2·9, … by adding or subtracting the nearest whole number and adjusting.

- Write up the numbers 1, 2, 3, 4, 5, leaving spaces between them. Choose volunteers to come and write the decimal number that is one tenth more or less than each of these. Ask some questions involving adding or subtracting these numbers, e.g. 58 + 4·9 or 36 + 5·1. Encourage children to explain their strategies and to add or subtract the whole numbers first, before adjusting. If appropriate, show the link between this and whole number questions where similar adjusting takes place, e.g. 368 + 69.
- In question 4, when children are investigating pairs of numbers with a difference of 7·9, encourage them to find solutions including numbers with 1, 2 or even 3 decimal places, e.g. 47 and 39·1, 48·15 and 40·25…
- Encourage children to spot that the difference is 1 more than in question 4 so that they can use their results from question 4. They need to realise that they must increase one of each pair of numbers by 1 or decrease one by 1 or split the 1 between the two numbers, e.g. increase one number by 0·7 and decrease the other by 0·3.

Strand: Calculations **Topic:** Mental calculation strategies (+ and −)

Things to say and ask
- Which strategy did you use to answer this question?
- What do you notice about the final number in the trail?

Addition and subtraction

Activity Sheet 22

Objectives
- Use the relationship between addition and subtraction.
- Explain methods and reasoning.

Vocabulary

add, subtract, solve, greater than, less than

Resources
none

Teaching support

The key idea is to use the inverse relationship between addition and subtraction by identifying and making use of related facts.

- Remind children that if we know one addition or subtraction fact, then we immediately know other related facts. Provide several examples, e.g. 3381 + 4836 = 8217, 4836 + 3381 = 8217, 8217 − 4836 = 3381, 8217 − 3381 = 4836. Draw attention to the largest number in each statement, highlighting that, for whole positive numbers, the largest is the answer for addition and the first number for subtraction.
- Question 3 includes 'I'm thinking of a number…' puzzles that involve more than one step. Encourage children to check their answer to each one by putting it back into the puzzle and seeing if the outcome matches the question. They should also explain how they solved the puzzles. As an extension activity children can devise their own puzzles like this to be used in a plenary.

Things to say and ask
- What are the other related facts?
- How can you check this without subtracting?

Calculations with several numbers

Pupil Book page 33

Objectives
- Consolidate all strategies from the previous year, including add several numbers.
- Solve mathematical problems or puzzles, recognise and explain patterns and relationships, generalise and predict.

Vocabulary

symbol, equation, total, sum, multiple, solution, consecutive

Resources
none

Strands: Calculations/Solving problems **Topics:** Mental calculation strategies (+ and –)/Making decisions

Teaching support

This page provides children with an opportunity to solve investigations and puzzles by adding several numbers, including multiples of 10, 1- and 2-digit numbers and consecutive numbers.

- Introduce a simple version of the first activity on the page by drawing these 5 symbols on the board:

Explain that each symbol represents a whole number between 1 and 5 inclusive. Introduce clues one at a time.

Clues:

If ⬡ plus △ equals ◇ what could they stand for?
Discuss possible solutions, e.g. that this represents 1 + 2 = 3 or 1 + 3 = 4 or 1 + 4 = 5 or 2 + 3 = 5 or the reverse of these, e.g. 2 + 1 = 3 …

If △ plus △ plus △ equals ◇ what could they stand for?
Discuss that this shows us which symbol represents 1 and which is 3, i.e. 1 + 1 + 1 = 3
This in turn tells us that the first clue is ⬡ + 1 = ◇
Encourage children to see that since we now know which symbol represents 3 then the other symbols in the first clue cannot be 3, so therefore it must be 4 + 1 = 5. List each symbol and its number and check these against each clue.

- Explain that question 1 involves the numbers 1 to 10.
- For question 4, remind children to look for quick strategies for adding several consecutive numbers, e.g. 18 + 19 + 20 + 21 can be found by multiplying 20 by 4 to give 80 and then adjusting by subtracting 2.

Things to say and ask

- *How did you work out which number this symbol represents?*
- *Let's make a list of all the solutions. Can anyone find any more?*

Mental methods of addition and subtraction (2)

Pupil Book page 34

Objectives

- Use known number facts and place value to consolidate mental addition/subtraction.
- Choose and use appropriate number operations to solve problems, and appropriate ways of calculating: mental, mental with jottings.

Vocabulary

prime, even, difference between, decimal

Resources
none

Strand: Calculations *Topic:* Pencil-and-paper procedures (+ and –)

Teaching support

Misconceptions

The most common error when adding decimals to make the next whole number is that the numbers in fact add to more than the whole number, e.g. 8·65 + 0·45. Show that, when adding, just as the partner to 100 of 65 is 35, the partner to 1 of 0·65 is 0·35.

This page provides practice in solving addition and subtraction calculations mentally, including 4-digit multiples of 100 and decimal fractions each less than 1 and with up to 2 decimal places. Children also find what to add to a decimal with units, tenths and hundredths to make the next higher whole number.

- For question 4 discuss the meaning of the term 'prime' by first listing the numbers from 1 to 20 on the board. Invite children in turn to come and rub out the multiples of 2 (but not the number 2 itself), then the multiples of 3 (but not 3 itself) and so on, up to 10. Under the remaining numbers show how each has only 2 factors, itself and 1. Show also that 1 has only 1 factor and so is not generally classed as a prime number, and rub 1 out.
- On completing the page, children should explain which operation they used to find the answers. Invite them to explain their strategies. Discuss which ones are most efficient for each type of question on the page. Encourage children always to make an approximation to gain a feel for the size of the answer, and to check the answer using a different method or operation.
- The largest possible number is 94 (47 + 47) if you are allowed to use the same number twice. There are a few even numbers less than this that cannot be made: 82, 86, 92. Children could also try: including all the primes to 100; investigating odd numbers; using 3 prime numbers.

Things to say and ask

- *Do you think you can make every even number using just prime numbers?*
- *What strategy did you use for this question?*

Written addition (1)

Pupil Book page 35

Objectives

Vocabulary

addition, subtraction, method

- Use informal pencil-and-paper methods to support, record or explain additions.
- Extend written methods to column addition of 2 integers less than 10 000.

Resources
2 sets of 0–9 digit cards (per pair)
squared paper (optional)

Teaching support

Misconceptions

Ensure children appreciate the importance of lining up numbers carefully in the correct columns. Working on squared paper can help to avoid errors.

The key idea is to use a written method to add 4-digit numbers where appropriate. Children can be asked to use the standard written method or a written method using an expanded form.

Children should be confident in using a written method for adding two 3-digit numbers or one 3-digit and one 4-digit number, with carrying.

- Begin by discussing an appropriate written method of addition for, e.g. 2475 and 4568. Encourage children to estimate before calculating and to check each calculation, e.g. using a different addition method:

approximate answer is 2500 + 4500 = 7000

```
   2475
 + 4568
   7043
```

check: 4568 + 2000 + 500 − 25 = 6568 + 500 − 25 = 7068 − 25 = 7043

- For the game, stress that children should always add 4687 to the number made with their digit cards.
- For question 2, revise the method of division you wish children to use.

Strands: Calculations/Solving problems **Topics:** Pencil-and-paper procedures (+ and –)/Checking results of calculations/Problems involving 'real life'

Things to say and ask

- What is the total? Are you sure?
- Did you approximate first?
- Have you checked? Which method did you use when checking?

Written addition (2)

Pupil Book page 36

Objectives

- Use informal pencil-and-paper methods to support, record or explain additions.
- Extend written methods to column addition of two integers less than 10 000.
- Choose and use appropriate ways of calculating.
- Identify and use appropriate operations to solve word problems involving numbers based on 'real life', using one or more steps.
- Check the sum of several numbers by adding in the reverse order.

Vocabulary

method, approximate

Resources
squared paper (optional)

Teaching support

Misconceptions

Ensure children appreciate the importance of lining up numbers carefully in the correct columns. Working on squared paper can help to avoid errors.

This page provides opportunities for adding several numbers using written methods, whether informal or formal. Word problems involving numbers and quantities based on real life and money are included.

Children should be familiar with using a written method for adding two 4-digit numbers, with carrying.

- Revise the written method of addition you wish the children to use to answer the questions on this page.
- Remind children to find an approximate answer before each one and to check each answer. Elicit that a suitable checking approach might be to list the set of numbers in a different order and to use a similar written method of addition.
- For question 1 they could add together all 4 numbers first, and then add rows or columns to make sub-totals when checking.

Things to say and ask

- What was your approximate answer?
- How are you going to check?

Strands: Calculations/Solving problems **Topics:** Pencil-and-paper procedures (+ and –)/Making decisions/Problems involving 'real life' and measures

Adding decimals

Pupil Book page 37

Objectives

- Extend written methods to column addition of numbers involving decimals.
- Choose and use appropriate ways of calculating.
- Identify and use appropriate operations to solve word problems involving numbers based on 'real life' and measures, using one or more steps.
- Check the sum of several numbers by adding in the reverse order.

Vocabulary

method, decimal, mass

Resources

squared paper (optional)

Teaching support

This page provides opportunities for adding at least 2 decimals using written methods, whether informal or formal. Word problems involving numbers and quantities based on 'real life' and measures are included.

Misconceptions

The most common error is not lining up the decimal point. Working on squared paper can help to avoid this.

Children should be familiar with using a written method for adding two 4-digit numbers, with carrying.

- Revise the written method of addition you wish the children to use to answer the questions on this page.
- Remind children to find an approximate answer before each one and to check each answer.
- For questions where decimals have different numbers of digits and decimal places, ensure children appreciate the importance of lining up numbers carefully in the correct columns. Stress that the decimal points must be in line. Some children may find it useful to write zeros on the end of decimals so that all have the same number of decimal places, e.g.

    changing   4·5   to   4·50
              + 3·68   + 3·68

- Discuss suitable checking approaches, e.g. listing numbers in a different order.

Things to say and ask

- *Always estimate the answers before calculating. This can help you to see when you make a mistake.*
- *What was your approximate answer?*
- *Have you lined up the numbers appropriately?*

Strands: Calculations/Solving problems *Topics:* Pencil-and-paper procedures (+ and –)/Making decisions/Checking results

Written addition (3)

Activity Sheet 23

Objectives

- Extend written methods to column addition of numbers involving decimals.
- Choose and use appropriate ways of calculating.
- Check with an equivalent calculation.

Vocabulary

method, total, digit, approximate, maximum, subtraction

Resources
none

Teaching support

This sheet provides a range of situations requiring written addition of whole numbers and decimals.

The first question involves using the standard written method and children should be familiar with this approach before starting this sheet.

- Revise the standard written method of addition with both whole numbers and decimals. Provide questions with more than 2 numbers to be added, including some with different numbers of digits, e.g. 385·4 + 52·58 + 0·65… Invite 3 children to come to the board to demonstrate the approximation, the written method and a checking strategy and to explain these to the rest of the group.
- For question 2, ensure children appreciate the meaning of 'maximum'. They should try to find which boxes can be taken to give the number closest to, but under, the maximum of 1000 kg.
- For question 3, children should be encouraged to work with a partner to share results and describe what they notice about solutions in each section of the sorting box, e.g. a 4-digit number and its reversal with a total between 16 000 and 17 000 have their first and last digits totalling 15.

Things to say and ask

- For question 1: *Which digit is missing from this question? How can you be sure?*
- *How can you check this answer?*

Written subtraction (1)

Pupil Book page 38

Objectives

- Use informal pencil-and-paper methods to support, record or explain subtractions.
- Extend written methods to column subtraction.
- Check with an equivalent calculation.

Vocabulary

subtraction, difference between, methods

Resources
none

Strands: Calculations/Solving problems **Topics:** Pencil-and-paper procedures (+ and –)/Checking results/Making decisions/Problems involving 'real life'

Teaching support

Misconceptions

In question 2, where children have to find the difference between 3773 and 37 735, watch out for children who think this is just simply 5 more. Remind them to set the numbers out correctly in columns, with the larger number first.

This page provides children with an opportunity to practise subtraction of numbers using a written method. Children can be asked to use the standard written method of subtraction, or if more appropriate, a written method using an expanded form.

Children should be familiar with using a written method for subtracting two 3-digit numbers, with carrying.

- Begin by discussing an appropriate written method of subtraction for, e.g. 7043 and 4568. Encourage children to estimate before calculating and to check each calculation, e.g. by using a different subtraction method, or by adding the second number in the question to the answer:

  approximate answer is 7000 – 4500 = 2500

  $$\begin{array}{r} 7043 \\ -\ 4568 \\ \hline 2475 \end{array}$$

- When exploring the patterns in question 3, children should focus on the pattern in the differences between the answers, and should notice that these are made from a number of the digits 1, 9 and/or 0 each time. Encourage them to describe any patterns they notice and to predict the next numbers in the sequence.

Things to say and ask

- How do you find the difference between these two numbers?
- Have you checked all your answers?
- For question 3: What patterns did you notice?

Written subtraction (2)

Activity Sheet 24

Objectives

Vocabulary

subtraction, difference between, method, operation

- Use informal pencil-and-paper methods to support, record or explain subtractions.
- Extend written methods to column subtraction.
- Choose and use appropriate ways of calculating.
- Identify and use appropriate operations to solve word problems involving numbers based on 'real life', using one or more steps.
- Explain methods and reasoning.

Resources
coloured pencils (per child)

Strands: Calculations/Solving problems **Topics:** Pencil-and-paper procedures (+ and –)/Making decisions/Problems involving measures

Teaching support

Misconceptions

The most common subtraction error is when children merely subtract the smaller digit from the larger digit and do not exchange, e.g. 9111 – 3999 = 6888. Give examples, find approximate answers and then look at each column in turn, e.g. *Can we subtract 9 units from only 1 unit?*

This sheet provides opportunities for solving word problems using written methods for subtracting numbers less than 10 000, whether informal or formal.

Children should be familiar with using a written method for subtracting two 4-digit numbers, with carrying.

- Begin by discussing an appropriate written method of subtraction for two 4-digit numbers. Encourage children to estimate before calculating and to check each calculation, e.g. by using a different subtraction method, or by adding the second number in the question to the answer.
- For question 1, children are required to solve the word problems and shade in the answers on the grids below. The unshaded sections should spell the word COT.
- In question 2, children should discover that, unless the starting number is palindromic, the pattern will reach a number with repeating digits of the 9× table, e.g. 3636, 1818, 6363, 2727, 4545 … and will then reach the palindromic number 909 that finally results in zero.

Things to say and ask

- *What is the value of this digit?*
- *Do you find this method easy?*
- *Have you checked your answers? Which method or operation did you use?*

Subtracting decimals

Pupil Book page 39

Objectives

Vocabulary

subtract, difference between, diameter

- Extend written methods to column subtraction of numbers involving decimals.
- Choose and use appropriate ways of calculating.
- Identify and use appropriate operations to solve word problems involving numbers based on measures, using one or more steps.

Resources
none

Teaching support

The key idea is that we can use written methods (informal or formal) to subtract decimal numbers in the same way as whole numbers. Word problems involving numbers and quantities based on measures are included.

- Revise the written method of subtraction you wish the children to use to answer the questions on this page, making the link with subtraction of whole numbers. Remind children to use approximation before a calculation and to check the answer. For questions where decimals have different numbers of digits and decimals places, ensure children appreciate the importance of lining up numbers carefully in the correct columns. Stress that the decimal points must be in line. Some children may find it useful to write zeros on the end of decimals so that all have the same number of decimal places, e.g.

    writing   4·5   as   4·50
              – 3·68   – 3·68

- Discuss the word 'diameter' and ensure children realise that this is the length from one side of the circle or sphere to the other through the centre, and that this is the widest point.

Strands: Calculations/Solving problems **Topics:** Using a calculator/Checking results of calculations/Making decisions

> Children will find that 6 calculations can be made and that, as with question 3, the answers can be placed in pairs with the same total. They may notice that the greatest answer pairs with the least, the next greatest with the next least, etc. The reason why the answers can be paired like this relates to the fact that the digits chosen are consecutive.

Things to say and ask

- *What was your approximate answer?*
- *Have you lined up the numbers correctly?*
- *Have you checked your answers using addition or by using another subtraction method?*

Using a calculator

Pupil Book page 40

Objectives

- Develop calculator skills and use a calculator effectively.
- Estimate by approximating, then check results.
- Choose and use appropriate number operations to solve problems, and appropriate ways of calculating.

Vocabulary

calculator, display, key, enter, clear, decimal place, estimate

Resources

calculator (per child)

Teaching support

This page develops calculator skills: entering money in pounds and pence and interpreting the display, e.g. 4·6 = £4·60; keying in a string of numbers carefully and in a particular order where brackets are used.

Children should be familiar with using a calculator for basic computation.

Misconceptions

To encourage quick and efficient use of a calculator, tell children to place the calculator on the table and press the keys using their non-writing hand so that they are free to write efficiently at the same time. As more complex calculations are tackled this will be a very useful skill.

- Ask some money questions involving adding pounds and pence. Elicit that the input amounts should either be in pounds or in pence, but not a mixture. Ensure that children interpret a display answer with 1 decimal place as a 2 decimal-place answer in pounds, e.g. 4·6 as £4·60.
- Remind children of the Clear Entry key on the calculator for cancelling mistakes, and introduce the idea of using the inverse operation to undo a mistake, e.g. 367 + 486 − 486 = 367. If you are in the middle of a long calculation it is useful not to lose all the steps already entered. Stress also the importance of intermediate numbers, e.g. in question 2.
- For question 2, encourage children to explore decimals with different numbers of decimal places, e.g. 7465·3, 7353·04, 7004·798, so that they can make accurate generalisations.

> Children may automatically choose to put the larger number of each pair at the beginning of the brackets so that they avoid negative numbers. But if they do create negative numbers, explore what happens when they are multiplied.

Things to say and ask

- *Have you estimated roughly what the answer will be?*
- *What can you do to undo this error?*
- *How can you check this answer?*

Strands: Calculations/Solving problems **Topics:** Checking results of calculations/Making decisions/Problems involving 'real life' and money

Checking addition and subtraction

Activity Sheet 25

Objectives

- Use knowledge of sums, differences and products of odd/even numbers.
- Choose and use appropriate number operations to solve problems.

Vocabulary

check, answer, total, sum, difference between, product

Resources

none

Teaching support

The key idea is that it is useful to use what you know about the sums, differences and products of odd/even numbers in checking answers.

Children should be familiar with written methods of addition and subtraction of 4-digit numbers.

- Compile a list of the rules for sums and differences of odd/even numbers on the board and ask children to provide examples to support each case:

    even + even = even   even − even = even
    odd + odd = even   odd − odd = even
    even + odd = odd   even − odd = odd
    odd + even = odd   odd − even = odd

- Write an addition, e.g. 3289 + 3754 and ask children to choose the most likely answer from a given set, e.g. 6077, 7043, 7254, 8546. Discuss that since the numbers in the question are odd and even, the answer must be odd, eliminating two possibilities from this given list. By looking at the units digits alone we can see that the answer should end with a 3, so the most likely answer is 7043.

- Ask children to give examples and complete the rules for the products of odd and even numbers:

    even × even = (even); odd × odd = (odd); even × odd = (even); odd × even = (even)

Things to say and ask

- *Will the answer be odd or even?*
- *What does this tell us about our answer?*
- *Will this always be the case?*

Solving problems involving 'real life'

Pupil Book page 41

Objectives

- Choose and use appropriate number operations to solve problems, and appropriate ways of calculating.
- Identify and use appropriate operations (including combinations of operations) to solve word problems involving numbers and quantities based on 'real life' and money, using one or more steps.
- Explain methods and reasoning.

Vocabulary

addition, altogether, total, method, average

Resources

calculator (per child)

Strands: Numbers and the number system/Solving problems **Topics:** Fractions, decimals and percentages/Making decisions/Problems involving 'real life' and money

Teaching support

This page provides practice in solving word problems involving all 4 operations and combinations of these.

Children should be familiar with addition and subtraction of numbers to 10 000 and multiplication by a single digit. They need to know how to find the mean of a set of data.

- ❏ To help children answer question 1, discuss real-life situations where decimals are used in recording, e.g. metres, kilograms, seconds, pounds… Think about appropriate question types for stories, e.g. *A shop has 32 CDs for sale at £8·46 each, totalling £270·72…*
- ❏ For questions 2–5, encourage children to look at the size of the numbers in the question and decide on the most appropriate method of calculating, e.g. mental with jottings, written method, calculator… Whichever method is used, children should record their working or note which mental strategy they used.

Things to say and ask

- ❏ *Can you give an approximate answer?*
- ❏ *How did you solve this question?*
- ❏ *Which operations did you use?*
- ❏ *Have you checked this?*

Solving percentage problems

Activity Sheet 26

Objectives

Vocabulary

per cent, %, fee

- ❏ Find simple percentages of small whole-number quantities.
- ❏ Choose and use appropriate number operations to solve problems, and appropriate ways of calculating.
- ❏ Identify and use appropriate operations to solve word problems involving numbers and quantities based on 'real life' and money, using one or more steps, including calculating percentages.
- ❏ Explain methods and reasoning.

> **Resources**
> calculators or OHP calculator
> red, yellow and blue pencils (per child)

Teaching support

This sheet provides practice in solving word problems involving percentages, particularly using mental methods.

Children should be familiar with finding percentages.

- ■ Revise how 50%, 25%, 10% … can be found by halving, doubling, dividing, adding or subtracting. Remind children that once these are known other related percentages can be found, e.g. 60% = 10% + 50% or 6 × 10%.
- ■ Discuss how other percentages such as 5% and then 15% can be found once 10% is known, e.g. finding 5% by halving 10% and then multiplying by 3 to get 15%. Provide a range of questions of this type for children to tackle mentally, e.g. *What is 5% of 260? … 15% of 260?*
- ■ Show children how to check these answers using a calculator, e.g. 15% of 260 can be found in this way: 15 ÷ 100 (to get the decimal 0·15) × 260.

Things to say and ask

- ❏ *How can we find 15% of a number?*
- ❏ *How did you work it out?*
- ❏ *How could you check this?*

Strand: Calculations *Topic:* Understanding multiplication and division

Relating multiplication and division facts

Pupil Book page 42

Objective

☐ Understand and use the relationships between the four operations, and the principles (not the names) of the arithmetic laws.

Vocabulary

multiplication, product, division

Resources
none

Teaching support

The key idea is that it is useful to look for related multiplication and division facts to help multiply and divide efficiently.

Children should be familiar with the principles (but not the names) of the commutative, associative and distributive laws as they apply (or not) to multiplication and division of 2-digit numbers by a single digit. They need to have some experience of using brackets.

- Revise the associative and distributive laws using questions, e.g. $6 \times 5 \times 20 = 6 \times (5 \times 20) = 600$ and $23 \times 6 = (20 \times 6) + (3 \times 6) = 138$. Include some questions with decimals and multiples of 10. Encourage children to look for the easiest way of multiplying and to use factors or partition numbers where this makes a calculation easier, e.g.
  $21 \times 25 = 21 \times (100 \div 4) = 2100 \div 4 = (2000 \div 4) + (100 \div 4)$
  $= \frac{1}{2}$ of $\frac{1}{2}$ of $2000 + \frac{1}{2}$ of $\frac{1}{2}$ of $100 = 525$
  or $21 \times 25 = 21 \times 5 \times 5 = 105 \times 5 = 525$ (using factors and then partitioning into hundreds, tens and units).

- For question 3, encourage children to think of many different ways to break up the numbers and multiply them separately, e.g. $3.6 = 3 \times 1.2$ or $(3 \times 1) + (3 \times 0.2)$ or $(3 \times 0.6) + (3 \times 0.6)$ or $2 \times 3 \times 0.6$ ... Remind children that this does not work for division, e.g. $3.6 = 18 \div 5$ but not $(18 \div 3) + (18 \div 2)$.

Things to say and ask

☐ How many different related facts have you managed to find?
☐ Does it matter in which order you multiply the numbers? Which is the quicker way?
☐ Can you partition division questions in the same way?

Using brackets

Pupil Book page 43

Objective

☐ Use brackets.

Vocabulary

brackets, order, equation

Resources
none

Strand: Calculations *Topic:* Understanding multiplication and division

Teaching support

Misconceptions
Children often forget that brackets are needed to define the order of operations. Remind them that brackets tell you which part to calculate first.

This page focuses on the use of brackets to indicate which part of a number calculation to work out first. The questions require children to use all 4 operations.

Children will find it helpful to know thoroughly all their times-tables facts to 10×10.

- Write the digits 4 5 9 5 on the board and the signs +, –, =, ×. Explain that by using the digits 4 5 9 5 in order, a question and answer can be created, e.g. $45 \div 9 = 5$. Ensure children realise that 2 digits have been pushed together to create a 2-digit number.
- Write 3 4 6 3 0 and ask children to work out how to keep the order and form a question and answer. If necessary, put the equals sign in so that it reads 3 4 6 = 30. Discuss ways in which 3, 4 and 6 can be combined to make 30, e.g. $3 \times (4 + 6)$. Point out that brackets need to be used since $3 \times 4 + 6$ equals 18, not 30.
- Provide similar questions, e.g. 1 8 4 1 6 or 4 9 5 2 7. ($49 \div (5 + 2) = 7$) Some may have more than one solution, e.g. $18 \div (4 - 1) = 6$ or $(1 + 8) - 4 + 1 = 6$…
- Note that the questions on Pupil Book page 43 do not allow you to create 2-digit numbers out of 2 single digits.

Things to say and ask

❑ Which part of this equation must you work out first?
❑ What is the value of the part in brackets?

Division and fractions

Activity Sheet 27

Objective

❑ Express a quotient as a fraction.

Vocabulary

fraction, mixed number, remainder, quotient, reduced to

Resources
2 dice (per pair)
coloured pencils (per pair)

Teaching support

The key idea is that if there is a remainder after a division has been performed, in some contexts it is better to give the quotient as a fraction or a mixed number.

Children should have had some experience of writing a quotient using fractions and should understand that, e.g. $16 \div 5$ is equivalent to $\frac{16}{5}$ or $3\frac{1}{5}$.

- Write several division questions involving remainders, e.g. $66 \div 7$, $46 \div 4$, $38 \div 6$, $39 \div 8$. Discuss how the answers can be given with whole-number remainders, e.g. 9 r 3. However in a real-life context this often does not make any sense, e.g. *If there were 66 packets of sweets to share between 7 people, how many would each get?* Point out how 9 r 3 means 9 packets with 3 left over, but that this is not a helpful answer if the packets themselves can be split further. Show how the 3 can be shared between 7 people, giving $\frac{3}{7}$ each. So the answer can be written as $9\frac{3}{7}$. This is the exact amount of packets that each person would get. Remind children that in the mixed number answer, the fraction's numerator is the whole-number remainder and the denominator is the divisor.
- Where appropriate, discuss that sometimes these fractions can be written in a simpler form, e.g. $46 \div 4 = 11\frac{2}{4}$ or $11\frac{1}{2}$.
- In question 2, encourage children to work backwards by choosing a whole-number part of the mixed-number answer and then multiplying it by 8, before adding the number of eighths.
- Encourage children to make a link with question 2. It would save them a lot of time to realise they can just add 2 to the answers from question 2.

69

Strands: Calculations/Solving problems **Topics:** Understanding division/Making decisions

Things to say and ask

- *How many are left over? Can we share these out too?*
- *Can you give this answer using a fraction rather than a whole-number remainder?*

Rounding to the nearest tenth

Pupil Book page 44

Objective

- Express a quotient as a decimal rounded to one decimal place.

Vocabulary

division, quotient, decimal, rounding, recurring

Resources

calculator (per child)

Teaching support

The key idea is that if there is a remainder after a division has been performed it can also be written as a decimal. The page begins with revision of rounding to the nearest tenth and also explores what sort of answer to expect from a division question, e.g. a whole number, a finite decimal or a recurring decimal.

Children need to be able to round a decimal to the nearest tenth and have some experience of giving a quotient as a decimal.

- Provide children with calculators and ask them to divide 22 by 5, 6, 7, 8, 9, 10, 11 and 12. List the answers on the board: 4·4, 3·666 666 6, 3·142 857 1, 2·75, 2·444 444 4, 2·2, 2, 1·833 333 3. Look for different kinds of answers together: whole numbers and decimals. Explain that the decimals fall into groups: decimals that end (4·4, 2·75 and 2·1) and decimals that have digits or groups of digits repeating (recurring). *What about 3·142 857 1?* Show how, if a calculator had more digits on the display, the group of digits 142 857 would keep repeating.
- Provide other division questions and invite children to say which 'type' each is, e.g. 55 ÷ 3, 16 ÷ 7, 27 ÷ 4, etc.
- Explain that, rather than writing down long decimals, it is often more useful to round the answer to the nearest tenth, e.g. writing 3·1 rather than 3·142 857 142 857...

Things to say and ask

- *Can you tell me about the decimal answer?*
- *Do you think the digits of this decimal keep on repeating? (recurring)*

Dividing money

Pupil Book page 45

Objectives

- Divide £·p by a 2-digit number to give £·p.
- Identify and use appropriate operations.
- Explain methods and reasoning.
- Choose and use appropriate number operations to solve problems and appropriate ways of calculating.

Vocabulary

share, divide, value

Resources

calculator (optional) (per child)

different size packets of the same cereal with prices (optional)

Strands: Calculations/Solving problems *Topics:* Understanding division/Problems involving money

Teaching support

Misconceptions
When working in pounds, children often forget that when an answer has only 1 decimal place in the display they should write it as a 2 decimal-place answer in pounds, e.g. 4·5 is £4·50.

This page explores dividing amounts of money given in pounds and pence and giving a suitable answer. Questions include comparing items in terms of value for money and other word problems.

- Discuss how items can be compared in terms of value for money, e.g. *If 2 tins cost 78p and 5 tins cost £1·90, which is the better value?* Show children how to compare by finding the cost for one item by dividing. Provide other non-discrete examples, e.g. *If a 500 g box of cereal costs £1·50, and a 750 g box costs £2, which is the better value for money?* Discuss alternative ways of comparing, e.g. cost per gram, cost per 100 g, using ratio to find the cost of 750 g if charged at the same rate as the first box (£2·25)…

- Encourage children to choose the most appropriate way of calculating for solving the problems on this page, e.g. using a mental method with jottings rather than a written method, or vice versa. If appropriate, children can be allowed to use calculators, but should be reminded of the importance of interpreting the display correctly in the context of money, e.g. where the display shows 0·4, this means £0·40 or 40p.

Things to say and ask

- How much money is that?
- Can you write it in pounds?

Rounding after division

Pupil Book page 46

Objectives

- Round up or down after division, depending on the context.
- Identify and use appropriate operations to solve word problems involving numbers and quantities based on 'real life', money and measures using one or more steps.
- Explain methods and reasoning.

Vocabulary

divide, division, remainder, fraction, decimal, rounding

Resources
none

Teaching support

The key idea is that whether you round up or down after division depends on the context of the question.

Children will have had experience of this idea. The page provides problems to solve with 2- and 3-digit numbers and amounts of money.

- Revise the idea of rounding up or down depending on a context:
  First provide situations where you need to round up the answer to solve the problem, e.g. *How many photo albums that hold 60 photos do I need to hold 259 photos?*
  Move on to situations involving rounding down, e.g. *How many tickets costing £1·20 can I pay for with £10?*

- Encourage children to realise that an answer with a remainder does not usually make sense, e.g. *How can you need 4 remainder 19 photo albums to hold your photos?*

Things to say and ask

- What does the question mean?
- How did you work this out? Did you round up or down? Why?
- Why do we have to round up or down?

Strand: Calculations *Topic:* Rapid recall of multiplication and division facts

Multiplying and dividing

Pupil Book page 47

Objectives

❏ Consolidate knowing by heart multiplication facts up to 10×10.
❏ Derive quickly: doubles of 2-digit numbers, doubles of multiples of 10 to 1000, doubles of multiples of 100 to 10 000, and the corresponding halves.

Vocabulary

double, halve, inverse, multiple

Resources

pack of playing cards with picture cards removed (per pair)

Teaching support

This page provides practice in recalling multiplication facts up to 10×10 and deriving doubles and halves quickly.

- The focus should be on deriving or recalling facts quickly. Discuss ways of using known facts to find new unknown ones.
- Remind children that once one fact is known many others can be derived from it directly, e.g. if $8 \times 2 = 16$ is known so are $2 \times 8 = 16$, $16 \div 8 = 2$ and $16 \div 2 = 8$; halve $16 = 8$, double $8 = 16$, $\frac{16}{2} = 8$…make even more. Link with place value, e.g. $80 \times 2 = 160$, halve $1600 = 800$…
- For the game, which involves speedy recall of multiplication facts up to 10×10, children should work in pairs.

Misconceptions

Children sometimes use, e.g. $6 \times 5 = 30$ to make the new, but incorrect, 'fact' $60 \times 50 = 300$. Ask them to break down the calculation into factors, e.g.
$6 \times 10 \times 5 \times 10 =$
$6 \times 5 \times 10 \times 10 = 30 \times 100$
to see that the correct answer is 3000.

Things to say and ask

❏ *How did you answer that question so quickly?*
❏ *Did you know the answer?*
❏ *Did you use another fact to help you?*

Division facts

Activity Sheet 28

Objective

❏ Derive quickly division facts corresponding to tables up to 10×10.

Vocabulary

divide, inverse, remainder, quotient

Resources

coloured pencils (per child)
2 dice (per pair)
a set of 2–10 number cards (per pair)

Teaching support

This sheet provides practice in speedy recall of division facts corresponding to tables up to 10×10.

- Talk about the link between multiplication and division using the vocabulary above. Write a range of numbers, e.g. 36, 54, 48… Call out numbers to be divided into these and ask children to state the complete fact, e.g. 6, $48 \div 6 = 8$ or $36 \div 6 = 6$.
- Write a zero (or zeros) on the end of each number and repeat, calling out single digits or multiples of 10, e.g. 6, $480 \div 6 = 80$; 60, $480 \div 60 = 8$; 6, $4800 \div 6 = 800$; 60, $4800 \div 60 = 80$…
- Remind children that division facts can also be expressed as fraction facts, e.g. one sixth of 36 is 6 and one eighth of 48 is 6… Provide further questions of this type, e.g. *What is one seventh of 56?*

Strand: Calculations **Topics:** Rapid recall of multiplication and division facts/Mental calculation strategies (× and ÷)

Things to say and ask

- Did you know this answer or did you use another fact to help you work it out?
- How could this multiplication fact be re-read as a division fact?
- Can you say this as a fraction fact?

Doubling, halving and squaring

Activity Sheet 29

Objectives

- Derive quickly: squares of multiples of 10 to 100.
- Derive quickly: doubles of 2-digit numbers, doubles of multiples of 10 to 1000, and the corresponding halves.

Vocabulary

double, twice, halve, square number, predict

Resources

counters or similar
calculator (per child)

Teaching support

This sheet provides opportunities for exploration of squares of numbers, including multiples of 10 to 100. Doubling and halving facts are also revised.

Children should already know by heart all the square numbers to 10×10.

- Ask volunteers to illustrate the square numbers using counters or similar. Discuss the meaning of the mathematical word 'square' in the context of 'squaring a number', e.g. 6 squared. Remind children that this means multiplying the number by itself. Introduce/revise square notation, e.g. 6^2.
- Point out how knowing the squares of numbers to 10 can help you to find the squares of multiples of 10 to 100, e.g. 3^2 is 9 and $30^2 = 30 \times 30 = 3 \times 10 \times 3 \times 10 = 3^2 \times 100 = 900$.
- For question 4, children may use a calculator. They should enter the calculation as a multiplication even if there is a 'square' key.
- When investigating squares of numbers such as 101, 1001, 10 001, encourage children to write about patterns they notice and how they can use these to predict, e.g. the tenth number in the sequence.

Misconceptions

Occasionally children make the mistake of forgetting a zero to the right of the answer, e.g. $30 \times 30 = 90$. This may show a confusion of multiplication with addition, e.g. the answer to $30 + 30$ has only one zero. Point out that squaring means 30 lots of 30, which is much more than 90, which equals 30×3 or 3×30.

Things to say and ask

- How did you answer that question so quickly?
- Did you know the answer?
- What is 70 squared? How can we write this?
- Did you use another fact to help you?

Using doubling and halving

Pupil Book page 48

Objective

- Use related facts and doubling or halving.

Vocabulary

double, twice, halve

Resources

none

Strand: Calculations **Topic:** Mental calculation strategies (× and ÷)

Teaching support

The key idea is that we can often use doubling and halving to work out a multiplication mentally rather than using a written method. The page provides opportunities to solve problems involving doubling and halving, exploring patterns created in related questions.

Children should be familiar with using this idea for 1- and 2-digit numbers.

- Write a sequence of questions where the first number doubles each time, e.g.
    $1 \times 13 =$
    $2 \times 13 =$
    $4 \times 13 =$
    $8 \times 13 =$
    $16 \times 13 = ...$

- Ask children to answer each question, starting at the top and doubling each answer to find the next one. Point out that if one number is doubled in a multiplication then the answer is doubled.

- Demonstrate how other × 13 multiplications can now be found easily, e.g. 12×13, by adding the answers to 4×13 and 8×13. Ask children to suggest their own questions that can be answered using those on the board, e.g. $18 \times 13 = (2 \times 13) + (16 \times 13)$.

- Write 5×86. Ask for suggestions for a quick way of finding the answer. Accept all suggestion and focus on using the equivalent multiplication 10×43. Point out that if you double one number in a multiplication and halve the other, the answer stays the same. This often helps you do a multiplication mentally.

- When using doubles such as 1, 2, 4, 8, 16... children should realise that all whole numbers can be made by adding two or more of these doubles, e.g. 19 is $16 + 2 + 1$, 20 is $16 + 4$, 21 is $16 + 4 + 1$ ... The Ancient Egyptians used this method of multiplying.

Things to say and ask

- *How did you double this number?*
- *Can we use this answer to find the next one?*
- *Which facts can we now find using these answers?*

Using factors

Activity Sheet 30

Objective

- Use factors (e.g. $35 \times 18 = 35 \times 6 \times 3$).

Vocabulary

factor, multiplication

Resources
none

Strand: Calculations *Topic:* Mental calculation strategies (× and ÷)

Teaching support

Misconceptions
The words 'factor' and 'multiple' are often confused. Remind children that you get a multiple when you have multiplied.

This sheet revises factors. It focuses on their use in multiplying and dividing efficiently, e.g. when multiplying 15 by 48 it is easier to rewrite it as 3 × 5 × 2 × 8 × 3 and to multiply the pairs 2 × 5 and 3 × 3, giving 10 × 9 × 8 = 720.

Children should be familiar with using factors to multiply and divide a 2-digit by a 1-digit number.

- Remind children of the term 'factor', e.g. that a factor is a number that divides exactly into another without a remainder. Choose a number, e.g. 36, and ask them to say all the factors of this number, i.e. 1, 2, 3, 4, 6, 9, 12, 18 and 36.
- Write the numbers 15 and 36 on the board and together identify all the factor pairs, i.e. 1 × 15 and 3 × 5, and 1 × 36, 2 × 18, 3 × 12, 4 × 9 and 6 × 6. Break down some of these factor pairs further, e.g. by showing that 2 × 18 can be written as 2 × 3 × 6 or even 2 × 3 × 2 × 3. Explain that multiplications can often be made easier by using pairs of factors. Write 15 × 36 and demonstrate that this could be solved easily by thinking of it as 3 × 5 × 2 × 3 × 6, which is the same as 10 × 9 × 6 = 540.

Things to say and ask

- What are the factors of this number?
- Can you give them in pairs?
- How did you work this out?

Using closely related facts

Activity Sheet 31

Objectives

- Use closely related facts.

Vocabulary

cost, adjust

Resources
none

Teaching support

Misconceptions
When multiplying by near multiples of 10, e.g. 49 and 51, some children find it difficult to make the final adjustment. Place the question in a context to help children see what adjustment to make.

The key idea is that a useful way of multiplying by a near multiple of 10 is to use the nearest multiple of 10 and then adjust the answer.

Children should be familiar with this idea for multiplying by 19 or 21.

- Revise suitable mental methods for multiplying numbers by 50, e.g. 42 × 50 = 42 × 100 ÷ 2 = 4200 ÷ 2 = 2100 or 42 × 50 = 42 × 5 × 10 = 2100. Explain that when we multiply by 51 we need an extra lot of 42, e.g. 42 × 51 is the same as 42 × 50 plus 42. Put this into a context if children are unsure, e.g. *A bottle of lemonade costs 42p. If we have 50 of them it is 2100p (or £21·00) and 51 of them is one more bottle, so that is an extra 42p, making £21·42.*
- For question 3, children explore multiplying by 39 and 41 and their relationship to multiplying by 40. Children should describe this relationship, e.g. that when a number is multiplied by 40 it is 'that number more' or 'that number less' than when multiplied by 39 or 41.
- The pattern is similar when multiplying by 49, 50 and 51. Encourage children to practise multiplying by 99 and 101 in the same way.

Things to say and ask

- How did you decide what to do?
- What method did you use for working this out?
- Can you explain your method to us?

Strands: Calculations/Solving problems **Topics:** Mental calculation strategies (× and ÷)/Making decisions

Partitioning

Pupil Book page 49

Objective

❏ Partition (e.g. 87 × 6 = (80 × 6) + (7 × 6)).

Vocabulary

partition

Resources
a 1–10 dice (per child)

Teaching support

Misconceptions
Occasionally children make a mistake with the place value of the answer to a decimal multiplication, e.g. 3·9 × 8 = 3·12. Remind children that they should always make an approximation first, e.g. 4 × 8 = 32, so they know the answer must be 31·2 rather than 3·12 or 312.

The key idea is to multiply by partitioning using the distributive law. This means splitting a 2-digit number into tens and units (or units and tenths), multiplying each separately and then adding the subtotals. Note that division is unlike multiplication in that it is not distributive over addition in this way.

Children should have some experience in multiplying a 2-digit number by a single-digit number, multiplying the tens first, and be confident with place value involving tens, units and tenths.

▪ Ask a range of questions to practise the skill of multiplying using partitioning, e.g. 39 × 8 = (30 × 8) + (9 × 8) = 240 + 72 = 312. These can be presented in a 'real-life' context, e.g. *How much will it cost for 8 radios at £39 each?* Remind children to approximate first before calculating.

▪ Demonstrate how similar questions involving decimals can also be solved in this way, e.g. 3·9 × 8 = (3 × 8) + (0·9 × 8) = 24 + 7·2 = 31·2. Discuss how tenths can be multiplied by whole numbers, e.g. by thinking of the tenth initially as a whole number, e.g. 9 × 8, and then making the answer ten times smaller.

Things to say and ask

❏ *What method did you use for working this out?*
❏ *Did you use partitioning?*
❏ *Can you explain your method to us?*

Using known facts

Pupil Book page 50

Objectives

❏ Use the relationship between multiplication and division.
❏ Use known number facts and place value to consolidate mental multiplication and division.
❏ Identify and use appropriate operations (including combinations of operations) to solve word problems involving numbers and quantities based on measures.

Vocabulary

multiply, divide, double, halve, mental calculation

Resources
none

Teaching support

This page provides practice with mental manipulation of decimal fractions with 1 or 2 decimal places: doubling, halving and multiplying by a single-digit number (1 decimal place); and with multiplying decimals with 1 or 2 decimal places by 10 or 100 or any single-digit number. Some problems are set in the context of measurement.

Strands: Calculations/Solving problems **Topics:** Mental calculation strategies (× and ÷)/Making decisions

Children should be familiar with multiplying mentally a 2-digit whole number by any single-digit number, crossing the tens boundary and doubling/halving/multiplying by multiples of 10.

- Encourage children always to make an approximation to gain a feel for the size of the answer before performing the calculation. They should check each calculation by using either a different method or a different operation, e.g. using multiplication to check division and vice versa.
- Remind children of the link between multiplication and division and that related facts can be written for any given fact. Ask children to explain their strategies for working out the answer.
- For question 4, remind children that they might need to use brackets to indicate which part of the calculation to work out first.
- Once children have realised that they can always make 1, e.g. 6 ÷ 6, they will be always be able to find the next number, though it may not be the neatest solution!

Things to say and ask
- How did you work it out? Did anyone work it out a different way?
- How could you check if you were right?

Multiplying and dividing mentally

Activity Sheet 32

Objectives

- Use known number facts and place value to consolidate mental multiplication and division.
- Choose and use appropriate number operations to solve problems, and appropriate ways of calculating.

Vocabulary

consecutive, square, approximate

Resources
none

Teaching support

This sheet focuses on patterns within consecutive whole numbers and 2-digit decimals with a difference of one tenth. Children are also required to choose the most appropriate method of calculation for each question, e.g. if multiplying 19 by 21 they may choose to multiply 21 by 20 and adjust.

Children should be familiar with the term 'consecutive' and have experienced the wide spread of mental strategies for efficient mental multiplication/division.

- Choose pairs of whole numbers with a difference of 2 and write them on the board as multiplication questions, e.g. 20 × 22, 12 × 14. Discuss appropriate strategies that children might use to solve these mentally, e.g. using partitioning or place value strategies.
- Remind children to make an approximation before doing the calculation mentally, and then to use a different method or operation to check their answers.
- Children may need to be reminded of the mathematical term 'square', i.e. multiplying a number by itself.
- Children should discover a difference of 0·01. Ask them to explain why this is 100 times smaller than in question 3 and to predict and investigate what would happen for 0·39, 0·4, 0·41. (The difference is 0·0001, a hundred times smaller again.)

Things to say and ask
- Did you know this answer or did you use another fact to help you work it out?
- What patterns did you find?

Strand: Calculations **Topic:** Pencil-and-paper procedures (multiplication)

Using short multiplication

Pupil Book page 51

Objectives

- Approximate first. Use informal pencil-and-paper methods to support, record or explain multiplications.
- Extend written methods to short multiplication ThHTU × U.

Vocabulary

multiplication, multiplied by, times, exchange

Resources

a set of 3–9 digit cards (per pair)

Teaching support

The key idea is that it is sometimes useful to use a written method for short multiplication. The page involves multiplication questions up to ThHTU × U. Ask children to solve these informally using a grid method or formally using the standard expanded or contracted form as you wish. The first question revises multiplication of multiples of 10, which is important for this method.

Children should be familiar with informal (grid) and standard written methods for short multiplication of HTU.

- Revise the appropriate written method, e.g.

Expanded		Expanded	Condensed (short method)
1431	or	1431	1431
× 5		× 5	× 5
5000		5	7155
2000		150	$_{2\ 1}$
150		2000	
5		5000	
7155		7155	

- Encourage children always to make an approximation to gain a feel for the size of the answer, e.g. *It's about 1500 times 5, so the answer should be about 7500.* Emphasise the importance of approximation as a means of allowing you to know whether your answer is sensible or not.
- Children can be asked to check each calculation using a different operation, i.e. division, or a different method, e.g. the grid method.
- For question 3, encourage children to think of all the ways you can end up zero units when you multiply 2 single digits.
- Children should use their answers to question 3 and factorise one of each pair of numbers further to produce a product of 3 numbers. This can be further extended to 4 or 5 numbers, if possible.

Things to say and ask

- *Can you see why this method works?*

Strand: Calculations *Topic:* Pencil-and-paper procedures (multiplication)

Multiplying decimals

Activity Sheet 33

Objectives

- ❏ Approximate first. Use informal pencil-and-paper methods to support, record or explain multiplications.
- ❏ Extend written methods to short multiplication of numbers involving decimals.

Vocabulary

short multiplication, decimal, decimal point, decimal place, multiplied by, exchange

Resources

sets of 0–9 digit cards (optional)

Teaching support

The key idea is to use place value and extend use of standard written methods of multiplication to short multiplication of a decimal number.

Children should be confident with multiplying whole numbers using this method.

Misconceptions

Ensure children make an approximation to decide where to place the decimal point. The 'rule' for lining up decimal points as used for addition and subtraction does not work for multiplication of 2 decimal numbers.

- ❏ Discuss the links between whole-number multiplication and decimal multiplication using a standard written method for multiplication, e.g.

$$\begin{array}{r} 532 \\ \times\ 4 \\ \hline 2128 \\ {\scriptstyle 1} \end{array} \qquad \begin{array}{r} 53\cdot2 \\ \times\ 4 \\ \hline 212\cdot8 \\ {\scriptstyle 1} \end{array} \qquad \begin{array}{r} 5\cdot32 \\ \times\ 4 \\ \hline 21\cdot28 \\ {\scriptstyle 1} \end{array}$$

- ❏ Rather than giving an explanation about where to insert the decimal point in the answer based on the numbers or position of digits, tell children to make an approximation to help them, e.g. *53·2 × 4 is about 50 times 4, so the answer should be about 200. So, in this case, the answer must be 212·8 and not 2·128 or 21·28.*
- ❓ Children should quickly realise that using the same arrangements of digits answers will be 10 times greater than those they have recorded for question 3. However, question 3 requires only 12 of the possible permutations. Children could be encouraged to find how many ways in total there are of arranging the digits (24).

Things to say and ask

- ❏ *Approximately how big is your answer going to be?*
- ❏ *Can you see why this method works?*

Strands: Calculations/Solving problems **Topics:** Pencil-and-paper procedures (multiplication)/Making decisions/Problems involving 'real life' and money

Converting currencies

Pupil Book page 52

Objectives

- Choose and use appropriate number operations to solve problems, and appropriate ways of calculating.
- Identify and use appropriate operations to solve word problems involving numbers and quantities based on 'real life' and money, using one or more steps, including converting pounds to foreign currency, or vice versa.

Vocabulary

currency, pound, convert, euro, exchange rate, equivalent, inverse

Resources

calculator (per child)

counters in 2 colours (per pair)

Teaching support

This sheet gives further practice in short multiplication of numbers involving decimals in converting pounds to euros and back again.

Children need to have completed Activity Sheet 33.

- Write the exchange rate £1 = 1·59 euros. Introduce the use of € to stand for euros. Elicit that if we know how many euros are equivalent to £1, then we can find £2, £3 and so on by multiplying, e.g. £2 is equivalent to €3·18 (1·59 × 2).
- Explain that when converting the other way, from euros to pounds, we use the inverse operation, division, e.g. €1112 = £ (1112 ÷ 1·59). Give some examples that can be done mentally, e.g. €159, €1590, €318...
- Talk about a useful approximation: *If there were 2 euros to each pound, 1 euro would be worth 50p. So 1 euro must be worth something between 50p and £1.* Ask a volunteer to use a calculator to divide 1 by 1·59 to find out that, at this exchange rate, a euro is worth about 63p. Tell children that exchange rates vary all the time, so there is a different rate to use on Pupil Book page 52.

Things to say and ask

- What is the exchange rate?
- If £1 is worth 1·59 euros how would we work out how many euros are worth the same as £5?

Using long multiplication (1)

Pupil Book page 53

Objectives

- Approximate first. Use informal pencil-and-paper methods to support, record or explain multiplications.
- Extend written methods to long multiplication of a 3-digit by a 2-digit integer.

Vocabulary

multiplication, multiplied by, times, exchange

Resources

none

Strand: Calculations *Topic:* Pencil-and-paper procedures (multiplication)

Teaching support

Misconceptions

Children sometimes confuse which digits are to be multiplied by which. Illustrate this using the grid method alongside the formal written method, to show how all digits of one number are multiplied by each digit of the second number.

The key idea is to extend long multiplication to HTU × TU. Children can attempt the questions on this page using the standard written method for long multiplication or alternatively complete this page using informal methods, e.g. the grid method.

Children should be familiar with informal (grid) and standard written methods for long multiplication of 2-digit numbers.

- Discuss the method of multiplication you wish children to use for this page, giving an example on the board to be used as a reference throughout the lesson, e.g.

$$
\begin{array}{r}
46 \\
\times 28 \\
\hline
46 \times 20 \quad 920 \\
46 \times 8 \quad 368 \\
\hline
1288
\end{array}
$$

or

	40	6
20	800	120
8	320	48

$$
\begin{array}{r}
920 \\
+ 368 \\
\hline
1288
\end{array}
$$

- Always encourage children to make an approximation to gain a feel for the size of the answer, e.g. *It's about 30 times 50, so the answer should be about 1500.* Emphasise the importance of approximation as a means of allowing you to know whether your answer is a sensible one or not.

- Children can be asked to check each calculation using a different operation, i.e. division, or a different method, e.g. the expanded form…

- In question 3, encourage children to describe which digits they placed in which positions in the number, e.g. the largest digit is the first digit of the 3-digit number, then the next largest is the first digit of the 2-digit number…

- Multiplication is commutative so a 2-digit × 3-digit calculation will give the same answer as the 3-digit × 2-digit calculation for the same numbers. It is useful for children to try these methods in a standard written form so they can decide which way round is more efficient (i.e. least likely to create errors).

Things to say and ask

- *How can we split up this number and multiply each part separately?*
- *Can you see why this method works?*

Using long multiplication (2)

Activity Sheet 34

Objectives

- Approximate first. Use informal pencil-and-paper methods to support, record or explain multiplications.
- Extend written methods to long multiplication of a 3-digit by a 2-digit integer.

Vocabulary

long multiplication, multiplied by, times, exchange

Resources

none

Strands: Calculations/Solving problems **Topics:** Pencil-and-paper procedures (division)/Checking results of calculations/Problems involving 'real life' and money

Teaching support

The key idea is to encourage children to make predictions about/investigate the values of missing digits in products before using a written method to check.

Children need to be familiar with long multiplication of TU × TU and to have encountered questions involving HTU × TU.

- Revise the long multiplication method for HTU × TU. Provide children with an example that they can use as a reference throughout the lesson, e.g. 346 × 28: approximate answer is 350 × 30 = 1050 × 10 = 10 500

$$\begin{array}{r} 346 \\ \times 28 \\ \hline 346 \times 20 \quad 6920 \\ 346 \times 8 \quad 2768 \\ \hline 9688 \\ {\scriptstyle 1} \end{array}$$

Check against approximate answer.

- For question 2, encourage children to use multiplication facts together with approximation to predict the missing digits. They should check their predictions by completing the multiplication.
- When investigating products of 58 212 in question 3, encourage children to think carefully about what the units digits must be in order to give this answer and to predict the approximate size of the numbers using rounding.
- Encourage children to realise that they just have to find single-digit factors of the 4-digit number.

Things to say and ask

- For question 2: *Which digit do you think is missing?*
- *Can you explain your thinking?*
- *If the digit was a 6, what would the answer be?*

Using short division

Pupil Book page 54   Activity Sheet 35

Objectives

Vocabulary

divide, share, quotient, remainder, mixed number

- Approximate first. Use informal pencil and paper methods to support, record or explain divisions.
- Extend written methods to short division of TU or HTU by U (mixed-number answer).
- Identify and use appropriate operations to solve word problems involving numbers and quantities based on 'real life' and money using one or more steps.
- Explain methods and reasoning.
- Check with the inverse operations or with an equivalent calculation.

Resources
For the Pupil Book:
  a set of 0–9 digit cards (per pair)
  calculator (per child)
For the Activity Sheet:
  coloured pencils (per child)
  0–9 dice (per pair)

Strand: Calculations *Topic:* Pencil-and-paper procedures (division)

Teaching support

This unit provides opportunities to practise written methods of short division for division of 3-digit numbers by single-digit numbers. Word problems, involving TU or HTU ÷ U are included on Pupil Book page 54 only.

Children should be familiar with using multiples of the divisor and have some experience in using standard written methods.

- Demonstrate and discuss the method of division that you wish children to use for completing either section, drawing attention to the importance of approximation and checking.
- Revise giving the answer as a mixed number, rather than with a whole-number remainder, e.g. giving the answer to this calculation as $26\frac{4}{5}$ rather than 26 r 4:

$$
\begin{array}{r}
134 \div 5 \quad\quad 26 \\
5\overline{)134} \\
-\underline{100} \quad\quad 20 \times 5 \\
34 \\
-\underline{30} \quad\quad 6 \times 5 \\
4
\end{array}
$$

- Encourage children to check each calculation by using multiplication, e.g. (26 × 5) + 4.

Things to say and ask

- How did you work it out?
- Did anyone work it out a different way?
- Can you see why this method works?

Using long division

Pupil Book page 55

Objectives

- Approximate first. Use informal pencil-and-paper methods to support, record or explain divisions.
- Extend written methods to long division of HTU by TU (whole-number answer).

Vocabulary

divide, share, quotient

Resources

a calculator (per child)

Strands: Calculations/Solving problems **Topics:** Pencil-and-paper procedures (division)/Problems involving 'real life' and money

Teaching support

The key idea is for children to develop and practise a standard written method for long division of HTU by TU (no remainder).

Children need to be familiar with using multiples of the divisor and a formal written method for short division.

- Write 972 ÷ 36. Ask children to give an approximate answer, e.g. 1000 ÷ 50 = 20 and to suggest a way to proceed. They may suggest trying a standard written method or using multiples of the divisor.

- Demonstrate whichever is suggested first, making links with children's experience of short division. Then bring in other methods, showing either of the two long division methods and multiples of the divisor side by side.

$$
\begin{array}{l}
36\overline{)972} \\
-720 \quad 20 \times 36 \\
\overline{252} \\
-252 \quad 7 \times 36 \\
\overline{0} \\
\text{answer : 27}
\end{array}
\quad \text{or} \quad
\begin{array}{l}
\phantom{36\overline{)}}27 \\
36\overline{)972} \\
-72 \\
\overline{252} \\
-252 \\
\overline{0}
\end{array}
\quad \text{and} \quad
\begin{array}{ll}
972 & \\
-360 & 10 \times 36 \\
\overline{612} & \\
-360 & 10 \times 36 \\
\overline{252} & \\
-180 & 5 \times 36 \\
\overline{72} & \\
-72 & 2 \times 36 \\
\overline{0} & \\
\text{answer: 27} &
\end{array}
$$

- For question 1, you may need to remind children that a missing-number division question, e.g. 527 ÷ ___ = 17 can be rearranged to form the question 527 ÷ 17 = ___. This can then be tackled using a long division method.

Things to say and ask

- What method did you use for working this out?
- Can you explain how it works?

Solving division problems

Activity Sheet 36

Objectives

Vocabulary

lots of, groups of, multiply, multiplied by, times, partitioning

- Approximate first. Use informal pencil-and-paper methods to support, record or explain divisions.
- Extend written methods to long division of HTU by TU (whole-number answer).
- Identify and use appropriate operations to solve word problems involving numbers and quantities based on 'real life' and money, using one or more steps.
- Explain methods and reasoning.

Resources
coloured pencils (per child)

Strands: Calculations/Solving problems *Topics:* Pencil-and-paper procedures (division)/Problems involving 'real life' and money

Teaching support

This sheet explores long division methods in the context of real life and money problems.

Children need to be confident using multiples of the divisor and a formal written method for short division and have some experience of these for long division.

- Revise the method of long division you wish the children to use for this sheet. Provide them with an example to use as a reference throughout the lesson, e.g. 972 ÷ 36: approximate answer is 900 ÷ 30 = 30

$$
\begin{array}{r}
36\overline{)972} \\
-720 \\
\hline
252 \\
-252 \\
\hline
0
\end{array}
\quad
\begin{array}{l}
20 \times 36 \\
\\
7 \times 36
\end{array}
\quad \text{or} \quad
\begin{array}{r}
27 \\
36\overline{)972} \\
-72 \\
\hline
252 \\
-252 \\
\hline
0
\end{array}
$$

answer: 27

- Ask children to check each calculation using a different operation, i.e. multiplication, or a different method.

Things to say and ask

- Can you see why this method works?
- Can you see a way to solve this mentally with jottings? Which way do you prefer?

Solving decimal problems

Pupil Book page 56

Objectives

Vocabulary

quotient, sum, product, remainder

- Approximate first. Use informal pencil-and-paper methods to support, record or explain divisions.
- Extend written methods to short division of numbers involving decimals.
- Identify and use appropriate operations to solve word problems involving numbers and quantities based on 'real life' and measures using one or more steps.
- Explain methods and reasoning.

Resources
none

Strand: Calculations **Topic:** Using a calculator/Checking results of calculations

Teaching support

Misconceptions
Stress the importance of approximating before calculating, e.g. 87·5 × 7 is about 90 × 7 = 630. This will assist children in placing the decimal point correctly in the answer.

This page provides opportunities to explore puzzles and problems including those requiring division of decimals.

Children need to be confident using multiples of the divisor and a formal written method for short division of whole numbers.

- Revise the terms quotient, product and sum, e.g. *If the product of two numbers is 10 and the sum is 7, what are the two numbers? If the quotient of two numbers is 3 and the product is 48, what are the two numbers?...*
- Demonstrate the method of recording you wish children to use for the decimal division. Provide them with an example that they can use as a reference throughout the lesson, e.g. 87·5 ÷ 7:

  approximate answer is 84 ÷ 7 = 12

  $$\begin{array}{r} 12{\cdot}5 \\ 7\,\overline{)87{\cdot}5} \\ -\,70{\cdot}0 \quad 10 \times 7 \\ \hline 17{\cdot}5 \\ -\,14{\cdot}0 \quad 2 \times 7 \\ \hline 3{\cdot}5 \\ -\,3{\cdot}5 \quad 0{\cdot}5 \times 7 \\ \hline 0{\cdot}0 \end{array}$$

  answer: 12·5

Things to say and ask

- If the quotient of two numbers is 9 and the sum is 30, what are the two numbers?
- Can you explain this method of short division to us on the board?

Developing calculator skills

Activity Sheet 37

Objectives

- Develop calculator skills and use a calculator effectively.
- Check with the inverse operation when using a calculator.

Vocabulary

calculator, display, key, enter, clear

Resources
calculator (per child)

Teaching support

This sheet explores using a calculator and includes problems and puzzles, including those in a real-life context.

Children should be familiar with using the ⊕, ⊖, ⊗ and ⊘ keys, the ⊜ key and the decimal point. They should know how to clear an accidental wrong entry. When they are working with a calculator encourage them to place it on a table and use their non-writing hand to press the keys. This enables children to have a pencil in one hand and to use the calculator with the other. As more complex calculations are tackled this will be a very useful skill.

- In question 1, encourage children to work out what each missing digit might be by using tables or addition facts.
- Children may choose to use a trial-and-improvement approach in question 2. They could also be encouraged to consider how many times the number sold on the first day has been added to give the 6-day total, e.g. on the first day x papers were sold, on the second 2x, on the third 4x, on the fourth 8x and so on, giving 63x. 252 can be divided by 63 to give the answer 4.

Strand: Calculations *Topic:* Checking results of calculations

Things to say and ask
- Have you estimated roughly what the answer will be?
- How can you check your answer?

Multiplication and tests of divisibility

Pupil Book page 57

Objective
- Use tests of divisibility.

Vocabulary
divisible by, tests of divisibility, multiple of, factor

Resources
up to 20 small counters and a calculator (per pair)

Teaching support

This page provides practice in using tests of divisibility.

- Ask children to help you make a list of tests of divisibility:

    In multiples of:
    - 100   the last two digits are 00
    - 25   the last two digits are 00, 25, 50 or 75
    - 10   the last digit is 0
    - 2   the last digit is 0, 2, 4, 6 or 8
    - 3   the sum of the digits is divisible by 3
    - 4   the last two digits are divisible by 4
    - 5   the last digit is 0 or 5
    - 6   the number is even and divisible by 3
    - 8   the last 3 digits are divisible by 8
    - 9   the sum of the digits is divisible by 9

- Check that children can apply them by writing a range of 2- and 3-digit numbers on the board and asking children to state which numbers will divide exactly into each number. Discuss the features of numbers divisible by 2, 3, 4, 5, 6, 8, 9, 10, 25 and 100. Encourage children to describe the features in their own words.

- Children should be encouraged to play the game several times to explore ways of preventing the other player from winning, e.g. by noticing that only two numbers in the grid have the factor 8 (360 and 64). If these are used first the other player may not be able to win.

Things to say and ask
- How can you tell if a number is exactly divisible by 2, 3, 4, 5, 6, 8, 9, 10, 25, 100?
- Is this number a multiple of 8?

Strands: Measures/Calculations *Topics:* Length/Using a calculator

Using metric units of length

Pupil Book page 58

Objectives

Vocabulary

kilometre, metre, centimetre, millimetre, thousandth, width, perimeter, approximately, operation key

- Use, read and write standard metric units (km, m, cm, mm), including their abbreviations, and relationships between them.
- Convert smaller to larger units (e.g. m to km, cm or mm to m), and vice versa.
- Suggest suitable units and measuring equipment to estimate or measure length.
- Develop calculator skills and use a calculator effectively.

Resources
calculator (per child)

Teaching support

Misconceptions

The most common errors are related to place value. Encourage children to work from the decimal point to identify tenths, hundredths, thousandths.

The key ideas are that 1 mm is 1 thousandth of 1 m and 1 m is 1 thousandth of 1 km.

Children should know that 1 km = 1000 m and 1 m = 1000 mm and be confident in their knowledge of place value for any whole or decimal number.

- Recall that the prefix 'kilo' means 'one thousand times' and that the prefix 'milli' means 'one thousandth part of'.
- Write: Distance to sports ground = 2479 m or 2·479 km. Elicit the distance to the nearest kilometre (2 km) and to the nearest tenth of a kilometre (2·5 km).
- Recall knowledge of place value to show that: 2·479 km = (1 km × 2) + ($\frac{1}{10}$ or 0·1 km × 4) + ($\frac{1}{100}$ or 0·01 km × 7) + ($\frac{1}{1000}$ or 0·001 km × 9)
- Write and discuss the relationships: 1000 mm = 1 m; 100 mm = 0·1 m; 10 mm = 0·01 m; 1 mm = 0·001 m
- Ask for suggestions of objects and distances that we might measure in $\frac{1}{10}$, $\frac{1}{100}$ and $\frac{1}{1000}$ of a metre or of a kilometre.
- In question 4, children may use a calculator. Talk about which operation key they need to use for each part.

Things to say and ask

- How many metre sticks placed end to end does it take to make 1 kilometre?... 10 kilometres?
- What is the value, in metres, of the 9 in 2·479 km ... 2·497 km ... 2·947 km?
- A sheet of card is 1 mm thick. What is the thickness of 100 ... 1000 ... 1 000 000 cards?
- How many books 1 cm thick are in a stack of 0·01 m ... 1·0 m ... 10 m?

Strand: Measures **Topic:** Length

Miles and kilometres

Activity Sheet 38

Objectives

- ❏ Know imperial units (mile).
- ❏ Know rough equivalents of miles and km.

Vocabulary

kilometre, metre, mile, estimate, ≈, is approximately equal to

Resources

road maps showing kilometre and mileage scales

OHT of a squared grid and OHT pens

calculator (per child) (optional)

Teaching support

Misconceptions
Some children do not appreciate that a mile is more than a kilometre.

The key idea is that 1 km ≈ $\frac{5}{8}$ mile so 8 km ≈ 5 miles.

Children should know that 1 km = 1000 m.

- Begin by asking children to name countries where distances by road are measured in kilometres, e.g. France, Spain; in miles, e.g. Great Britain, United States; and in both kilometres and miles, e.g. Canada.
- In a tournament the competitors cycled 5 km and then ran 5 km. Is the total distance more or less than 10 miles? How can you check?
- Explain that 1 mile > 1·5 km ≈ 1600 m. Note the use of the ≈ sign to mean 'approximately equal to'. Refer to the conversion scales on a road map. Draw 2 parallel lines. Label the ends 0 m and 1600 m, and 0 miles and 1 mile. Estimate and mark 8 equal divisions on both lines. Establish that a distance of 8 km ≈ 5 miles and derive the relationship 1 km ≈ $\frac{5}{8}$ mile.
- Refer to question 1 and show that if 5 miles ≈ 8 km then 10 miles ≈ 16 km because (10 × 8) ÷ 5 = 16.
- Discuss ways to convert kilometres to miles, e.g. 12 km = (12 × 5) ÷ 8 miles = $7\frac{1}{2}$ miles.

Things to say and ask

- ❏ Write on the board: 40, 80, 120, 160, 200, 400, 800.
- ❏ How many miles are equivalent to 80 km/160 km/800 km?
- ❏ How many kilometres are equivalent to 40 miles/120 miles/400 miles?
- ❏ The 10 000 m race is run at the Olympics. About how many miles is this?

Strands: Measures/Solving problems *Topics:* Length/Making decisions/Words problems involving length

Estimating and measuring length

Pupil Book page 59

Objectives

- Suggest suitable units and measuring equipment to estimate or measure length.
- Measure and draw lines to the nearest millimetre.
- Record estimates and readings from scales to a suitable degree of accuracy.
- Identify and use appropriate operations (including combinations of operations) to solve word problems involving length, using one or more steps. Explain methods and reasoning.
- Choose and use appropriate number operations to solve problems, and appropriate ways of calculating: mental, mental with jottings, written methods, calculator.

Vocabulary

diameter, kilometre, metre, centimetre, millimetre, inch, estimate, approximately

Resources

coins, counters, small circular lids, rulers, base-10 rods
callipers (optional)
calculator (per child)

Teaching support

This page provides practice in measuring the diameter of circular objects to the nearest millimetre. The results are used to solve problems.

- Begin by posing the problem of how to measure the diameter to the nearest millimetre of a circular object, e.g. a coin or medal. Trial suggestions. Elicit the importance of finding objects to enclose the circular object at its widest point and make a right angle with a ruler, as callipers do.
- Provide children with coins, counters, circular lids, rulers and base-10 rods. Use 'trial and improvement' to establish that the best position for the left-hand rod is not 0 cm but 1 cm.
- Encourage children to estimate before measuring and to use previous results to predict for other diameters, e.g. a 1p coin has a diameter of 2 cm. A 2p coin is larger so its diameter will be more than 2 cm.

Misconceptions

Check that children place the leading edge of the left-hand rod at the 1 cm mark, keep the rods perpendicular to the ruler, read the measurement shown by the right-hand rod to the nearest millimetre and then remember to subtract 1 cm from the reading.

Things to say and ask

- Why is it important to ensure that both rods are perpendicular to the ruler?
- The left-hand rod is at 1 cm and the right-hand rod indicates 4·6 cm. What is the diameter? Who can explain why it is 3·6 cm?
- What is 3·6 cm in millimetres … in metres?
- Imagine a straight line of ten 3·6 cm tin lids. How long is it in centimetres … in metres?

Strands: Measures/Calculations **Topics:** Mass/Checking results of calculations

Converting masses

Pupil Book page 60

Objectives

Vocabulary

kilogram, gram, round to the nearest 10, 100

- Use, read and write standard metric units (kg, g), including their abbreviations, and relationships between them.
- Convert smaller to larger units (e.g. g to kg), and vice versa.
- Suggest suitable units and measuring equipment to estimate or measure mass.
- Estimate by approximating (round to nearest 10, 100 or 1000), then check result.
- Identify and use appropriate operations to solve word problems involving mass.

Resources
1 g, 10 g, 100 g, and 1 kg standard masses

Teaching support

Misconceptions

Encourage children to recognise that 5·2 kg is 5200 g, not 5002 g. Note that 5240 g can be written as either 5·24 kg or 5·240 kg and that the zero in 5·240 kg does not affect the value of the mass.

The key idea is that 1 g is one thousandth or 0·001 of 1 kg.

Children should know that 1 kg = 1000 g and be confident in their knowledge of place value for any whole or decimal number.

- Show the standard masses and ask children to say the smaller ones as fractions of a kilogram.
- Write the relationships, highlighting the place value of each standard mass:

  1 kg $\qquad\qquad\qquad\qquad\qquad$ = 1·0 kg
  100 g = 1 tenth of 1 kg $\quad$ = $\frac{1}{10}$ kg $\;$ = 0·1 kg
  10 g = 1 hundredth of 1 kg = $\frac{1}{100}$ kg = 0·01 kg
  1 g = 1 thousandth of 1 kg = $\frac{1}{1000}$ kg = 0·001 kg

- Establish that to convert kilograms to grams you multiply by 1000 and to convert grams to kilograms you divide by 1000.
- Write: 3579 g = 3·579 kg and discuss the masses you would use to show this, e.g. (1 kg × 3) + (0·1 kg × 5) + (0·01 kg × 7) + (0·001 kg × 9). Discuss rules for rounding 3579 g to the nearest 10, 100 and 1000 g.

Things to say and ask

- *The third place to the right of the decimal point represents 1 g, the second place to the right represents 10 g and the first decimal place represents 100 g.*
- *A plastic 1 cm cube has a mass of 1 g. What is the mass of a bag of 50/500/5000 cubes? How would you write that in kilograms?*

Kilograms and pounds

Pupil Book page 61

Objectives

Vocabulary

kilogram, gram, pound (lb), metric/imperial unit, ≈, is approximately equal to

- Know imperial units (lb).
- Know rough equivalents of lb and kg.
- Record estimates and readings from scales to a suitable degree of accuracy.

Resources
kitchen scales displaying imperial and metric units
1 kg bag of sugar or flour
a 454 g jar of jam

Strands: Measures/Solving problems *Topics:* Mass/Problems involving measures

Teaching support

Misconceptions
In the spoken form, one pound (£1) is easily confused with one pound (1 lb).

The key ideas are that 1 kg ≈ 2 lb, that $2\frac{1}{4}$ lb ≈ 1 kg and that 1 lb ≈ 454 g.

- Elicit places children might visit on holiday where imperial units are used, e.g. the United States.
- Use the kitchen scales and bag of sugar/flour to show how the two systems are related, e.g. 1 kg ≈ 2·2 lb. The rhyme, '$2\frac{1}{4}$ lbs of ham is round about 1 kg' may help children recall the relationship.
- Show the jar of jam. Explain that jam was normally sold in 1 lb jars and that this is the closest metric equivalent. Say that 1 lb is not exactly equal to 454 g so we use the sign '≈' meaning 'is approximately equal to' and write the relationship as 1 lb ≈ 454 g.
- Draw this conversion table on the board and invite children to complete the grams:

pounds	1	$\frac{1}{2}$	$\frac{1}{4}$	$\frac{3}{4}$
grams	454	227	113	340

Things to say and ask

- About how many pounds are equivalent to 10 kg?
- Imagine 2 bags of jellybeans both priced at 50p. One weighs 100 g and the other $\frac{1}{4}$ lb. Which is the better buy? Why?
- Look at the conversion table. Round the grams to the nearest 10 g.

Grams and ounces

Activity Sheet 39

Objectives

Vocabulary

kilogram, gram, pound (lb), ounce (oz), metric/imperial unit, ≈, is approximately equal to

- Know imperial units (lb, oz).
- Know rough equivalents of lb and kg, oz and g.
- Suggest suitable units and measuring equipment to estimate or measure mass.
- Record estimates and readings from scales to a suitable degree of accuracy.
- Explain methods and reasoning.

Resources
kitchen scales displaying imperial and metric units (optional)
OHT of a square grid and OHT pen

Strands: Measures/Solving problems *Topics:* Mass/Problems involving measures/Making decisions

Teaching support

Misconceptions
Check that children do not mix metric and imperial measures.

The key idea is that 1 ounce is between 25 g and 30 g.

Children should have some experience of converting metric to imperial units and know that 1 kg ≈ 2 lb, $2\frac{1}{4}$ lb ≈ 1 kg and 1 lb ≈ 454 g.

- Elicit some of the imperial units of mass that were in use in the past.
- Write: 16 ounces (16 oz) = 1 pound (1 lb).
- Draw this conversion table on the board and invite children to complete the ounces.

pounds	1	$\frac{1}{2}$	$\frac{1}{4}$	$\frac{3}{4}$
ounces	16	8	4	12
grams	454	227	113	340

    Establish that 1 oz ≈ 28 g by dividing 454 by 16.

- Show the OHT of the square grid. Label and number the axes as shown on the sheet. Plot the points (0 oz, 0 g), (8 oz, 227 g), (16 oz, 454 g). Join them and extend the straight line as far as it will go. Use the graph to check the equivalent grams for $\frac{1}{4}$ lb or 4 oz (between 100 and 125 g) and $\frac{3}{4}$ lb or 12 oz (between 325 and 350 g).
- Write the sequence: 1, 2, 4, 8, 16, ___, ___ and ask children to continue it. Explain that the imperial system used this sequence of standard balance masses and people could use them to balance any mass in whole pounds and ounces, e.g. 1 oz, 2 oz, 4 oz, 8 oz, 16 oz (1 lb), 32 oz (2 lbs), 64 oz (4 lbs) and so on.

Things to say and ask

- How many ounces are equivalent to $\frac{1}{2}$ lb? To 454 g?
- Look at the graph. What is 200 g to the nearest ounce?...12 ounces to the nearest 25 g?
- Which weighs more, 4 oz or 100 g? How did you work it out?

Solving mass problems

Pupil Book page 62

Objectives

Vocabulary

tonne, kilogram, pound (lb), percentage, ≈, is approximately equal to

- Know imperial units (lb, oz).
- Know rough equivalents of lb and kg, oz and g.
- Identify and use appropriate operations (including combinations of operations) to solve word problems involving mass, using one or more steps, including calculating percentages. Explain methods and reasoning.
- Choose and use appropriate number operations to solve problems, and appropriate ways of calculating: mental, mental with jottings, written methods, calculator.

Resources
calculator (per child)

Strands: Measures/Solving problems **Topics:** Capacity/Problems involving measures

Teaching support

Misconceptions
Check that children use the correct units when recording their answers.

The key idea is that 1 tonne = 1000 kg. Children are asked to interpret tables correctly to solve problems.

- Explain that the metric tonne is equivalent to 1000 kg and should not be confused with the imperial ton (2240 lb). Write 1 t = 1000 kg and elicit suggestions for what might be measured in tonnes, e.g. large mammals, cars, lorries…
- Give children practice in converting tonnes to kilograms and vice versa.
- Recall and discuss this 4-step model for solving word problems:
  - read the question and identify any important information
  - identify the calculation needed
  - find the answer to the calculation
  - find the answer to the problem.
- Before children begin Pupil Book page 62, check that they understand and can explain the terms 'average body mass' and 'average mass of food at a meal'. Ensure children are aware that animals in the wild may not eat every day.
- Encourage children to use their calculators to check answers.

Things to say and ask

- A male killer whale weighs about 9000 kg. About how many killer whales are in a school of 100 tonnes? How did you work it out?
- The female killer whale weighs about 60% of the male's mass. What is her mass in tonnes?

Litres, centilitres and millilitres

Pupil Book page 63

Objectives

Vocabulary

litre, centilitre, millilitre, percentage

- Use, read and write standard metric units (l, ml, cl), including their abbreviations, and relationships between them.
- Convert smaller to larger units (e.g. ml to l), and vice versa.
- Record estimates and readings from scales to a suitable degree of accuracy.
- Identify and use appropriate operations (including combinations of operations) to solve word problems involving capacity, using one or more steps. Explain methods and reasoning.

Resources
a drink bottle labelled 50 cl or 70 cl (optional)

Teaching support

Misconceptions
The most frequent errors are related to place value.

The key ideas are that 1 ml = 0·001 l, that 100 cl = 1 l and that 1 cl = 10 ml.

Children should be able to derive $\frac{1}{10}$ litre and $\frac{1}{100}$ litre in millilitres and be confident in their knowledge of place value for any whole or decimal number.

- Recall the relationships between 10 ml, 100 ml and 1000 ml and write, in fraction and decimal notation:
  1000 ml = 1 l = 1·0 l
  100 ml = $\frac{1}{10}$ l = 0·1 l
  10 ml = $\frac{1}{100}$ l = 0·01 l
  Elicit that 1 ml = $\frac{1}{1000}$ l = 0·001 l
- Introduce the term 'centilitre' and write 100 cl = 1 l. Explain that some drinks are labelled in centilitres. Elicit that 1 cl = $\frac{1}{100}$ of 1 litre and 1 cl = 10 ml.

Strand: Measures **Topic:** Capacity

- Give children practice in converting millilitres to litres, centilitres to litres and to millilitres and vice versa. For example, using the digits 2, 6, 7 and 0, write several 4-digit numbers as millilitres and ask children to convert them to centilitres and litres, e.g. 2760 ml = 276 cl or 2·76 l.

Things to say and ask

- What fraction of a litre is 1 cl/10 ml?
- How many millilitres are equivalent to 10/20/50 centilitres?
- How many centilitres are in 1·5 l/660 ml?
- The supermarket offers a standard 500 ml carton of orange juice with 50% extra free. You buy 2 cartons. How many litres is that?

Litres, pints and gallons (1)

Pupil Book page 64

Objectives

- Know imperial units (pint, gallon).
- Know rough equivalents of litres and pints or gallons.
- Record estimates and readings from scales to a suitable degree of accuracy.

Vocabulary

pint, gallon, litre, imperial, metric, conversion graph

Resources

2-litre and 4-pint milk containers
OHT of pints-to-litres conversion graph from Pupil Book page 64

Teaching support

The key ideas are that 1 litre is approximately $1\frac{3}{4}$ pints and 8 pints equal 1 gallon.

Children should recognise that pints and gallons are imperial units of capacity.

Misconceptions
Check that the children interpret the litres-to-pints conversion graph correctly.

- Discuss why most containers for soft drinks (cans, bottles and cartons) are sold in multiples of 250 ml or 330 ml.
- Display and compare the 2-litre and 4-pint milk containers. Elicit that they hold approximately the same amount of milk. Show that the label on the 4-pint container reads '2·272 litres/4 pints'. Establish that 4 pints ≈ 2·3 litres to the nearest $\frac{1}{10}$ of a litre and that 4 pints > 2 litres. Check that children understand the need for the approximation sign. Write 1 litre ≈ $1\frac{3}{4}$ pints.
- Show the OHT of the pints-to-litres conversion graph. Use the graph to find the equivalents of 0·6 litres (≈ 1 pint) and 8 pints (≈ 4·5 litres). Explain that 8 pints = 1 gallon or about 4·5 litres. Some children may need further practice in converting from imperial to metric units. Encourage children to give answers to the nearest $\frac{1}{10}$ litre or $\frac{1}{2}$ pint.

Things to say and ask

- *If the 2-litre and 4-pint cartons of milk both cost 99p, which is the better buy? Why?*
- *Approximately how many litres, to the nearest $\frac{1}{10}$ of a litre, are equivalent to 2 pints?*
- *About how many pints, to the nearest $\frac{1}{2}$ pint, are there in 3 litres?*
- *What fraction of a gallon is 3/4 pints? What is that as a percentage?*
- *How many pints are equal to 50% of 4/8/10 gallons?*

Strands: Measures/Solving problems *Topics:* Capacity/Problems involving measures

Litres, pints and gallons (2)

Activity Sheet 40

Objectives

Vocabulary

pint, gallon, litre

- Know imperial units (pint, gallon).
- Know rough equivalents of litres and pints or gallons.
- Suggest suitable units and measuring equipment to estimate or measure capacity.
- Record estimates and readings from scales to a suitable degree of accuracy.

Resources
OHT of litres-to-gallons conversion scale from Activity Sheet 40
coloured pencils (per child)

Teaching support

Misconceptions
Check that children read the divisions on the scale correctly.

This sheet provides further practice in finding rough equivalents of litres, pints and gallons.

Children should have completed Pupil Book page 64 and should be able to recognise square numbers.

- Begin by recalling the relationships between pints and gallons and between litres and pints or gallons.
- Show the OHT of the litres-to-gallons conversion scale and elicit that we can often find this scale on display at the pumps at petrol stations. Use the scale to give children practice in converting litres to gallons and vice versa.
- Encourage children to use the key conversion factors to help them estimate answers.

Things to say and ask

- *I filled my tank with petrol. I put in more than 8 gallons and less than 40 litres. How many litres might I have bought?*
- *A litre of water has a mass of 1 kilogram. What is the mass of water in a full 5-gallon drum?*
- *Which is more, 32 pints or 20 litres? What is the difference in litres?*

Solving capacity problems

Pupil Book page 65

Objectives

Vocabulary

pint, gallon, litre, percentage

- Know imperial units (pint, gallon).
- Know rough equivalents of litres and pints or gallons.
- Record estimates and readings from scales to a suitable degree of accuracy.
- Identify and use appropriate operations (including combinations of operations) to solve word problems involving capacity, using one or more steps, including calculating percentages. Explain methods and reasoning.

Resources
OHT of litres-to-gallons conversion scale from Activity Sheet 40 (optional)
OHT of pints-to-litres conversion scale from Pupil Book page 65 (optional)

Strands: Measures/Solving problems *Topics:* Area and perimeter/Reasoning and generalising about numbers or shapes

Teaching support

This page provides practice in using and applying knowledge of rough equivalents of litres, pints and gallons to solve word problems.

- Begin by recalling the relationships between pints and gallons and between litres and pints or gallons. You could use the OHT of the litres-to-gallons conversion scale or the OHT of the litres-to-pints conversion scale.
- Remind children of the key steps in solving word problems:
  - read the problem to identify the important information
  - identify the calculation needed
  - find the answer to the calculation
  - find the answer to the problem.
- Encourage children to make rough estimates of the answer and, where necessary, to make jottings or diagrams to help them see the route to the solution. Discuss ways in which they might check their answers.

Misconceptions
Check that children work out the divisions on the scales correctly.

Things to say and ask

- *What clues do you look for in the wording of the question?*
- *Did anyone work out the answer in a different way?*

Perimeter puzzles

Activity Sheet 41

Objectives

- Calculate the perimeter of simple compound shapes that can be split into rectangles.
- Solve mathematical problems or puzzles, recognise and explain patterns and relationships, generalise and predict. Suggest extensions asking 'What if…?'.

Vocabulary

perimeter, distance, edge, concave

Resources
16 small, identical Geostrips and fasteners
1 cm square dotty paper (per child)
scissors and ruler (per child)

Teaching support

The key idea is that you total the lengths of all the sides to find the perimeter of a compound shape.

Children should know that the perimeter is the distance around an enclosed shape.

- Join the 16 Geostrips to form a 3 × 5 rectangle. Discuss ways of calculating the perimeter of the rectangle. Highlight any quick ways, e.g. perimeter equals twice length plus twice breadth, and perimeter equals 2 times length plus breadth. Using the distributive property of multiplication, show that (5 × 2) + (3 × 2) = 2 × (5 + 3) leads to the rule $P = 2(l + b)$
- Push in one corner of the rectangle to make it concave. Establish that the length of the perimeter is unchanged.
- Re-form the Geostrips as a 4 × 4 square. Ask children to explain why the rule for the perimeter of a square is $P = 4l$.
- Push in one corner of the square. Sketch the L-shape on the board and show 3 squares with sides of 2 units with dotted lines. Elicit that the area of the L-shape is reduced but the perimeter is unchanged at 16 units.

Misconceptions
Perimeter is a linear measure, has one dimension and is recorded in units of length. Area is a square measure, has two dimensions and is recorded in square units of length.

Things to say and ask

- *Why is the perimeter of this shape still 16 units?*
- *Imagine a rectangle with a perimeter of 20 units. What might its dimensions be?*

Strands: Measures/Solving problems **Topics:** Area and perimeter/Reasoning and generalising about numbers or shapes

Investigating perimeters

Pupil Book page 66

Objectives

- Calculate the perimeter of simple compound shapes that can be split into rectangles.
- Develop from explaining a generalised relationship in words to expressing it in a formula using letters as symbols (e.g. the cost of *n* articles at 15p each).

Vocabulary

perimeter, distance, edge, isosceles, formula

Resources
OHT of a square grid and OHT pens
interlocking square tiles, equilateral triangle tiles, hexagonal tiles
ruler (optional)

Teaching support

The key idea is that you total the lengths of all the sides to find the perimeter of a compound shape.

Misconceptions
Perimeter is a linear measure, has one dimension and is recorded in units of length. Area is a square measure, has two dimensions and is recorded in square units of length.

Children should know that the perimeter is the distance along the edge of an enclosed shape.

- Use interlocking square tiles to make a 4 × 2 rectangle and a 3 × 5 rectangle. Elicit the perimeters as 12 units and 16 units respectively. Ask volunteers to join the rectangles to make different compound shapes.
- Draw the compound shapes on the OHT, marking the join with a dotted line. Ask children to explain why the perimeter of the compound shape is always less than the total of the individual rectangles, e.g. less than 28 units (12 + 16).
- Show that the regular polygons have uniform sides of, e.g. 5 cm. Discuss quick ways to calculate their perimeters, e.g. 5 cm × 3, 5 cm × 4 and 5 cm × 6.
- Challenge children to work out the perimeter of a joined strip of 1, 2, 3 and 4 equilateral triangles (3/4/5/6 × 5 cm = 15/20/25/30 cm). Ask them to explain the general relationship in words, e.g. constant difference of 5, and elicit the rule for the perimeter of the *n*th shape as $P = 5(n + 2)$

Things to say and ask

- *Form a compound shape by pushing together two rectangles. How would you go about calculating the perimeter of the compound shape?*
- *What if you join the rectangles in a different way? Will the perimeter be the same?*

Finding areas (1)

Pupil Book page 67

Objective

- Calculate the area of simple compound shapes that can be split into rectangles.

Vocabulary

area, square centimetres (cm²), formula

Resources
OHT of a square grid and OHT pens

Strands: Measures/Calculations *Topics:* Area and perimeter/Using a calculator

Teaching support

Misconceptions
Check that children measure areas in square units and read such measurements correctly, e.g. 54 m² as '54 square metres', not '54 metres squared'.

The key idea is that by splitting a compound shape into rectangles you can find its area.

Children should know that area is the amount of surface enclosed within a 2-D shape and that it is measured in square units.

- Recall the generalised rule (formula) for calculating the area of a rectangle as 'length times breadth'. Write: $A = l \times b$.
- Draw a rectangle 18 cm × 7 cm on the OHT. Ask children to calculate its area. Compare methods. Focus on applying the distributive property of multiplication for ease of mental calculation, e.g. (10 cm × 7 cm) + (8 cm × 7 cm) = 70 cm² + 56 cm² = 126 cm².
- On the OHT, outline 2 rectangles, 2 cm × 4 cm and 3 cm × 5 cm. Invite children to draw different compound shapes formed by the 2 rectangles and to show the steps in finding out their areas.
- Outline an L-shape on the OHT. Show that there are 2 ways to split the shape into rectangles and that the sum of the rectangular areas is the same for both ways.

Things to say and ask

- *Imagine two different rectangles. Push them together to form a compound shape. How might you find the area of the compound shape?*
- *Why is it a good idea to split the shape into rectangles to find its area?*
- *What happens to the area if you join the rectangles in a different way? Why is the area unchanged?*

Finding areas (2)

Pupil Book page 68

Objectives

Vocabulary

area, covers, surface, square centimetres (cm²), formula

- Calculate the area of simple compound shapes that can be split into rectangles.
- Develop calculator skills and use a calculator effectively.

Resources
OHT transparency and pens
OHT of a squared grid
calculator (per child)

Teaching support

Misconceptions
Check that children measure areas in square units and read such measurements correctly, e.g. 54 m² as '54 square metres', not '54 metres squared'.

The key idea is that by splitting a compound shape into rectangles you can find its area.

Children should know that area is the amount of surface enclosed within a 2-D shape and that it is measured in square units.

- Recall the generalised rule (formula) for calculating the area of a rectangle as 'length times breadth'. Write: $A = l \times b$.
- Discuss how to find the missing measurement when you know the area of a rectangle and the length of one side. Elicit ways to use the calculator to check answers.
- Outline an L-shape on the OHT square grid. Show that there are 2 ways to split the shape into rectangles and that the sum of the rectangular areas is the same for both ways. Show a third method that involves enclosing the shape in a larger rectangle, finding that area and then subtracting the area of the 'missing' part.
- Draw a square on the OHT transparency. Write: Area = 40 cm². Ask children to use a 'trial and improvement' strategy with their calculator to find the length of each side to 1 decimal place (6·3 cm).

Strands: Measures/Solving problems **Topics:** Time/Problems involving measures

Things to say and ask

- Why is it a good idea to split the shape into rectangles to find its area?
- How would you go about calculating the dimensions of the rectangles? Of the compound shape? Of the missing length?
- What happens to the area if you join the rectangles in a different way? Why is the area unchanged?

Times around the world

Activity Sheet 42 Pupil Book page 69

Objectives

- Read the time on a 24-hour digital clock and use 24-hour notation, such as 19:53.
- Appreciate different times around the world.
- Identify and use appropriate operations (including combinations of operations) to solve word problems involving numbers and quantities based on measures (including time), using one or more steps. Explain methods and reasoning.

Vocabulary

Greenwich Mean Time (GMT), Prime Meridian, British Summer Time, time zone, 24-hour clock

Resources
globe
OHT of Activity Sheet 42 and OHT pen
copy of Activity Sheet 42 (per child)
scissors and glue (optional)

Teaching support

The key idea is that all places in the same time zone have the same clock time.

Children should be familiar with using 24-hour notation.

- Use the globe to show that when the sun is directly overhead in Britain it is dark over the Pacific. Explain that the Earth is divided into 24 time zones, one for each hour of the day and that clocks in the places in a time zone are set to the same time.
- Show the OHT of world time zones. Explain that the Prime Meridian is an imaginary line of longitude that runs from the North Pole to the South Pole and, passing through Greenwich, London, gives us the standard time, Greenwich Mean Time (GMT). Talk about variations from this time in Britain for British Summer Time.
- On the OHT circle the 'L' for London. Discuss the scales at the top and bottom of the map. Establish that if it is noon or 12:00 in London then it is morning in the Americas, evening in a large part of Asia and night in Australia. Show children how to work out the time in Tokyo (12:00 + 9 h = 21:00) and New York (12:00 − 5 h = 07:00).
- You may wish to show children how to glue the ends of the sheet together to make a cylinder. If so, check that children can locate the key cities on the flat map before you introduce the cylindrical version.
- Practise finding the local time in cities when it is noon in London or when local time in, e.g. Athens, is 16:00. Avoid choosing times or cities that will involve a date change.
- Some children will notice that not all countries adhere to the time(s) for their zone(s). For example, the same time is used throughout China, although the country spans several zones.

Misconceptions

Check that children interpret the scales correctly. Turning the cylinder clockwise or anticlockwise may help them to work out the relative times in other time zones.

Strand: Measures **Topic:** Time

Things to say and ask

- It is 12:00 GMT in London. Name a city where the time is 5 hours later/earlier… where the local time is 04:00/20:00…
- What is a good time for someone living in Britain to phone a relative in Sydney?
- Your cousin phones from Vancouver. Your watch shows 6:30 pm. What time is it in Vancouver?

Solving time problems

Pupil Book page 70

Objectives

- Use units of time.
- Read the time on a 24-hour digital clock and use 24-hour notation, such as 19:53.

Vocabulary

24-hour clock, units of time from seconds to millennium

Resources

analogue teaching clock
circle of card cut into sectors of 180°, 90° 60°, 30°
Blu-tack

Teaching support

The key idea is for children to use the 24-hour clock to calculate duration of time.

Children should be confident with these units of time: minute, hour, day.

Misconceptions
Check that children add 12 hours to pm times to write 24-hour clock times.

- Quickly revise units of time, from seconds to millennium.
- Discuss situations where you need to know how long an event will last or how long something will take to complete. Encourage a wide range of ideas and suggestions.
- Show the analogue clock face. Name the hours as 1 am, 2 am…12 noon. Elicit that most children are asleep from midnight to 7 am. Attach the sectors for 180° and 30° to the clock face from 12 to 7. *The card represents how much of today you have spent sleeping.* Write 'sleep' on the card. Attach the 90° card to cover the sector from 9 am to noon and label it 'school'. Elicit that we spend about 3 hours of the morning in school.
- Remove the cards from the clock face. Take suggestions for things children might do on a Saturday from noon to midnight. Use the 30°, 60° and 90° cards to represent the durations, e.g. attach the 60° card from 1:30 to 3:30 to show the time spent at the swimming pool, …

Things to say and ask

- *Roughly how long does it take to go to town from your home…to fly to Spain…to play a computer game?*
- *Estimate how much time you would need to pack a bag for your holidays…to bake a cake…to do your homework…to boil an egg.*
- *Why is it important to have a rough idea of how long something will last or take to complete?*

Strand: Shape and space **Topic:** Properties of 3-D and 2-D shapes

Polyhedra

Pupil Book page 71

Objective

- Describe and visualise properties of solid shapes such as parallel or perpendicular faces or edges.

Vocabulary

polyhedron, octahedron, dodecahedron, parallel, perpendicular, congruent

Resources

large cuboid and hexagonal prism

regular polyhedra made with interlocking tiles: cube, tetrahedron, octahedron, dodecahedron

reference material (optional)

Teaching support

The key idea is that children can identify pairs of parallel and perpendicular faces and edges in polyhedra and some of the properties of regular polyhedra.

- Show a large cuboid and elicit properties such as the number of faces, vertices and edges, and whether or not any face is right angled.
- Establish that a table has a horizontal surface with legs perpendicular to the surface. Place the cuboid on the table. Ask the children to identify faces and edges that are parallel/perpendicular to the tabletop.
- Label the vertices of one face A, B, C and D. Begin at the vertex A and follow the edge with a finger to B. *This is the edge AB.* Repeat for the edge DC. Explain that both edges run in the same direction and are parallel.
- Ask children to find and name pairs of edges that meet at right-angled vertices. *The edge DA is perpendicular to DC.*
- Stand the hexagonal prism on its base on the table. *How many faces/edges are horizontal?* (2/12) *How many are vertical?* (6/6) Turn the prism so that a rectangular face is on the table. *What can you say about the number of horizontal/vertical faces/edges now?*
- Display the 4 shapes made with interlocking tiles. *What is the same about the faces of these polyhedra?* (regular, congruent) Elicit the names of the tetrahedron, cube and octahedron and introduce the dodecahedron. *What is the same about the vertices of these regular polyhedra?* (same number of edges meet at each vertex)
- Children will need to look closely at these 4 regular polyhedra for the investigation in question 3. They may need additional reference material (books, CD-ROMs, the Internet) to find the fifth polyhedron (icosahedron). They could then attempt to make this shape using 20 interlocking triangular tiles.

Misconceptions

Some children may need help in identifying a pair of perpendicular edges when the face is not perpendicular to a horizontal surface.

Things to say and ask

- *How can you describe this shape?*
- *What can you say about a pair of horizontal/vertical edges?* (always parallel) *About a pair of edges that are at right angles to each other?* (always perpendicular)

Strand: Shape and space **Topic:** Properties of 3-D and 2-D shapes

Parallelogram and rhombus

Pupil Book page 72

Objectives
- Classify quadrilaterals, using criteria such as parallel sides, equal angles, equal sides.
- Make shapes with increasing accuracy.

Vocabulary
rhombus, parallelogram, parallel, quadrilateral, perpendicular, regular, irregular, polygon, acute, obtuse, opposite, adjacent, line of symmetry

Resources
Geostrips and fasteners

Blu-tack

1 cm square dotty paper and ruler (per child)

Teaching support

The key idea is that children know and can compare the properties of a rhombus and a parallelogram with those of a square and a rectangle.

- Make a rectangle and a square from Geostrips. Ask children to compare the 2 shapes, saying how they are similar/different. (Same: 4 right angles, opposite sides parallel, 2 pairs of perpendicular sides. Different: square: regular, all sides equal; rectangle: irregular, opposite sides equal.)
- Make another congruent rectangle. Demonstrate the shear movement to transform it into a parallelogram. Attach the rectangle and the parallelogram to the board. Discuss and compare the opposite sides (equal, parallel) and angles. Elicit that in a parallelogram one pair of opposite angles is acute and one pair is obtuse.
- Make another congruent square. Repeat the shear movement to transform the square into a rhombus. Blu-tack the square and rhombus shapes to the board and compare them. Elicit that a rhombus is a parallelogram with 4 equal sides.

Misconceptions
The most common errors are confusing diagonals with lines of symmetry and thinking that the diagonals of a rectangle and parallelogram are lines of symmetry.

Things to say and ask
- *In what ways are these two shapes similar/different?*
- *Imagine a shape. Its adjacent sides are unequal and its opposite sides are parallel. What shape do you see?*
- *Imagine a rhombus made with Geostrips. Push the opposite acute angles towards each other until the sides are perpendicular. Name your shape.* (square) *Continue to push these angles closer together. What shape do you have now?* (rhombus) *What will happen if you continue in this way?*

Kite and trapezium

Activity Sheet 43

Objectives
- Classify quadrilaterals, using criteria such as parallel sides, equal angles, equal sides.
- Make shapes with increasing accuracy.

Vocabulary
parallelogram, arrowhead, kite, trapezium, quadrilateral, parallel, perpendicular, opposite, adjacent, concave, convex, isosceles, reflex

Resources
a pin board and rubber bands

A4 white and coloured paper (per child)

Strand: Shape and space **Topic:** Properties of 3-D and 2-D shapes

Teaching support

The key idea is that children know and can compare the properties of a trapezium and a kite with those of other quadrilaterals.

Children should have completed Pupil Book page 72.

- Use the pin board to show a rectangle. Pull the band down from a vertex to form a trapezium (Fig. 1). Elicit the properties 'one pair of opposite sides parallel' and '2 right angles' then give the name 'trapezium'.
- Make a parallelogram on the pin board. Stretch the band from a vertex to form an isosceles trapezium (Fig. 2). Elicit the properties 'one pair of opposite sides parallel' and 'one pair of equal sides' then give the name 'isosceles trapezium'.
- Use the pinboard to make a quadrilateral with 1 pair of parallel sides and no other special properties (Fig. 3). Establish that this shape is also a trapezium.
- Display a square on the pin board. Ask children to predict the shape when you stretch the band in the direction of an extended diagonal at a vertex (Fig. 4). Elicit that the shape has no parallel sides but adjacent sides are equal. Give the name 'kite'. Re-form the square on the pin board and pull the band diagonally towards the centre, transforming the convex kite to a concave arrowhead (Fig. 5).

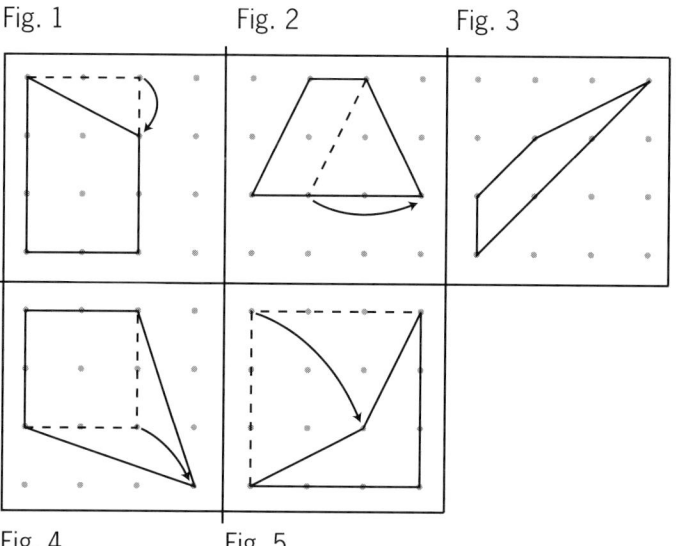

Fig. 1 Fig. 2 Fig. 3

Fig. 4 Fig. 5

Things to say and ask

- *In what way is this trapezium similar to a rectangle/parallelogram?*
- *Can you make a kite with no right angles on the pin board?*
- *Which of the five shapes we made together have line symmetry? How can we check?*
- *What is the difference between an arrowhead and a kite?* (The former is concave, with a reflex angle. The latter is convex.)

Strands: Shape and space/Solving problems *Topics:* Properties of 3-D and 2-D shapes/Reasoning and generalising about shapes

Polygon puzzles

Pupil Book page 73

Objectives

- Classify quadrilaterals, using criteria such as parallel sides, equal angles, equal sides.
- Make shapes with increasing accuracy.
- Solve mathematical problems or puzzles, recognise and explain patterns and relationships, generalise and predict. Suggest extensions asking 'What if…?'.

Vocabulary

rhombus, parallelogram, kite, trapezium, quadrilateral, parallel, perpendicular, opposite, adjacent, isosceles, regular, irregular, polygon, reasoning

Resources
4 isosceles right-angled triangles, a square and a rectangle with side(s) of the same length, e.g. Mathematical Activity Tiles (per pair)
2 sheets of A4 paper and 1 sheet of 1 cm squared paper (per child)
scissors, ruler and pen (per child)

Teaching support

The key idea is that the matching edges of shapes made by dissecting a square can be joined to form quadrilaterals and other polygons.

Children should know some of the properties of a parallelogram, a rhombus, a trapezium and a kite.

- Begin with 2 isosceles right-angled triangles. Ask each pair to make these shapes: large isosceles triangle, square, parallelogram.
- Now include the square as well. Using the square and the 2 triangles ask each pair to investigate ways to form a rectangle, a parallelogram and an isosceles trapezium. Repeat, substituting the rectangle for the square.
- Ask children to find how many different shapes they can make using 4 triangles and to explain their reasoning.

Misconceptions
Check that children join matching edges.

Things to say and ask

- *Use a triangle and a square to make a trapezium.*
- *Using your four triangles, can you make an isosceles triangle…a square… a parallelogram…an isosceles trapezium?*
- *Join three triangles and a square to make a pentagon.*

Circle patterns

Activity Sheet 44

Objectives

- Make shapes with increasing accuracy.
- Solve mathematical problems or puzzles, recognise and explain patterns and relationships, generalise and predict. Suggest extensions asking 'What if…?'.
- Develop from explaining a generalised relationship in words to expressing it in a formula using letters as symbols (e.g. the cost of n articles at 15p each).

Vocabulary

circle, circumference, construct, predict, formula

Resources
ruler (per child)

Strands: Shape and space/Solving problems *Topics:* Properties of 3-D and 2-D shapes/Reasoning and generalising about shapes

Teaching support

Misconceptions
Check that children understand that the letter *n* represents any numbered point on the circumference.

The key idea is for children to investigate simple relationships expressed using letters.

Children should have some experience in explaining a generalised relationship in words and then expressing it in a formula using letters as symbols.

- Draw a diagram for the long jump, marking a scale of 1–10 along the sandpit board (Fig. 1). Build up the results table (Fig. 2). Explain that these are the distances jumped by 5 competitors in Round 1. Write the scores for Round 2 and elicit that each athlete's jump improved by 2 units. Repeat for Round 3.
- Explain that we can express this relationship using letters as symbols. Substitute *n*, *n* + 2 and *n* + 4 for Rounds 1, 2 and 3. Ensure that children understand that *n* is the distance jumped by each athlete in Round 1. *Let's check that the rule/formula works.*
- Using the data for *n* → *n* + 4, show how you can create a line pattern within a circle. Introduce/revise the meaning of 'circumference'.

Fig. 1

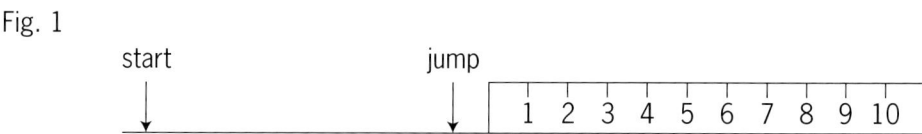

Fig. 2

	Competitor				
	A	B	C	D	E
Round 1 (*n*)	1	2	3	4	5
Round 2 (*n* + 2)	3	4	5	6	7
Round 3 (*n* + 4)	5	6	7	8	9

Things to say and ask

- Why is it important to check that the rule works?
- You want to join *n* to *n* + 4. If *n* equals 3, what number do you join 3, 6… to?

Diagonals in quadrilaterals

Activity Sheet 45

Objectives

Vocabulary

rhombus, parallelogram, kite, trapezium, square, rectangle, quadrilateral, diagonals, opposite, adjacent, intersecting, bisect, line of symmetry

- Explain methods and reasoning, orally and in writing.
- Solve mathematical problems or puzzles, recognise and explain patterns and relationships, generalise and predict. Suggest extensions asking 'What if…?'.
- Make and investigate a general statement about familiar shapes by finding examples that satisfy it.

Resources
Geostrips and fasteners
string, scissors and Blu-tack
set square
ruler and red pencil (per child)

Strands: Shape and space/Solving problems *Topics:* Properties of 3-D and 2-D shapes/Reasoning and generalising about shapes

Teaching support

The key ideas are that the diagonals of some quadrilaterals bisect each other and for some quadrilaterals the diagonals intersect at right angles.

Children should know some of the properties of a parallelogram, a rhombus, a trapezium and a kite.

- Make a rectangle with Geostrips. Demonstrate measuring and cutting lengths of string to represent the diagonals of the rectangle. Show that the cut strings are the same length and attach them to the rectangle with Blu-tack. Explain that the diagonals cut across each other and introduce the term 'bisect'.
- Repeat the above steps for a square.
- Compare the angle sizes of the rectangle and square at the point of intersection. Use the set square to confirm that the diagonals of the square intersect at right angles.
- Before you transform the rectangle into a parallelogram, ask children to predict what will happen to the strings. Demonstrate and elicit that the diagonals of the parallelogram are different lengths.
- Elicit predictions before you transform the square into a rhombus. Test whether the diagonals intersect at right angles.

Things to say and ask

- *What can you say about the diagonals of a rectangle? Will this be true for any rectangle?*
- *What do you think will happen to the diagonals when I turn the Geostrip square into a rhombus?*
- *Imagine a kite shape. What can you say about its diagonals? What about a trapezium?*

Finding and using patterns

Activity Sheet 46

Objectives

- Recognise and extend number sequences.
- Explain methods and reasoning, orally and in writing.
- Solve mathematical problems or puzzles, recognise and explain patterns and relationships, generalise and predict. Suggest extensions asking 'What if…?'.

Vocabulary

predict, reasoning

Resources

9 carpet tiles or hoops
coloured pencils (per child)

Strands: Shape and space/Solving problems **Topics:** Properties of 3-D and 2-D shapes/Reasoning and generalising about shapes

Teaching support

This sheet is about looking for patterns in shapes and numbers and using the patterns to solve a problem.

- Write the following sequences on the board. Ask children to discover the pattern and to give the next 2 terms in each sequence. Encourage explanations and reasoning that refers to the difference between terms.

  1, 2, 4, 7, 11 ___, ___   (16, 22)
  4, 7, 10 13, ___, ___   (16, 19)
  7, 21, 14, 28, 21, ___, ___ (35, 28)

- Clear a space on the floor. Place 6 of the carpet tiles in a 3 × 2 rectangle (Fig. 1). Indicate the 'start' and 'finish' corner carpet tiles. Ask a child to stand on the 'start' tile and to walk to the 'finish' tile. Explain that they can only go forwards, to the left or to the right and not backwards or diagonally. Invite ideas for other routes. Test and record them.

- Lay all the carpet tiles to form a 3 × 3 square (Fig. 2). Invite children to trial different ways from 'start' to 'finish'. Continue until you have found and recorded all 6 ways.

Fig. 1

S		
		F

Fig. 2

S		
		F

Things to say and ask

- *Is there another way to walk from 'start' to 'finish'?*
- *How can we be sure we have found all the ways?*
- *What patterns do you notice in our results for 6 carpet tiles? For 9 tiles?*

Nets of a closed cube

Pupil Book page 74

Objectives

- Visualise 3-D shapes from 2-D drawings and identify different nets for a closed cube.
- Make and investigate a general statement about familiar shapes by finding examples that satisfy it.

Vocabulary

net, closed, base, regular, vertex, cube

Resources
a cube made with interlocking square tiles: base – blue; lid – red; 4 sides – green
interlocking square tiles (per child)
large dice
2 cm squared paper, scissors and glue (per child)

Strands: Shape and space/Solving problems *Topics:* Properties of 3-D and 2-D shapes/Reasoning and generalising about shapes

Teaching support

The key idea is that there are 11 hexominoes (out of a set of 35) which form nets of closed cubes.

Children should know that a cube has 6 faces, 8 vertices and 12 edges.

- Hold up the cube. *This cube has a red lid and a blue base. Its sides are green.* Ask children to visualise opening the cube until they see a flat net. Elicit a range of descriptions of nets and encourage clear explanations.
- Distribute the interlocking tiles. Ask children to make a closed cube and then to choose a vertex and open up the cube to make the net. Compare nets made by children. Check for duplications by placing nets on top of one another to eliminate reflections and rotations. Explain that hexominoes are patterns made by joining 6 squares.
- Ask children to test the generalisation, 'All nets of cubes are hexominoes', by making closed cubes and checking whether they open out to form hexominoes.
- Hold up the initial cube and a dice. *Suppose the blue square has 6 dots. How many dots has the red square?* Elicit that in a dice opposite faces add to 7. Invite suggestions for the green faces. Open the cube to form a T-shape net. Discuss the relationship between the red and blue squares. Repeat several times for other nets.

Things to say and ask

- ❑ All nets of cubes are hexominoes. Are all hexominoes nets of cubes?
- ❑ Who can explain why we only need 7 tabs on the net of a cube? How many edges has a cube? (12) How many are joined in the net? (5)

Solving cube problems

Pupil Book page 75

Objectives

- ❑ Visualise 3-D shapes from 2-D drawings.
- ❑ Solve mathematical problems or puzzles, recognise and explain patterns and relationships, generalise and predict. Suggest extensions asking 'What if…?'.

Vocabulary

cube, cuboid, length, breadth, height, pattern, base, face

Resources
large cuboid
interlocking cubes
about 60 interlocking cubes in 2 colours (per child)

Strand: Shape and space **Topic:** Reflective symmetry, reflection and translation

Teaching support

Misconceptions

If children have difficulty with question 3, ask them to build models of each skeletal cube, making the base and top layers in a different colour from the edges.

This page is about developing children's thinking processes of abstraction, generalisation, prediction and deduction, and applying these processes to solve problems. The activities will help children to see the connection between the answer and the question asked.

- Use the large cuboid to revise that a 3-D shape has the three dimensions of length, breadth/width and height.
- Make and display 3 models of 2-layer shapes with cubes of 1 colour (Fig. 1). *How many cubes do you need to add to this shape to make it into a cuboid? How many cubes will be in its length…width…height?* Ask a child to build the cuboid. Discuss ways to predict and check the answer. *For a 3 × 2 × 2 cuboid there are 6 cubes on the base and 2 layers, making 12 cubes in total. We began with 5 cubes and need 7 more.*
- Make and display the U-shaped model (Fig 2). *Imagine you are a bricklayer. This shape is part of a window frame. What is the smallest number of cubes you will need to cover the two end faces and complete the frame?* Ask a child to complete the loop with cubes of a different colour.
- For questions 1 and 2, review the completed shapes. Discuss how the use of coloured cubes links the answer to the question.

Fig. 1 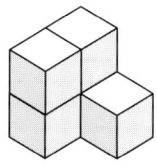 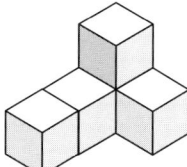 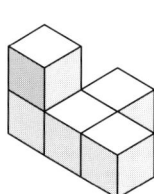   Fig. 2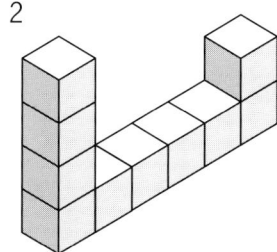

Things to say and ask

- *Why do shelf stackers in supermarkets create large cuboid shapes of cartons and boxes?*
- *Imagine a box. It is three cubes long, three cubes wide and three cubes high. How many cubes make up the box? What shape is the box? How do you know it is a cube?*

Reflective symmetry

Pupil Book page 76

Objectives

Vocabulary

line of symmetry, mirror line, reflection, reflective symmetry, parallel, perpendicular, formula

- Recognise reflective symmetry in regular polygons: for example, know that a square has four lines of symmetry and an equilateral triangle has three.
- Recognise where a shape will be after reflection in a mirror line touching the shape at a point (sides of shape not necessarily parallel or perpendicular to the mirror line).

Resources

OHT of a squared grid and OHT pens

paper squares and equilateral triangles (per child)

1 cm squared paper and ruler (per child)

mirror (per child) (optional)

Strand: Shape and space **Topic:** Reflective symmetry, reflection and translation

Teaching support

The key ideas are that the number of lines of symmetry of any regular polygon is equal to the number of sides and that placing the mirror line across a polygon makes overlapping reflections.

Children should be confident in sketching the reflection of a simple shape in a mirror line parallel to one edge, where the edges of the shape or the lines of the pattern are parallel or perpendicular to the mirror line.

- Ask children to find, by folding the paper shapes, the number of lines of symmetry of an equilateral triangle. Elicit that an equilateral triangle has 3 equal angles, 3 equal sides and 3 lines of symmetry. Encourage children to see that each line of symmetry is perpendicular to the base and bisects the angle opposite the base.
- Repeat for the square. Use the fold lines on the square to establish that 2 lines of symmetry bisect and are perpendicular to the opposite sides and 2 lines of symmetry bisect the opposite angles.
- Outline a 4 × 4 square on the OHT square grid. Draw a mirror line and outline the reflected shape (Fig. 1). Investigate for other 4 × 4 squares, drawing the mirror line in different positions and invite children to complete the overlapping reflection.

Fig. 1

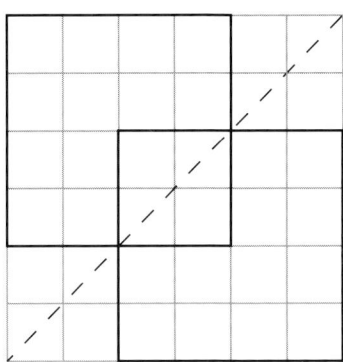

Things to say and ask

- What general rule can we make about the symmetry of regular triangles and squares?
- Will this be true for any regular polygon?
- Can you predict the position of the overlapping reflection with the mirror line in this position?

Symmetry in designs

Activity Sheet 47

Objectives

- Complete symmetrical patterns with two lines of symmetry at right angles (using squared paper or pegboard).
- Recognise where a shape will be after reflection in a mirror line touching the shape at a point (sides of shape not necessarily parallel or perpendicular to the mirror line).

Vocabulary

line of symmetry, mirror line, reflection, reflective symmetry, parallel, perpendicular

Resources

OHT of a square dot grid and OHT pens

drawing pin

ruler and coloured pencils (per child)

Strand: Shape and space **Topic:** Reflective symmetry, reflection and translation

Teaching support

Misconceptions
Some children confuse the 'flip' movement of reflection with the 'slide' movement of translation.

This sheet provides practice in reflecting patterns in mirror lines that are at right angles.

Children should be confident in sketching the reflection of a simple shape in a mirror line parallel to one edge, where the edges of the shape or the lines of the pattern are parallel or perpendicular to the mirror line.

❑ Draw dotted mirror lines to quarter the OHT of the square dot grid. Start at the left-hand side of the grid. Ask a child to toss the drawing pin. If it lands 'point up', mark the upward diagonal dot and draw the diagonal line. If it lands 'point down', mark the downward diagonal dot and draw the diagonal line (Fig. 1). Continue until you reach the right-hand side of the grid or the other mirror line.

❑ Take each 'turning' point in turn; reflect first in the vertical mirror line, then in the horizontal mirror line. Encourage children to check that the point and its reflected position are equidistant from the mirror line. Draw lines to connect the points and complete the reflected pattern.

Fig.1

Things to say and ask

❑ Tell me a way to check that we have the correct reflected position for this point.
❑ This point is 5 dots to the right of the mirror line. How many dots to the left is its reflected position?
❑ What can you say about any point and its reflected position in the mirror line?

Strand: Shape and space **Topic:** Reflective symmetry, reflection and translation

Reflection in 2 mirror lines

Pupil Book page 77

Objective

- Recognise where a shape will be after reflection:
  - in a mirror line touching the shape at a point (sides of shape not necessarily parallel or perpendicular to the mirror line)
  - in two mirror lines at right angles (sides of shape all parallel or perpendicular to the mirror line).

Vocabulary

line of symmetry, mirror line, reflection, *x*-axis, *y*-axis, quadrant, parallel, perpendicular, adjacent, coordinates, origin

Resources

20 interlocking square tiles
OHT of Activity Sheet 50 and OHT pens
1 cm squared paper and ruler (per child)
Copy of Activity Sheet 50 (per child)

Teaching support

The key idea is that you can reflect a shape in 2 mirror lines at right angles.

Children should have completed Pupil Book page 76 and be familiar with using a 4-quadrant coordinate grid.

Misconceptions

Check that children reflect the sloping side(s) of shapes correctly.

- Make 4 P-shape pentominoes with interlocking tiles. Show the OHT of the 4-quadrant coordinate grid. Place one pentomino at random in the 1st quadrant so that the sides are all perpendicular to the *x*- and *y*-axes. Explain that you can reflect the P-shape in the vertical mirror or *y*-axis. Place a pentomino in the reflected position in the 2nd quadrant. Reflect both shapes in the horizontal mirror or *x*-axis.
- Select a vertex and ask children to count the squares from the mirror line. Establish that corresponding vertices are the same distance from the mirror line and that all sides are parallel/perpendicular to the mirror line.
- Place the P-shape in the 1st quadrant so that a vertex touches the *y*-axis and the adjacent sides lie on diagonal lines from the point of contact with the *y*-axis. Invite children to place the reflected shape in the other 3 quadrants.

Things to say and ask

- *What can you say about the relationship between corresponding vertices and the mirror line? What instructions would you give to someone to reflect this shape?*
- *Describe the pentomino when it is reflected into the second quadrant.*
- *In which quadrant is the P-shaped pentomino inverted and back to front?*
- *Why are shapes more difficult to reflect when they have a sloping or diagonal side?*

Translating a shape

Activity Sheet 48

Objective

- Recognise where a shape will be after two translations.

Vocabulary

translation, *x*-axis, *y*-axis, coordinates, parallel, horizontal, vertical, vertex, vertices

Resources

OHT of 1st quadrant grid and OHT pens
ruler and coloured pencils (per child)

Strand: Shape and space **Topic:** Position and direction

Teaching support

Misconceptions
Check that children make the horizontal translation first.

The key idea is that a translation is a transformation where every point moves the same distance in a parallel direction.

- Briefly discuss moves on popular board games, e.g. chess, ludo, Connect. Elicit the knight's move as 2 squares to the left or right and 1 square up or down or 1 square to the left or right and 2 squares up or down.
- On the OHT, circle the point (4, 5). Recall the rule that the x-coordinate comes first then the y-coordinate. Invite children to find 'knight's moves' from this position. Encourage descriptions of the translation, giving the horizontal or x-axis move first.
- Wipe clean the OHT. Draw parallelogram P with vertices at (1, 4), (4, 4), (5, 2), (2, 2). Translate the shape 7 units to the right to make parallelogram Q. Elicit its vertices as (8, 4), (11, 4), (12, 2), (9, 2). Compare corresponding vertices and establish that the x-coordinate is 7 more each time.
- Draw these translations: parallelogram P, 1 unit right, 1 unit down; parallelogram Q, 1 unit left and 1 unit down (Fig. 1). Discuss the relationship between the coordinates and the direction and distance of moves.

Fig. 1

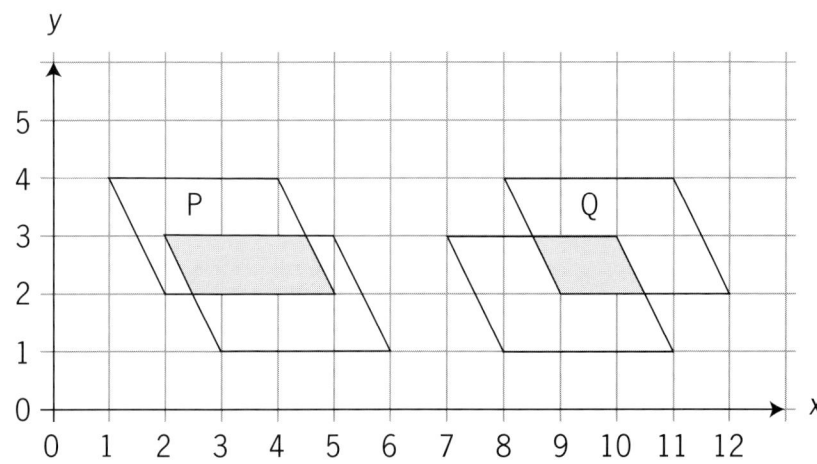

Things to say and ask

- The point (6, 4) is 2 units to the right and 1 unit down.
- Name the shape in the overlap.
- Who can explain why the parallelograms overlap?
- We must slide the shape along the same number of squares and in the same direction each time.

Coordinates in the first and second quadrants

Pupil Book page 78

Objectives

- Read and plot coordinates in 1st and 2nd quadrants.

Vocabulary

origin, coordinates, x-axis, y-axis, quadrant, negative, vertex, vertices, reflection

Resources
OHT of a squared grid and OHT pens

Strand: Shape and space *Topic:* Position and direction

Teaching support

Misconceptions
The most common error is transposing the coordinates of a point.

The key ideas are that we use negative numbers when we extend the x-axis to the left beyond zero and that we can plot points in the 1st and 2nd quadrants.

Children should be able to use negative integers in contexts such as temperature.

- Prepare an OHT of a 2-quadrant grid. Reveal the 1st quadrant. Label the x-axis and y-axis from 0 to 6, emphasising that the numbers are written below the x-axis and to the left of the y-axis. Recall the term 'origin'.
- Discuss the use of negative integers in recording temperature. Point to 6 on the x-axis and as children count back to zero and beyond, reveal the 2nd quadrant. Encourage children to say 'negative 1, negative 2 …' and so on. Introduce the term '2nd quadrant' and label the x-axis from 0 to $^-6$.
- Mark 3 points at random in the 1st quadrant. Elicit and write their coordinates, e.g. (3, 5). Ask children to find the reflection of each point in the 2nd quadrant, e.g. ($^-3$, 5). Emphasise that the points are equidistant from the y-axis and that the value for y is unchanged. Join up the 3 points in each quadrant to show a triangle and its reflection.

Things to say and ask

- *What name do we give to the point where the x- and y-axes intersect?*
- *What are the coordinates of the origin?*
- *In the second quadrant the value of x is always negative.*
- *The phrase 'along the corridor then up the stairs' reminds us that we give the x-axis coordinate first.*
- *Predict the shape we will make by joining the points we have plotted in the second quadrant.*

Coordinates in all 4 quadrants

Pupil Book page 79

Objective

- Read and plot coordinates in all 4 quadrants.

Vocabulary

origin, coordinates, x-axis, y-axis, quadrant, plane

Resources
OHT of Activity Sheet 50 and OHT pens

Strand: Shape and space **Topic:** Position and direction

Teaching support

Misconceptions
The most common error is transposing the coordinates of a point.

The key idea is that extending both the x-axis and y-axis to include negative integers allows us to plot any point in the plane.

Children should be able to read and plot points in the 1st and 2nd quadrants.

- Prepare an OHT of a 4-quadrant grid (Activity Sheet 50). Display the OHT. Draw children's attention to the y-axis extending down from zero into negative integers and to the numbering to the left of the y-axis. Point out that, because it is difficult to fit in a zero for the x-axis and one for the y-axis, an alternative is to wrap a zero around the origin. Explain that the axes have quartered the flat surface or plane of the grid, dividing it into 4 quadrants that are numbered in an anticlockwise direction (Fig. 1).
- Mark at random 12 points, 3 per quadrant, and label them A, B, ... L. Explain that the grid shows the guesses 12 children made at a treasure hunt game at the school fete. Invite children to point to and read the coordinates of each guess.
- Ask children to plot these points: P1 (⁻3, 5), P2 (⁻2, ⁻6), and P3 (4, ⁻4). Explain that prizes are at points P1, P2 and P3. Elicit which guess, A to L, is closest to each point.
- Wipe clean the OHT. Repeat the activity to give children further practice in reading and plotting coordinates in the 4 quadrants if necessary.

Fig. 1

	y	
2nd quadrant		1st quadrant
3rd quadrant		4th quadrant

→ x

Things to say and ask

- ❏ The x- and y-axes extend for ever so the grid can stretch out in all directions.
- ❏ A flat surface is called a plane. The x- and y-axes divide the plane into four quadrants.
- ❏ What can you say about the values for x and y in the third quadrant? In the fourth quadrant?
- ❏ The most valuable prize is buried at the origin. Which child's guess is closest?

Coordinates of shapes

Activity Sheets 49 and 50

Objectives

Vocabulary

origin, coordinates, x-axis, y-axis, quadrant, vertex, vertices, parallel, perpendicular

❏ Read and plot coordinates in all 4 quadrants.
❏ Recognise perpendicular and parallel lines.

Resources
OHT of Activity Sheet 50 and OHT pens
ruler (per child)

Strand: Shape and space *Topic:* Position and direction

Teaching support

This unit is about using and applying knowledge of the properties of quadrilaterals to reading and plotting coordinates of 2-D shapes in all 4 quadrants.

Children should be able to read and plot points in the 1st and 2nd quadrants and have begun to work in all 4 quadrants.

- Display the OHT of Activity Sheet 50. Recall that the y-axis extends down from zero into negative integers and that the axes have divided the plane into 4 quadrants, numbered in an anticlockwise direction.

- Draw a square that has a vertex in each quadrant and that is centred on the origin, with sides parallel to the axes. Elicit and write the coordinates of each vertex. Draw children's attention to the pattern of coordinates.

- Use the square you have drawn to establish that:
  - for any point in the 1st quadrant, both coordinates are positive
  - for any point in the 2nd quadrant, the x-coordinate is negative and the y-coordinate is positive
  - for any point in the 3rd quadrant, both coordinates are negative
  - for any point in the 4th quadrant, the x-coordinate is positive and the y-coordinate is negative.

- Ask children to plot these points on the grid and to join them up in order: A (1, 3); B (4, 4); C (4, 1); D (1, 1). Ask a child to reflect the shape in the y-axis. Discuss and name pairs of parallel and perpendicular sides. *Suppose I want to turn this trapezium into a rectangle. Which vertex must I move?* (A) *What are its new coordinates?* (1, 4)

Things to say and ask

- A square has vertices at (0, 0), (3, 3). Give 3 possible answers for the other 2 vertices.
- You know 3 vertices of a rectangle. What clues do you look for in plotting the fourth vertex? What patterns do you notice in the coordinates for the vertices of a square?
- How might the words 'parallel' and 'perpendicular' help you to check that you have plotted a quadrilateral shape correctly?
- What must you remember when you reflect a shape in the y-axis?

Finding angles

Pupil Book page 80

Objectives

- Understand and use angle measure in degrees.
- Recognise and estimate angles.
- Use a protractor to measure and draw acute and obtuse angles to the nearest degree.

Vocabulary

acute, obtuse, reflex, degree, protractor, define, intersect, intersection

Resources

blank OHT transparency and OHT pens

transparent circular protractor and ruler (per child)

Strand: Shape and space **Topic:** Angle and rotation

Teaching support

Misconceptions
Failing to place the protractor correctly is a common error and children need individual support to build their confidence in measuring with this tool.

The key ideas are that an acute angle is less than 90°, an obtuse angle is greater than 90° and less than 180° and that an angle of 180° is a straight line.

- Recall the definitions for acute and obtuse angles. Introduce the term 'reflex' for all the remaining angles. *How can we 'define' a reflex angle?* (between 180° and 360°)
- Revise the key points in using a protractor to measure an angle:
  - accurately place the 'cross wires' of the centre on the vertex of the angle
  - align the 0°–180° baseline with 1 arm of the angle
  - count from 0° to the other arm.
- Draw 3 acute and 2 obtuse angles on the OHT. Choose an acute angle and elicit estimates of its size. Demonstrate how to use the protractor to measure the angle. Ask some children to measure the remaining angles on the OHT, assisting where necessary.
- Wipe clean the OHT. Draw a blue and a red line intersecting at ≈ 60°. Explain the terms 'intersect' and 'intersection'. Label the missing angles formed at the intersection a, b and c. Elicit that the red line is equal to the sum of 2 right angles or 180° and ask for ways to calculate angle b. (180° − 60°) Repeat for the blue line.
- Discuss the sizes of the acute and obtuse angles.

Things to say and ask

- *Always place the scale with 0° on one of the arms of the angle.*
- *Why should we estimate the size of an angle before we measure it?*
- *How can we use what we know about a straight line to calculate the size of angle b?*
- *What important tips about using a protractor would you give to your friend?*

Calculating angles

Pupil Book page 81

Objectives

Vocabulary

acute, obtuse, degree, protractor, scalene triangle, equilateral triangle, trapezium

- Use a protractor to measure and draw acute and obtuse angles to the nearest degree.
- Check that the sum of the angles of a triangle is 180°; for example, by measuring or paper folding.
- Calculate angles in a triangle or around a point.

Resources
4 squares, 3 equilateral triangles and Blu-tack
scrap paper, ruler and scissors (per child)
protractor (per child)

Strand: Shape and space **Topic:** Angle and rotation

Teaching support

Misconceptions

A common error is reading the wrong scale on a protractor. Check that children count on from 0°.

The key ideas are that the sum of the angles of any triangle is 180° and that the sum of the angles around a point is 360°.

Children should be able to measure acute and obtuse angles with a protractor and classify triangles.

- Rule a straight line on the board and mark 2 points on it. Attach 2 squares and 3 equilateral triangles such that the vertices of the squares meet at one point and the vertices of the triangles meet at the other point (Fig. 1). Use discussion of regular shapes to elicit that 2 × 90° = 180° and 3 × 60° = 180°.
- Lead children through these steps (Fig. 2):

  Draw a large triangle on your sheet of scrap paper and cut it out. Label the vertices A, B and C. Tear off the 3 angles. Fit the 3 angles along the straight edge of your ruler.

- Demonstrate an alternative method (Fig. 3). Draw any triangle and cut it out. Label the vertices A, B and C on both sides of the triangle. Fold vertex B to meet the opposite side of the triangle. Fold in vertices A and C to fit along the straight side.
- Make a large square with the 4 squares. Elicit that the sum of the angles around a point is 4 × 90° = 360°. Use the 2 squares and 3 equilateral triangles to find different angle combinations around a point, e.g. 2 × (90° + 60°) + 60° = 360°.

Fig. 1

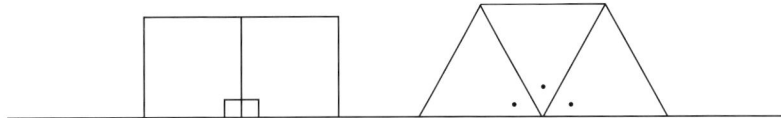

Fig. 2

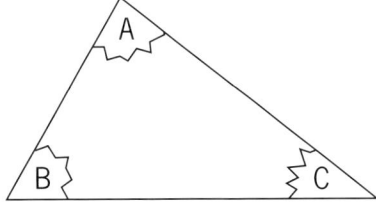 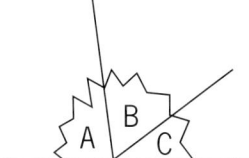

Fig. 3 Fold at dotted lines →

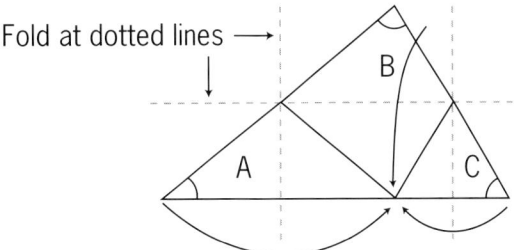 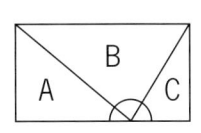

Things to say and ask

- *What can you say about the sum of the three angles of your triangle?…about the sum of the angles around a point?*

Strand: Shape and space *Topic:* Angle and rotation

Angles in regular polygons

Activity Sheet 51

Objectives

Vocabulary

acute, obtuse, degree, protractor, intersect, intersection

- ❏ Recognise and estimate angles.
- ❏ Use a protractor to measure and draw acute and obtuse angles to the nearest degree.
- ❏ Calculate angles in a triangle or around a point.

Resources

blank OHT transparency and OHT pens

protractor (per child)

Teaching support

Misconceptions

A common error is reading the wrong scale on a protractor. Check that children count on from 0°.

This sheet gives children opportunities to apply what they know about the sum of the angles in a triangle or around a point to calculating angles in regular polygons.

- ❏ Ask children to imagine themselves on the helicopter pad of an oil rig in the North Sea. *The Shetland Isles are to the north, Norway is to the east, London is to the south and Scotland is to the west.* Recall that the N–S and E–W axes intersect at right angles.
- ❏ Copy the diagram on to the OHT sheet (Fig. 1). Establish that the helicopter pad is at the point of intersection. *Face oil rig Charlie. Turn to face oil rig Beta and continue turning in the same direction until you face the supply ship coming from Aberdeen. Through how many degrees will you turn to face oil rig Charlie once more?* Discuss ways of calculating the missing angle, e.g. 360° − (90° + 130°) = 140°.
- ❏ Form a triangle by joining the points for A (Aberdeen), B (Beta) and C (Charlie). Ask children to estimate and measure the angles at A and B. Invite suggestions of ways to calculate the angle at C, e.g. C = 180° − (A + B). Check the calculation by measuring.

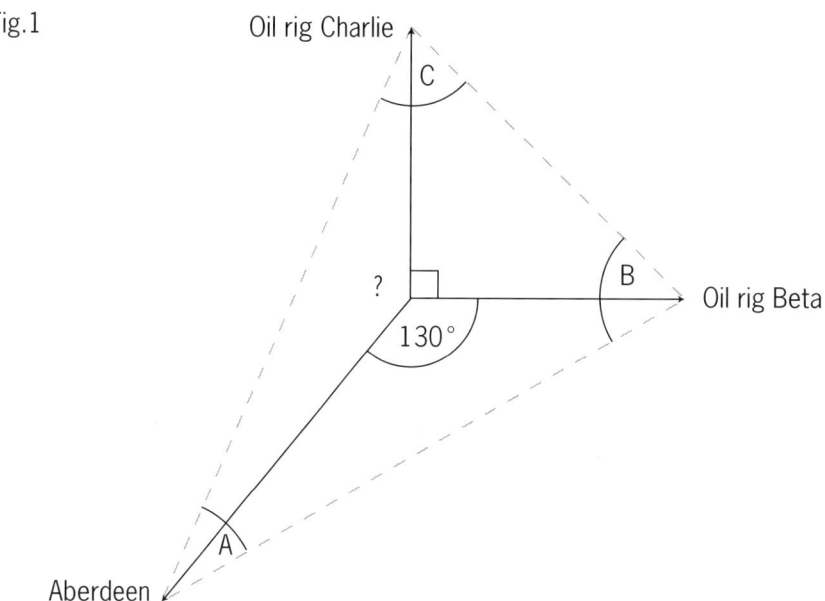

Fig.1

Things to say and ask

- ❏ What can you say about the sides and angles of a regular polygon?
- ❏ How many degrees are in one full turn? How many right angles is that?
- ❏ You have turned through 315°. How many degrees must you turn to get back to your starting position?
- ❏ In a triangle, one angle is 62° and another is 90°. Tell me two ways I can calculate the size of the third angle. (180° − (62° + 90°) = 28° or 90° − 62° = 28°)

Strands: Shape and space/Handling data **Topics:** Angle and rotation/Probability

Rotating shapes

Activity Sheet 52

Objective

- Recognise where a shape will be after a rotation through 90° about one of its vertices.

Vocabulary

rotate, rotation, point, vertex, vertices

Resources
OHT of a 4-quadrant grid and OHT pens
interlocking square tiles
ruler and coloured pencils (per child)
examples of logos and motifs that show turning patterns

Teaching support

The key idea is that as you rotate a shape about a vertex, the position of the vertex remains the same.

Children should be familiar with 4-quadrant coordinate grids.

Misconceptions

The most common errors are in confusing rotation with reflection and in transposing the coordinates of a point.

- Discuss motifs and logos that show turning patterns, e.g. recycling logo, Isle of Man motif...
- Make 4 L-shapes with interlocking tiles. Position an L-shape in the 1st quadrant on the OHT grid, with a vertex at the origin. Elicit that all sides are parallel or perpendicular to the x-axis.
- Ask children to visualise rotating the L-shape through 90°, in an anticlockwise direction and about the vertex at the origin. Establish that the shape is rotated into the 2nd quadrant with the coordinates of the vertex unchanged and place an L-shape in its rotated position in the 2nd quadrant. Elicit and position the shape rotated through 90° into the 3rd and 4th quadrants.
- On the OHT draw the L-shape rotated through 90° in the 4 quadrants. Mark a vertex C and write its coordinates (2, 3). *Tell me the coordinates of vertex C in the second quadrant* (⁻3, 2), *third quadrant* (⁻2, ⁻3) *and fourth quadrant* (3, ⁻2). Draw children's attention to the coordinates of each vertex after a rotation of 180°.

Things to say and ask

- What do you notice about the coordinates of the vertex at the origin when we rotate the shape about that vertex?
- When you rotate a shape through 180° does it matter whether you turn clockwise or anticlockwise? Why not? What about a rotation through 90°?
- Look at the coordinates for vertex C in each quadrant. What patterns do you notice?

Equally likely outcomes

Pupil Book page 82

Objective

- Use the language associated with probability to discuss events, including those with equally likely outcomes.

Vocabulary

event, certain, uncertain, even chance, fifty-fifty chance, equal chance, equally likely, outcome

Resources
none

Strand: Handling data **Topic:** Probability

Teaching support

Misconceptions

It is easy to decide that outcomes are equally likely, e.g. when throwing a dice, you are as likely to throw a 1 as a 2, as a 3 ..., but then to assume that this means that an associated outcome, e.g. that a number rolled on a dice will be less than or greater than 2, must also be equally likely. In this case there is 1 way of rolling a number less than 2 and 4 ways of rolling a number more than 2, so rolling a number more than 2 is more likely.

The key idea is for children to consider and discuss events with 2 or more possible outcomes. Their discussion should focus on whether or not the outcomes are equally likely.

Children need to be familiar with simple ideas and vocabulary about chance and likelihood, including placing statements on a simple probability scale.

- Revise ideas and language about probability, e.g. fair/unfair, likely/unlikely, certain/uncertain, possible/impossible, chance/good chance/poor chance/no chance/even chance. Put some events on a simple probability scale with 'even chance' marked as the centre point.

- Discuss events when there is an even or fifty-fifty chance of something happening, e.g. when tossing a coin there are only 2 possible outcomes. Talk about each outcome being equally likely or having an equal chance.

- Look at question 1 together. *How do we know when outcomes are equally likely?* First you have to decide what the outcomes are and then whether there is an equal chance of each one of them happening. Sometimes, when there are 2 or more possible outcomes, which one it is that actually occurs is a random event, e.g. when throwing a dice, you are as likely to throw a 1 as a 2, as a 3 .... For other situations, e.g. when considering whether left- and right-handedness are equally likely, you will need to find out how many people are left-handed and how many are right-handed.

- In question 2, children begin to think about the difference between theoretical probability and experimental probability: the difference between the expectation that the paper will land an equal number of times on the picture side and the plain side and the actual experiment results. Children may need support in ensuring that their experiment is fair, in the same way as scientific tests must be fair: how should the paper be held to start?...should it always start at the same height?...what if there is a breeze?

- When they have completed the question, encourage a discussion about theory and practice in this probability experiment, and about the benefit of using a larger sample made by adding together all their scores.

Things to say and ask

❏ *What do you expect the results to be?*
❏ *Why do the actual results not match your expectation?*

Considering likelihood

Activity Sheet 53

Objective

❏ Use the language associated with probability to discuss events, including those with equally likely outcomes.

Vocabulary

event, outcome, even chance, fifty-fifty chance, equal chance, good chance, poor chance, equally likely, fair

Resources

a dice and 2 counters (per pair)

Strand: Handling data **Topic:** Probability

Teaching support

Misconceptions
Encourage children not to be too hasty about making decisions about the likelihood of events. They may well be affected by their own experience.

This sheet asks children to consolidate their ideas about what is more likely and to focus on probability in the context of a game.

Children need to understand the concept of an even chance.

- Begin by considering events that have 2 possible outcomes that are equally likely, e.g. tossing a coin and getting a head or a tail, taking a card from a pack of playing cards and finding that it is red or that it is black ....
- Extend the discussion by asking children to contribute ideas for pairs of events where one is more likely than the other, e.g. it is more likely that the temperature will be less than 30 degrees tomorrow than more than 30 degrees; it is more likely that you will throw a number greater than 2, than a number less than 2 on a 1–6 dice.
- Explain that Activity Sheet 53 begins by considering pairs of events that do not have an equal chance of happening.
- As children play the game, or at the end, encourage them to discuss whether the game is fair or not, and why.
- This is a situation where outcomes are equally likely and there is an even chance of either happening. Encourage children to play the game several times. If one child happens to win all/most of the games, take the opportunity to talk about fairness and ensure through discussion that children realise that the result of one game has no effect on the result of the next. There is always an even chance of winning. Put together results from all children to see if the experimental probability comes closer to the theoretical probability.

Things to say and ask

- *Can you think of two similar events where the likelihoods will be very close?*
- *Can you think of some rules for a game where one person is more likely to win than the other?*

Expected and experimental probability (dice and cards)

Pupil Book pages 83 and 84

Objective

- Use the language associated with probability to discuss events, including those with equally likely outcomes.

Vocabulary

event, outcome, expected probability, impossible, certain, equal/even chance, good chance, poor chance, equally likely, frequency, probability scale

Resources

For Pupil Book page 83:
  a dice (per child)
For Pupil Book page 84:
  a pack of playing cards with the picture cards removed (per pair)

Strand: Handling data **Topic:** Probability

Teaching support

Misconceptions

When placing probabilities on a probability scale, encourage children to compare the probability they are considering with what they estimate to be the nearest neighbour, e.g. are you more likely to roll an odd number or to roll a 1 or a 2?

The key idea is to develop understanding of expected (theoretical) probabilities and how they may differ from experimental probabilities.

Children should have worked with events and games where there are 2 equally likely outcomes, and also compared the probabilities of different events.

Pupil Book page 83

- Use a dice to introduce the game. Elicit that there is an even chance (3 out of 6 or 1 half) of rolling an odd or an even number. Write $\frac{3}{6} = \frac{1}{2}$. *Is there an equal chance of rolling any number on the dice, or is it more likely that you will roll, e.g. a 6 than a 4? Experiment by rolling the dice 6 times, to see if one of each number is rolled. How many rolls do you think we need to do before the frequency of each number is the same?* Elicit that the more rolls, the closer the scores are likely to be. *What is the expected probability for each number?* ($\frac{1}{6}$) *If we roll the dice 36 times, how many 5s would we expect?* (6)

- Remind children about using a probability scale to compare probabilities. Elicit that we place an even chance (1 in 2 or $\frac{1}{2}$) at the middle of the scale, so the 'impossible' end of the scale must be 0 and the 'certain' end 1. Ask a volunteer to place the probability of rolling a 6 with a 1–6 dice.

- Suggest that children work in pairs to think about the possible outcomes of rolling 2 dice. They need to consider all the ways to throw each possible total before they can find an expected probability for each total and then apply this to the outcomes in the table from question 2. As they work or when they have finished, support children in turning the probabilities into fractions and placing them on the line.

Pupil Book page 84

- Explain that this page is also about experimenting to find probabilities and how close these are to the expected probability.

- Children need to realise that there are a total of 40 cards in a pack of playing cards with the picture cards removed (Ace = 1), 2 red suits (hearts and diamonds) and 2 black suits (spades and clubs).

- Children should realise that the probabilities in this question will be exactly the same as in question 2.

Things to say and ask

- *How many different possible outcomes are there? How many of them do we need to think about?*
- *How many cards are in the pack? How many are red? How many are not red?*

Expected and experimental probability (coins)

Activity Sheet 54

Objective

- Use the language associated with probability to discuss events, including those with equally likely outcomes.

Vocabulary

event, outcome, expected, predict, impossible, certain, equal/even chance, good chance, poor chance, equally likely

Resources

20 counters and a coin (per pair)

Strand: Handling data **Topic:** Probability

Teaching support

The key idea in this activity is for children to think about more complicated outcomes in the context of an experiment in order to develop their understanding of expected (theoretical) probability.

The children should be familiar with representing simple probabilities as fractions on a probability scale.

- Explain that the activity is about working out more complicated probabilities through experimenting.
- Establish with children that there is an even chance of getting a head or a tail when you toss a coin. In pairs, ask them to try to work out the probability of tossing a coin twice and getting 2 heads. Accept all suggestions and record them. If they have only one suggestion, offer some others, including $\frac{1}{2}$ and $\frac{1}{4}$. Explain that the experiment on Activity Sheet 54 may help them decide which one is the correct expected probability.
- Children will need to be systematic as they work. Encourage them to make sure they both have a clear task as they move the counters around.
- When children have completed the experiment, give them the opportunity to compare their results with other pairs. Elicit that there are 2 ways of getting to the circle and only 1 way of getting to either the square or the triangle. So there are 4 routes (or outcomes) altogether, giving the probability of tossing 2 heads as $\frac{1}{4}$.

Things to say and ask

- How many different possibilities are there?
- Is there the same chance of getting 2 heads as getting 2 tails?

Expected and experimental probability (cubes)

Pupil Book page 85

Objective

- Use the language associated with probability to discuss events, including those with equally likely outcomes.

Vocabulary

expected, probability, impossible, certain, equal/even chance, equally likely, random

Resources
coloured cubes in 2 colours and an opaque bag (per pair)
extra coloured cubes

Teaching support

The key idea is that we can predict a probability through sampling.

The children should be familiar with representing simple probabilities as fractions.

- Prepare for the session by placing 4 red cubes and 4 yellow cubes in a bag. Tell children there are 8 cubes in the bag and there are two colours. Ask a volunteer to select one cube at random, without looking, record the colour and replace it. Repeat another 23 times. Remind children that there are 8 cubes in the bag. Ask them to discuss in pairs how to use the data collected to estimate the probability of each colour being picked and to predict how many of each are in the bag.
- Repeat with a bag with 2 green cubes, 1 blue and 1 yellow. Ask children to predict how many are blue. Note: it is of no consequence what colour the other cubes are, so the prediction will be clearer to make if colours are recorded as blue/not blue.

Strand: Handling data **Topic:** Probability

Things to say and ask

- How can you prepare a bag with 24 cubes of mixed colours so that the probability of picking each colour is $\frac{1}{12}$?
- Can you use this idea to make a game?

Expected and experimental probability (spinners)

Activity Sheet 55

Objective

- Use the language associated with probability to discuss events, including those with equally likely outcomes.

Vocabulary

equally likely, biased, random, expected, fair

Resources

a paper clip (per pair)

Teaching support

The key idea is that when outcomes are not equally likely then results will be biased towards the most likely outcome.

The children will need to have considered expected and experimental probabilities using coins and dice where the outcomes are equally likely. They should be familiar with representing probabilities as fractions on a probability scale.

- Confirm with children that on a dice there is an equal chance of throwing any of the numbers 1–6. *It is completely random which number will be thrown.*
- Draw a spinner with 6 equal (but empty) spaces and give children the opportunity to discuss whether or not the spinner is 'fair' with an equal chance of spinning each number from 1–6. Whether they decide 'yes' or 'no' or 'depends', write '7' in five of the spaces and '8' in the last one. Confirm that this is not a fair spinner if an equal chance of spinning 1–6 is required: there is no chance of spinning the numbers 1–6. Explain that the spinner is biased in favour of spinning 7.
- When children have completed Activity Sheet 55, discuss any differences between the experimental and expected probabilities. Discuss any bias that may have been introduced by the method of spinning.

Things to say and ask

- Are there any other numbers that it is impossible to spin?
- Can you make a spinner with four spaces where there is an equal chance of spinning 1, 2 or 3?

Expected probability (spinners)

Pupil Book page 86

Objective

- Use the language associated with probability to discuss events, including those with equally likely outcomes.

Vocabulary

equally likely, biased, random, expected

Resources

protractor (per child)

Strand: Handling data *Topics:* Probability/Organising and interpreting data

Teaching support

The key idea is that we can find expected probabilities where outcomes are not equally likely and there is bias.

The children will need to have considered probabilities using coins and dice, where the outcomes have an equal chance. They should have completed Activity Sheet 55.

- Draw these 2 spinners:

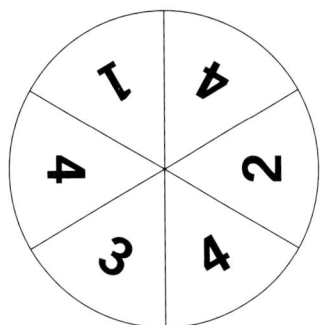 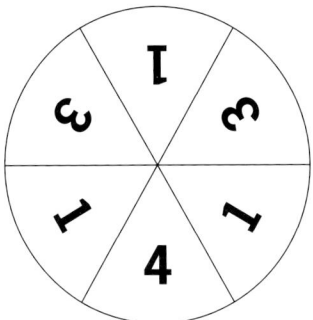

Ask children to discuss, decide and explain the best choices for the following questions:
If I want the best chance of scoring 2, which spinner should I use?
If I want the best chance of scoring 3, which spinner should I use?
If I want the best chance of scoring 4, which spinner should I use?
If I want the best chance of scoring 1, which spinner should I use?

- On the first spinner rub out the lines dividing the '3' from the two '4' sectors and replace the numbers with '3'. Reconsider the questions. Stress that you must take account of the size of each sector as well as how many times a number appears.

Things to say and ask

- For question 1: *Which spinner gives the best chance of scoring a 4? ... a 3?*
- For question 3: *Do you think your spinners would give the expected results if you tested them? Why? Why not?*

Interpreting a line graph

Pupil Book page 87

Objective

- Solve a problem by extracting and interpreting data in a line graph where intermediate points may or may not have meaning.

Vocabulary

line graph, maximum/minimum value

Resources
A4 graph paper and ruler (per child)

Strand: Handling data *Topic:* Organising and interpreting data

Teaching support

The key idea is that the only reason for representing data diagrammatically is to make information clear and easy to understand and interpret. Most graphs are produced by computer, so the critical skill children need to develop is that of understanding what a diagram does or does not show.

Children should be familiar with reading a line graph where intermediate points may or may not have meaning.

- Ask children when they might use a line graph. Accept their suggestions and encourage them to explain why a line graph is a good way to represent the data they have identified, e.g. if they suggest that a line graph can be used to show the growth of a plant over a period of time, encourage them to acknowledge that a line graph is useful because there are two bits of information, time and height, one for each axis.
- In question 2, children are asked to produce a graph, not from data, but to comply with information given about the graph. Support them through discussion about how the graph might look, e.g. *Will the line be above or below 18 degrees? When are the children likely to be in school?*
- When children have completed Pupil Book page 87, ask them to compare their graph with others'. Help them to establish that they all fulfil the same criteria, although they probably look different in some ways.

Things to say and ask

- *How high does the scale need to go?*
- *Why might the temperature go up and down in a classroom?*

Using straight line graphs

Activity Sheet 56 Pupil Book page 88

Objective

- Solve a problem by extracting and interpreting data in a line graph where the intermediate points have meaning.

Vocabulary

line graph, conversion graph, scale, axes

Resources

For the Activity Sheet
  OHT square grid
  ruler and sharp pencil (per child)

For the Pupil Book
  a clothes or toy catalogue, with prices in pounds sterling

Strand: Handling data *Topic:* Organising and interpreting data

Teaching support

Misconceptions
Accuracy is important in constructing line graphs. Encourage children to be precise when plotting coordinates and always to use a ruler.

The key idea is to develop children's understanding of straight line graphs and their uses. In the case of these graphs, all points on the lines do have meaning.

Children should be familiar with reading a line graph where intermediate points do not have meaning.

Activity Sheet 56

- Introduce the activity by asking children to say the 3× table. As they say it, record the numbers:

1	3
2	6
3	9
4…	12…

- Demonstrate on the OHT how to construct a line graph using the numbers as coordinates and joining them with a ruler to make a straight line: (1, 3), (2, 6), (3, 9), (4, 12)… Explain that the line can be continued in both directions indefinitely.
- Show children how to 'read' answers to tables from the graph, e.g. the answer to 3×5 can be found by reading up from 3 on the horizontal axis to the 5× line, and then reading across to the answer on the vertical axis.

Pupil Book page 88

- Introduce the idea of using a straight line graph for converting one currency to another.
- When children have completed Activity Sheet 56 and Pupil Book page 88, discuss values for and interpretation of intermediate points: all points on the line on these graphs have meaning.

Things to say and ask

Activity Sheet 56:
❏ *How could you work out what the answer to $^-2 \times 3$ is?*

Pupil Book page 88:
❏ *How much in pounds sterling is 1 euro? Tell me about the scale.*

Using a frequency table

Activity Sheet 57

Objective

Vocabulary

frequency table

❏ Solve a problem by representing, extracting and interpreting data in a frequency table and bar chart with grouped data.

Resources
$\frac{1}{2}$ cm squared paper or graph paper (per child)
calculator (per child)

Strand: Handling data **Topic:** Organising and interpreting data

Teaching support

The key idea is for children to understand that grouping data can make the representation of data in a chart easier and clearer to interpret.

Children should be familiar with representing discrete data on a frequency bar chart.

- Introduce the activity by making a simple birthday chart to show in which season children in the class have their birthdays. Use the following groups of months. Complete the table by asking children to find the relevant information from a class list.

Winter Dec-Feb	Spring March-May	Summer June-August	Autumn Sept-Nov

Draw a bar chart and show children how to label the range of each bar. Note that the divisions between the bars are not labelled.

- Explain that numerical data can also be grouped in this way. Make it clear that for a fair representation each group must be the same size.

- Make sure that children are familiar with the idea of a national lottery where 6 random numbers between 1 and 49 are chosen each week as prize winners. Encourage them to offer their ideas about how it can be guaranteed that the numbers are random.

- Explain that the (fictional) 'Euro lottery' has run each week for the past 7 years with numbers 1–50. Ask children to look at the data and to decide whether it seems truly random which numbers have been drawn. (They will spot that 38 has occurred more frequently than all the other numbers.) *Would it help to represent the data in a chart? How could you do this?* Establish that there is rather too much data to make representation and interpretation straightforward, and that grouping should help to give a clearer, if simplified, picture.

Things to say and ask

- ❑ *If you were going to play the 'Euro lottery', which 6 numbers would you choose? Why?*
- ❑ *What is the difference between the most and fewest numbers of times a number has been drawn?*

Strand: Handling data **Topic:** Organising and interpreting data

Collecting, representing and interpreting real data

Pupil Book page 89

Objective

- Solve a problem by representing, extracting and interpreting data in a table and bar chart.

Vocabulary

bar chart, axes, random, statistics

Resources

television listings for sports channels (per pair)

Teaching support

The key idea is to gather and interpret 'real-life' data.

Children should be able to organise data appropriately and have some experience of justifying their conclusions.

- Look at the relevant sections of the television listings with children and ensure they can identify the majority of sports featured.
- Ensure children realise that finding the number of times a given sport is shown may not, on its own, determine whether Maia is right or not. The length of each programme is also significant.
- Encourage children to focus on their more important findings and to consider how best to present their information.
- Discuss how important sporting events (World Cup football, tennis at Wimbledon, ...) could affect their findings.

Things to say and ask

- Do you think that Maia would be right (or wrong) whichever day you looked at?
- What other sports get a lot of coverage?

Using pie charts

Pupil Book page 90 Activity Sheet 58

Objective

- Solve a problem by representing, extracting and interpreting data in a pie chart.

Vocabulary

pie chart

Resources

For the Pupil Book and Activity Sheet:
  protractor or paper circle with 10° intervals marked (per child)

For the Activity Sheet:
  coloured pencils (per child)
  reading books (per child)

Strand: Handling data **Topic:** Organising and interpreting data

Teaching support

Misconceptions

Constructing a pie chart is more difficult than reading one. Children may need support in focusing on the relationship between the numbers in each group and the total number of children and then the fractional part of the whole circle in degrees.

The key idea is for children to be able to interpret information in a pie chart using their understanding of fractions.

Children should be familiar with a range of charts and graphs, and should also understand fractions and be able to apply their understanding of them to circles. They should know how to use a protractor.

- Introduce pie charts by telling the children a story about a class with 24 children. Draw a circle on the board. *We can call this circle a pie because some pies are circular. The pie represents the whole class.* Then draw a line across the 'pie' and ask how many children half the pie would represent. Then suggest other fractions and ask the children to discuss and agree on the number of children each fraction of the pie would represent. *A diagram like this is called a pie chart.* Encourage them to draw the fractions on the pie chart and label them.

- Explain that pie charts are frequently used to represent data about a group of people, e.g. *If 12 of the 24 children have brown eyes, 6 have green and 6 have blue, then we can draw a pie chart like this:*

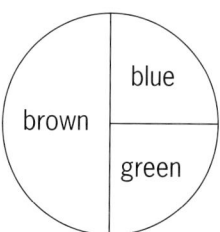

- Ask children if they can work out how many degrees represent 1 person, e.g. 90 ÷ 6 = 15. *So how many degrees would represent 3 people, 10 people...?*

- For question 3 in the Pupil Book, children may need support to draw their own pie chart. You could provide paper circles with 10° intervals already marked for their use.

Things to say and ask

Activity Sheet 58:
- For question 2: *Suppose only 6 children were in one of the groups. How would you decide where to draw the line?*
- *Can you estimate the approximate fraction?*

Interpreting data and finding the mode and range

Pupil Book page 91   Activity Sheet 59

Objectives

Vocabulary

mode, range

- Solve a problem by extracting and interpreting data in tables, graphs, charts and diagrams.
- Find the mode and range of a set of data.

Resources
For the Pupil Book:
  graph paper (per child)
For the Activity Sheet:
  squared paper and ruler (per child)

Strand: Handling data *Topic:* Organising and interpreting data

Teaching support

Misconceptions

Children may think that the range of the data in Pupil Book page 91 question 2c is 7 because the information was gathered over a 7-day period. Remind children that it is the difference between the largest and smallest values in the data collected. Note that this is the only chart where the data is not given in terms of its frequency.

The key idea is to find the mode and range of a set of data presented in a variety of forms.

Children should be familiar with interpreting data presented in a variety of forms.

Pupil Book page 91

- Gather information quickly about the number of buttons children are wearing and record in a frequency table.
- Elicit that there are several pieces of useful information children can find from the data including the **range** (the difference between the largest and smallest numbers in the set) and the **mode** (the most common/popular number or item). (There may be 2 or more modes with equal frequency.)

Activity Sheet 59

- Ensure children are able to extract information from the table in question 1.

Things to say and ask

Pupil Book page 91:
- *What is the mode of the ages in our class?*
- For question 2: *What is the greatest number in the set? What is the smallest?*

Activity Sheet 59:
- *What was the fastest time in the first heat of the semi-finals?*
- *Which race produced the fastest time?*
- *Which country came second in Round 1 Heat 3?*

Finding the median

Pupil Book page 92

Objective

- Find the median of a set of data.

Vocabulary

median, mode, range

Resources

none

Teaching support

Misconceptions

Stress that to find the middle number the set must be put in order first. Mistakes happen when children try to find the median without recording the ordered list.

The key idea is to identify the median of a set of data and begin to understand what this number represents.

Children should have completed Pupil Book page 91 and Activity Sheet 59.

- Discuss how, when extracting information and seeking to draw conclusions about a set of data, finding the mode and range can be helpful. Explain that another useful indicator is the median: the middle number in a set of data that has been put in numerical order. It can be thought of as representing a typical value for the set. It is especially helpful when there is no clear mode.
- Ask children to think of a number. Let 5 children tell you their numbers and record them. Ask for a volunteer to write the numbers in order, smallest to largest, and then ask children to identify the range and the median. Repeat the exercise with 5 new numbers twice more. Describe the 3 sets of numbers using their range and median and ask children to identify and compare them. *Is there a clear mode for each set?*
- You may wish to discuss children's ideas for finding a median when there is an even number of data values in the set. Show them/highlight the accepted procedure of taking the two middle numbers and finding the number half way between them.

Things to say and ask

- *Were there any results that surprised you?*
- *Can you also calculate the range for each set of data?*

Strand: Handling data **Topic:** Organising and interpreting data

Finding the mean

Activity Sheet 60

Objective
- Find the mean of a set of data.

Vocabulary

average, median, mode, mean, range, adjust

Resources
interlocking cubes

Teaching support

The key idea in this activity is for children to calculate the mean of a set of data and to begin to understand what this number represents.

Children should be able to identify the mode and median of a set of data.

- Remind children that the range, mode and median all provide useful information about a set of data.
- Introduce children to the mean. It is helpful to show the mean as a balancing or sharing average using interlocking cubes and/or a chart. Arrange cubes of 4 different colours into blocks of 8, 2, 5 and 9. Then reposition cubes to create blocks of equal height:

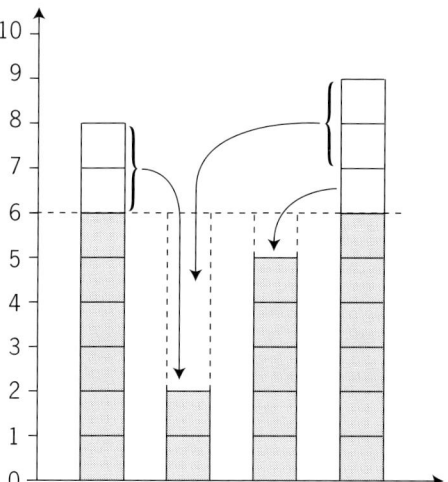

- Now explain that the most common way of finding the mean (average) is to add all the members of the set and divide by the total number in the set.
- Encourage children to realise that they need to use negative numbers and/or decimal fractions to find a set of numbers with a mean of 1.

Things to say and ask

- What do you think the mean would be for a set of consecutive numbers, e.g. 2, 3, 4, 5, 6 or 2, 3, 4, 5?
- What is the mean for this set: 54, 54, 54, 54, 54?